The Untold Story of Shirley Mason, Her Multiple Personalities and Paintings

SYBIL

in her own words

Patrick Suraci, Ph.D.

SYBIL IN HER OWN WORDS
THE UNTOLD STORY OF SHIRLEY MASON, HER MULTIPLE PERSONALITIES AND PAINTINGS

Published by Abandoned Ladder
http://www.abandonedladder.com

Printed in the United States of America

ISBN-13: 978-0615560472 (Abandoned Ladder)
ISBN-10: 0615560474

10 9 8 7 6 5 4 3 2 1

Dedication

To Josephine, Frank and Lorrine Suraci.

CONTENTS

Preface

I met Flora Schreiber in 1973 shortly after the publication of her book *Sybil.* Working together and living near each other, we quickly became friends. She often spoke about the therapy and recovery of Sybil. She remained in contact with Sybil and kept me informed about her.

After Flora's death I discovered the identity of Sybil—Shirley Ardell Mason. In 1993 I called her and we formed a distinctive relationship. She verified that Flora's book was accurate. After years of conversations she agreed to have me write about her life after the book *Sybil.* This part of her life as an artist and teacher has never been told. She was pleased that I would let people know of her long-term recovery from Multiple Personality Disorder, as well as the benefits of therapy.

She planned to send me the paintings she and her alternate personalities created while in therapy with Dr. Cornelia Wilbur. She hoped that the paintings would aid others in early diagnosis of mental disorders. These paintings are reproduced in color in this book. My interpretations of the paintings offer a portrait of the various personalities who painted them.

This book provides an update and insight acquired from the documentation of my personal relationship with Shirley Mason.

I use the name "Sybil" to refer to the person with Multiple Personality Disorder, described by Flora Schreiber, the main persona in the book *Sybil.* Otherwise, I use the name Shirley to refer to the real-life person I knew.

In order to ensure accuracy, all Shirley's direct quotations are from our taped conversations. Quotes from Shirley's diary, which she gave me, are verbatim. I received extensive material from Naomi (whose father Virgil and Shirley's mother Mattie were first cousins, making Naomi and Shirley second cousins) and her husband Jim Rhode. I interviewed Professor Daniel Houlihan, Wilma Bode, Betty Christensen and Patricia Alcott, all of whom gave me permission to record them. Other descriptions are based on my contemporaneous notes.

Readers are referred to the book *Sybil* for what I consider to be an accurate account of Shirley's history of Multiple Personality Disorder and her treatment.

While Shirley was undergoing analysis, she made a painting for Flora Schreiber called *New York City*. It appears on the Introduction page.

Patrick Suraci, Ph.D.

Acknowledgments

The late Shirley Mason, Naomi and Jim Rhode, Betty Christensen, Patricia Alcott, the late Wilma Bode, Professor Daniel Houlihan, Dr. Leah Dickstein, Pauline Miller, Jeanne Cohen, Jeff and Janet Ware, Lucca, Dr. Gregory Lehne, Basia Kapolka, Carroll Baker, Stewart Stern, Tony R. Perkins, Thom Rivera, Christopher Rozzi, Joe Romanaskas, Diane Sawyer, Ellen Belcher (Special Collections Librarian at Lloyd Sealy Library), Helen Vogel (Executrix of Flora Schreiber's will), and Kristopher Clark (author's headshot photographer).

The letters and diary entries in Chapter 5, *Remembering Flora*, are from:

The Papers of Flora Rheta Schreiber
Special Collections, Lloyd Sealy Library
John Jay College of Criminal Justice.

The remaining Sybil paintings shown in Chapters 12, 13, 14, 15, and 16 are printed with the permission of Naomi Rhode.

The audio tape cited in Chapter 19 is in:

Addition to the Schreiber Papers
Gift of Dr. Robert Rieber, 2006
Special Collections, Lloyd Sealy Library
John Jay College of Criminal Justice.

Shirley Mason's painting in Appendix G is owned by Patricia Alcott. Shirley gave it to Patricia's mother in 1953.

All excerpts quoted from *Sybil* are from the first edition Published by Henry Regnery Company, 114 West Illinois Street, Chicago, Illinois, 60610, Copyright 1973 by Flora Rheta Screiber, Library of Congress Catalogue Card Number:72-11188, ISBN 0-8092-0001-5.

O. Aldon James, President of The National Arts Club, Linda Zagaria, Babette Bloch, and Joan Meyer of the Roundtable for their encouragement and assistance with this book.

Introduction

I was always fascinated by the painting. It caught my attention the first time I walked into Flora Rheta Schreiber's office at John Jay College in 1973. As a new instructor at the college, I was grateful for our budding friendship as colleagues and as neighbors on Gramercy Park in New York City. Whenever I had a chance to visit Flora in her office, I found myself staring at the painting on the wall behind her desk. It served as a backdrop for our conversations about the psychological phenomena with which I was engaged in my doctoral program.

There was an aura of mystery about the painting. It had no signature.

It is acrylic on cardboard, thirty inches wide and twenty-four inches high. The sky has streaks and swirls of shades of blue and green with two dominant white clouds framed by pale green. One of the clouds is pierced by the steeple of the Empire State Building forming a small cloud which is descending toward the city. Dark blue and purple form an ominous background to the Empire State Building, highlighting the white buildings of the city. A jumble of skyscrapers is softened by hints of turquoise but threatened by deep purple foliage which tapers down to a light-colored earth at the center of the picture. At this point the light filters into the turquoise water and the land on the opposite shore in the foreground. Two white seagulls safely land on the shore. A large skeletal version of the Staten Island Ferry followed by three similar but smaller boats sails to the right of the painting.

My eyes are drawn to the Empire State Building. This impressionistic image reminds me of a wax model of that building which I treasured during my childhood in Rochester, New York. While constantly handling it and dreaming of escaping to New York City, I had distorted it. The second focal point is the Staten Island Ferry, which appears to be in the lake in Central Park instead of where it belongs in the Atlantic Ocean.

I feel peaceful as my eyes rest on the two seagulls. The larger one is leading the smaller one to shore. When I learned the artist was Sybil, I was then able to fully interpret the painting. Sybil had painted it for Flora Schreiber while undergoing psychoanalysis with Dr. Cornelia Wilbur in New York City. At that time, Flora was writing the book *Sybil.*

The two large white clouds at the top represent Sybil's parents producing the small cloud, Sybil. She is immersed in the cacophony of New York City during her therapy. Her chaotic state of mind is manifested in the distorted Empire State Building, the morphing skyscrapers, and the boats in the wrong waters. I see the larger seagull representing Dr. Cornelia Wilbur, the psychiatrist who treated her with psychoanalysis, leading the smaller seagull, symbolizing Sybil, to shore and safety after traversing her therapy in New York.

• • •

On November 1, 1988, Flora lay in a bed at Beth Israel Hospital in Manhattan. She had been treated unsuccessfully for cancer that year. Since she disliked doctors intensely, she had not been to one for thirty-five years.

With death in the air, Flora said, "If anything happens to me I want you to have Sybil's painting."

I replied, "Florabelle, you're not going anywhere. If you survived all the battles over your books, you're going to hang around, so I'll have to take care of you."

She said, "I'm glad I won those battles, but I'm really most proud of taking care of Joe Kallinger's son."

Much to the chagrin of many of her friends, Flora had taken Kallinger's son into her home and supported him through his teenage years. Joe Kallinger was the murderer and the subject of Flora's next book *The Shoemaker: The Anatomy of a Psychotic*.

I said, "You gave him a wonderful opportunity to have a good life."

She replied, "I know people thought I was crazy. But I'm glad I did it."

I agreed, "You did real good, Florabelle. I'll see you tomorrow."

She quipped, "Merry Christmas." That was her unique salutation to me, the Catholic. Regardless of the time of year, whenever we had a heavy or disturbing conversation, she would smile and end it by saying "Merry Christmas." It sounded more like "Good luck in solving that one." It was her way of ameliorating a dark situation with a happier one. I knew her black sense of humor would give her strength to get through her final ordeal.

On November 3, 1988, the day the hospital had planned to discharge her, Flora got her final revenge on the doctors—she died.

Shortly after her funeral I received the painting. After I became a therapist it hung on my office wall as an inspiring reminder of Flora's contribution to the field of psychology and Dr. Cornelia Wilbur's successful and innovative therapy with Sybil. It gave me and my patients hope knowing that someone as depleted as Sybil could recover.

• • •

To be able to wake up in the morning and know that you have the entire day before you. To know that you will be aware of what happens to you today. To know that you will be able to make choices, however difficult they may be. To know that you have some control over your thoughts. To know who you are every minute of the day. This knowing is taken for granted by most of us. This was not the case for Sybil.

Shirley Ardell Mason, called "Sybil" in the book, was born on January 25, 1923 in Dodge Center, Minnesota. She was an artistically gifted child, but shy and withdrawn. These characteristics became more pronounced as she grew. She appeared to be timid and forgetful. When her mother, Mattie, and her father, Walter, agreed to take her to medical doctors, the vague diagnosis was "nervousness." Finally, on August 10, 1945, when Shirley was 22, she saw a psychiatrist in Omaha, Nebraska—Dr. Cornelia Wilbur. After several sessions, she developed a rapport with Dr. Wilbur, who told Shirley that there was help for her. Shirley realized that this caring doctor might be able to solve the mystery of her illness. Dr. Wilbur told Shirley that eventually she was moving to Chicago to pursue her analytic training. She advised Shirley to go to Chicago or New York to be analyzed.

On October 6th, Shirley could not get out of bed due to pneumonia. She asked her mother to telephone Dr. Wilbur to cancel her appointment that day. She heard her mother speaking on the phone, not knowing that her mother had not actually placed the call and was only pretending to speak to Dr. Wilbur. She asked her mother what Dr. Wilbur said. Mattie told Shirley that Dr. Wilbur did not say anything. Shirley was shocked by the apparent lack of concern of Dr. Wilbur and was later shattered by her abrupt departure for Chicago.

Sporadically, over the years she saw a few other therapists who were never able to solve the mystery of her illness. Fortunately, in 1954, Shirley discovered that Dr. Wilbur was in New York, and she moved there to continue her therapy.

During her psychoanalysis Shirley discovered that she had fifteen personalities in addition to her own, who was called "Sybil" in the book. A total of sixteen personalities inhabited the frail body of Sybil Isabel Dorsett: Vicky; Marcia; Vanessa; Mary; Helen; Clara; Sybil Ann; The Blonde; Peggy Ann; Peggy Lou; Mike; Sid; Nancy Lou Ann; Marjorie; and Ruthie. After eleven years of intensive psychoanalysis, she accepted her alternate personalities caused by abuse from her mother. Shirley was finally integrated into one whole human being.

Flora's best-seller *Sybil* was made into an Emmy Award-winning TV movie which aired in 1976. Sally Field won an Emmy for her portrayal of Sybil and Joanne Woodward was nominated for her portrayal of Dr. Cornelia Wilbur.

The movie brought to the general public an awareness of Multiple Personality Disorder. Despite the rarity of this mental disorder, many people identify with the dynamics of it because they also have many facets to their own personalities. These facets are manifested in a variety of behaviors with particular people and in different environments. Sometimes a person is shocked by his or her own behavior. However, most people remain aware of their own identity even though they may be puzzled by their uncharacteristic behavior.

Sometimes we wake up and wish that we could be a different person; we would like to escape from our troubled lives. This daydreaming is an escape mechanism that we use. In Multiple Personality Disorder, the defense mechanism is so extreme that the person dissociates and develops an "alternate personality." This survival technique is used to combat severe childhood abuse.

Sybil used this survival mechanism. However, Sybil, the waking self, was neither aware of her other personalities nor aware that they took over her body. Sybil had no knowledge of what happened during these times. The other personalities were aware of each other and of Sybil. All that Sybil knew was that she "lost time."

The fascination with this case continues thirty-five years after the original movie. Recently, CBS produced a new TV movie starring Jessica Lange as Dr. Wilbur and Tammy Blanchard as Sybil based on Flora Rheta Schreiber's book.

• • •

While taking a photograph of Sybil's painting to send to my sister, Lorrine, I noticed white streaks forming on the lower portion of it. I became concerned about preserving this painting by a woman for whom I had such an affinity. I was struck by her ability to persevere in her treatment until she was cured. I marveled at her intelligence in grasping the concept of her various personalities and her ability to integrate them. My own sister was not so fortunate in overcoming her mental illness—Schizophrenia. In this psychotic condition, she had a split from reality rather than a split in her personality. Whenever Lorrine had hallucinations, she was not aware of her reality being interrupted, in the same way that Sybil was not aware during her dissociative states. Lorrine also "lost time," as did Sybil.

The deterioration of the painting renewed my fear that Sybil might possibly deteriorate as well. While Flora was alive, I was continually reassured that Sybil had not had a relapse and that she was living a productive life. Flora informed me that Sybil was in constant contact with Dr. Wilbur. Unknown to the public, Sybil and Dr. Wilbur had developed a friendship after Sybil's therapy terminated.

The coming together of Sybil, Flora and Dr. Wilbur proved to be a life-shaping event for each of them. They all became famous after the book was published. Unfortunately, that fame also brought them heartaches. They provided support for each other during those trying times. These shared experiences created a bond that lasted until their deaths.

• • •

In the 1950s when Flora was writing psychiatric articles and was Psychiatry Editor for *Science Digest*, she met Dr. Cornelia Wilbur.

During the ensuing years Dr. Wilbur came to admire Flora's

writing skills. In the early 1960s Dr. Wilbur asked Flora if she would like to write a book about one of her patients. Flora was intrigued by this case of Multiple Personality Disorder. After getting permission from her patient, Dr. Wilbur arranged a meeting at a restaurant on Madison Avenue in New York City.

In 1962, Flora sat in the restaurant anticipating the arrival of this interesting subject, but feared she would not show up. She devoured the bread as she envisioned writing this important case study. She relied on Dr. Wilbur to give her credentials to her patient and hoped that she would be accepted by her. When Flora saw Dr. Wilbur approaching, she rose from her seat. Accompanying Dr. Wilbur was a demure young woman with downcast eyes.

Flora was struck by this plain, unassuming woman who nevertheless had such a complex psyche. Shirley later told me she was somewhat overcome by Flora's dowager-empress demeanor. Flora spoke with a broad, Oxford English accent left over from her days of studying acting in London.

During their dinner Flora spoke of her research of Multiple Personality Disorder beginning with Morton Prince's book *The Dissociation of a Personality*. Dr. Wilbur thought that Flora could write a knowledgeable book about Shirley. Shirley believed that her story could help others, clinicians as well as patients. So she gave permission to Flora to have full access to her life as long as her identity was not revealed.

Years after this fateful meeting, during one of our conversations, Shirley told me that she was impressed with "Flora's ability to grasp an intellectual concept and run with it."

Shirley gave Dr. Wilbur permission to give Flora audio tapes of their therapy sessions. Some of them had been used by Dr. Wilbur to introduce Shirley to her alternate personalities.

When Flora listened to the tapes, she was struck by this pleasant woman manifesting such contradictory and bizarre behavior and speech during her dissociative states. Each alter (alternate personality) had her or his (there were two male alters) own speech pattern and behavior.

Flora agreed to write the book on the condition that Shirley's treatment was successful and she was completely cured.

Thus, the three women embarked on a journey with an unknown destination. Dr. Wilbur successfully integrated all sixteen personalities and Flora published the book *Sybil* in 1973.

• • •

That year, I received the book from Flora at John Jay College of Criminal Justice, City University of New York, where I began teaching. At a faculty orientation Flora strode over to me. She was enveloped in a cloud of smoke which emanated from the cigarette she ground between her teeth. Her flamboyantly-printed dress was covered in ashes. Her eyes were particularly captivating with one eyelash jetting off to her left. I later learned that she regularly had the eyelashes applied by a cosmetician at Saks Fifth Avenue. Her hair was puffed up in a sweeping 1970s style. It was often washed and coifed by a stylist on Gramercy Park. She never washed it herself.

Introducing herself, Flora said, "I think that it's important for us older professors to meet the new ones. I'm Flora Rheta Schreiber. I'm in the Speech and Theatre Department and the Director of Public Relations."

I replied, "It's nice to meet you. I'm Patrick Suraci and I'm in the Speech Department also. I was lucky to get the position based on my experience as a professional actor. Now I'm working on my Ph.D. in Psychology."

"Oh!" she exclaimed. "You'll be interested in a book I wrote about Multiple Personality Disorder. It's called *Sybil.* Come to my office and I'll give you a copy."

Discovering that we were neighbors on Gramercy Park paved the way to our blossoming friendship and to my first contact with Sybil.

After reading the book, I was fascinated; Sybil became flesh and blood for me, not merely a case study. Flora told me about Sybil's new life as an integrated person. I imagined the new Sybil teaching art and painting. I was intrigued by Sybil's continuing association with her therapist Dr. Wilbur. What kind of relationship was it?

Also, my scientific curiosity was aroused by the book. Was it completely factual? I knew that Flora had altered situations and changed names to protect people. Was the essence of the case preserved? Years later I witnessed Flora's dedication to research when I worked with her on her next book, *The Shoemaker*. I saw first hand how she disguised certain facts to protect the anonymity of people while keeping the essence of those facts. Her dedication to writing the truth about unusual human behavior was also evident in her book *Sybil*.

Shortly after meeting Flora, a scathing review of *Sybil* appeared in the Book Review in the Sunday edition of The New York Times. Even though the reviewer was a psychiatrist, he objected to Flora's writing about the abuse perpetrated by Sybil's mother. He failed to understand the importance of tracing Sybil's Multiple Personality Disorder to its genesis. If the case history of Sybil's illness did not include the abuse from her mother, heinous as it was, it would not have been a valid and complete research study.

I was upset over this senseless critique. How could one comprehend this extreme dissociation of a personality without understanding the underlying causation as uncovered by the therapist? I was in a quandary over calling Flora to extend my sympathy. I decided to wait until I saw her before I expressed my dismay over the review. Although hurt by the uninformed criticism, Flora put it into perspective by recognizing how difficult it was for most people to accept such cruel behavior from a mother toward her child.

This difficulty of acceptance was reiterated in an Abnormal Psychology class that I taught for police officers at the 6th Precinct in Greenwich Village. Upon the occasion of Flora being the guest speaker, some of the officers brought their wives to the class. Flora was eloquent in answering their questions about the case.

During the discussion, one of the officers who had brought his wife asked Flora how she could say these terrible things about Sybil's mother. It had become unbearable for him and his wife, the mother of his children, to hear about these atrocities committed by Sybil's mother. Flora explained to him that she had to report that behavior in order to fully explain how Sybil's personality fragmented into the various alters.

Embarrassed by my student, I attempted to apologize to Flora over lunch after the class. She took the student's objections in stride, realizing the impact that seldom reported child abuse had in the 1970s.

Neither my student nor *The New York Times* review was able to keep the book off *The New York Times* Bestseller List. It is still in print with over six million copies sold.

Eventually the public and the psychiatric community became more knowledgeable about child abuse. In 1994 the American Psychiatric Association published the *Diagnostic and Statistical Manual of Mental Disorders, Fourth Edition*, changing Multiple Personality Disorder to Dissociative Identity Disorder stating that the major cause is "severe physical and sexual abuse, especially during childhood."

• • •

I was constantly amazed by the remarkable recovery and accomplishments of Sybil, despite the atrocities and damage caused by her mother. This compelling story was portrayed in the TV movie written by Stewart Stern. Authenticity was provided by Dr. Wilbur as consultant. I went with Flora to meet them when it was being filmed in New York City. On a summer evening we found ourselves on the set in the subway station under Carnegie Hall.

Dr. Wilbur was a tall, trim and vivacious redhead. She wore a colorful dress, platform shoes, and big earrings, reminding me more of a Miami Beach matron than a Park Avenue psychiatrist. She was assisting the film director, or rather, exuberantly expounding to the director. A crew member looking at Dr. Wilbur said to me, "Can you imagine being distraught and going to a psychiatrist's office and finding her!" Dr. Wilbur's behavior on the set was contradictory to her therapeutic manner during the taped sessions with Sybil, which I heard. During those sessions her manner was warm and compassionate, often calling Sybil "sweetie" and "honey." After years in my own therapeutic practice, I came to appreciate that same difference in my own behavior. Constantly monitoring my behavior in service to the therapeutic relationship with patients caused me to behave more aggressively in my everyday encounters with non-patients.

In the Russian Tea Room, Flora and I met Stewart Stern, who displayed a thoughtful, calm, and serious demeanor. He was courteous to us while he poured over his script.

Sally Field was attempting the nearly impossible task of recreating Sybil. That night, they were filming the scene of Sybil getting sick in the subway. Ms. Field sat quietly knitting until it was time for her to act. After shooting the scene we had a chat about New York. She said that it was the first time she had been in the subway, having grown up in California. Joanne Woodward was not filming that night. However, after attending the ballet, she graciously came to the subway station in order to pose for a publicity photo with Flora.

Hoping that Sybil might be on the set, I was disappointed by her absence. Flora told me that Sybil couldn't risk being identified.

When they filmed the scene in the subway car filled with extras, the director asked Flora, Dr. Wilbur, and me if we would like to be passengers. Although the air-conditioned car was freezing, Flora, shivering in her chiffon gown, leapt at the chance. Flora and Dr. Wilbur sat in the subway car until 4 a.m. Being a true New Yorker, Flora thought she would read a book, as many people do on the subway. After the first take the director screamed, "Flora what are you doing?!" She replied, "I'm trying to blend into the crowd by reading." The exasperated director spouted, "You can't sit there reading the book *Sybil*. It hasn't been written yet!"

My desire to learn Sybil's identity was fulfilled when I became concerned about preserving Sybil's painting. I took it to be reframed. When the framer removed the old frame, I saw "Shirley Mason" written on the inside of it. I snatched the frame from the hands of the startled man and gasped, "I have to keep the frame." I took it home and quickly erased the name and destroyed the frame. I had done my part in preserving the anonymity of Sybil. Her identity would not be revealed by me in spite of inquiring reporters and tabloids offering considerable amounts of money.

Despite knowing Sybil's identity, I resisted the temptation to contact her. I knew that as long as Dr. Wilbur was alive, Sybil had a benefactor. When Dr. Wilbur died in 1992 I became concerned about her. What if she were alone and in need of help? Did anyone know her identity besides me? Did she have any relatives or friends? If she had a relapse, would anyone know how to treat her?

Although most of my time was occupied with my patients, I was haunted by the specter of Shirley Mason. She had been a part of my life for the past twenty years. Having taught my students about Multiple Personality Disorder by using the book about her life, I felt a personal attachment to and responsibility toward Shirley Mason. Yet, Ms. Mason did not even know of my existence.

I agonized for months trying to develop a plan for contacting Ms. Mason without upsetting her. I knew only that she was seventy years old and living in Lexington, Kentucky. I worried about her perceiving me as an aggressive New Yorker. I thought I might soften my approach by introducing myself and sharing some background. I would explain that I'd been raised in Rochester, New York, (I later learned that she was born near Rochester, Minnesota), I'd attended Catholic schools and that I had a strong desire to do the "right thing" by preserving her anonymity. Obviously, I was floundering and in danger of regressing into a pool of fear, which would prevent my contacting her. There was no failsafe method of reaching out to her. A letter might be too impersonal and it could be thrown away without a response. I thought that a telephone call, hearing my voice, might convey my sincerity and concern for her. Calling her in the afternoon seemed the best course of action. Early in the morning might disturb her and later in the evening might frighten her.

On December 1, 1993, at 2:38 pm, with perspiration dripping from my upper lip, tension constricting my chest, and my pulse accelerating, I touched the telephone numbers 606-268-3304.

CHAPTER 1

A Moment of Fulfillment

As I listened to the ringing of the telephone, I rehearsed what I was going to say. Knowing that Flora Schreiber and Dr. Cornelia Wilbur had been fiercely protective of Shirley's identity, I wanted to introduce myself in as non-threatening a manner as possible; I didn't want her to hang up before I had a chance to explain why I was calling. Shirley had never appeared on any television show nor granted any interview in an effort to live as normal a life as possible. I was worried that she might misinterpret my good intentions about her well-being, since they were tempered by my scientific curiosity about her psychological state. I was prepared to help her in any way that I could, but I had also always wanted to conduct a follow-up on her case to discover if she had maintained her complete integration. However, no matter the cost to my clinical investigation, I didn't want to invade her privacy and make her feel as if I were examining her in a laboratory.

A fragile, gentle, soft voice answered, "Um, hello." I couldn't believe I was going to talk to this woman who had occupied my thoughts for the past twenty years.

I gasped, "Hello, is this Ms. Mason?"

"Yes."

"This is Patrick Suraci in New York. I'm a friend of Flora Schreiber."

"Yes."

"I was just wondering how you were doing."

Fearfully she asked, "Are you a reporter?"

"Oh, no. I was a good friend of Flora's. I taught with her at John Jay College and we lived next to each other on Gramercy Park. I'm now a psychologist so I was wondering if you need anything. I'd be glad to help any way I can."

"That's very kind of you."

"I thought that since Dr. Wilbur has died that you might need some help."

Again, she suspiciously asked, "Are you a reporter?"

"No, I promise you I'm not. I'm only concerned about you and wish to offer my help if you need anything. I've always been concerned about Sybil since I read the book. And Flora always gave me information on how you were doing."

"What makes you think that I am Sybil?"

"After Flora died I received the painting that Sybil made for her. It's hanging in my office. A few months ago I noticed that there were some streaks, maybe water marks on the painting. So I took it to be reframed under glass. When they took off the old frame I saw your name written on it. I took the old frame home so no one could see it. I had Flora's address book, so I found your number. I was worried about you and so I called."

"Well, I'm all right. I have retired, of course, so I don't get out too often. I have my house and garden to take care of. So that keeps me busy."

She sounded composed and cheerful—a remarkable contrast to the tortured woman I remembered from the book. I was touched by her apparent enjoyment of life.

"Do you have any friends you can call if you need anything?"

"Oh, I have friends from the church who visit me."

"What church do you belong to?"

"I'm a Seventh Day Adventist."

I was shocked to learn that she had returned to the religion of her childhood—the strict, dour religion which had provided fertile ground for the blossoming of her mental disorder. Evidently, she now derived something positive from this church in Lexington, Kentucky. She had found dependable friends. Perhaps this branch of the Seventh Day Adventist religion was more nurturing than the one during her youth in Dodge Center, Minnesota.

"I'm happy to hear that you have friends, but may I call you once in a while to see if everything is okay?"

"Since you're a friend of Flora, it would be nice to talk with you. It has been lonely since Connie [Dr. Cornelia Wilbur] died."

"I miss Flora too. She was a good friend. Did you ever see her obituary from *The New York Times*?"

"No, I wasn't able to go to the funeral. I had the flu at that time."

"Would you like me to send it to you?"

"Oh yes, I would like that."

"I have a story about the obituary. Would you like to hear it?"

"Sure."

"Flora died on Thursday morning, November 3, 1988, just before she was supposed to be discharged from the hospital. Her doctor called me with the news and I said, 'How could it happen, when you were going to discharge her?' He said, 'Well, we couldn't predict that she would die.' I could see that she was going to die, but he couldn't. She always hated doctors."

"I know that she did. She would never go to a doctor when she got the flu or anything."

"I was so angry with the doctor, but I knew I had to fulfill Flora's wish about her obituary. New Yorkers say that you are not officially dead until you're dead in *The New York Times*. So I had to call the newspaper. I got a young woman in the Obituary Department who did not know who Flora was and never heard of the book *Sybil.* I told her that Flora had written several articles for *The New York Times* and that there probably was an obituary on file. The woman couldn't find anything. I called Ralph Blumenthal, a reporter for *The Times*, whom Flora had known. I asked if he could get them to write an obituary for her. He said he would try."

"Later that day, a man from the Obituary Department called and told me to give him the information immediately so they could print it the next day. If I couldn't do it at the moment, he couldn't guarantee that it would get in the paper if someone 'more famous' died within the next few hours."

"Isn't that something!" exclaimed Shirley. "Flora was so dedicated to her writing. When she was interested in a topic, she researched it to death. She made sure that she knew it thoroughly and if she didn't know a particular aspect of it she would find an expert who did know it. She wouldn't give up on it, but kept at it until she had the answer."

"That's right. That's why I knew I had to get them to mention her books in her obituary. Fortunately, I had a break between patients and I had a copy of *Who's Who*, so I read him Flora's biographical sketch."

"It's a good thing you were able to do that for Flora," said Shirley.

Then, I read Shirley the obituary from *The New York Times*:

> *"November 4, 1988*
> *Flora Schreiber, 70, The Writer of 'Sybil' and of 'Shoemaker'*
> *By ANDREW L. YARROW*
>
> *Flora Rheta Schreiber, the author of "Sybil," a best-selling book about a woman with multiple personalities, and "Shoemaker," a portrait of a Philadelphia murderer, died of a heart attack yesterday at Beth Israel Hospital in Manhattan. She was 70 years old.*
>
> *Miss Schreiber, a professor of English and speech at John Jay College of Criminal Justice, first gained renown with "Sybil," her 1973 case study chronicling the life and psychoanalysis of a woman with 16 clinically distinct personalities. The book became a best seller and was turned into a two-part NBC television movie in 1976...*

> *...Like "Sybil," the new book by Miss Schreiber provoked considerable controversy. After "Shoemaker" was published in 1983, she was sued by the family of one of Kallinger's victims under a so-called Son of Sam law in New Jersey that required that money owed to a criminal or his representatives as a result of his crimes go to the victims. A Superior Court ruled that not only the 12.5 percent promised to Mr. Kallinger but also money earned by Miss Schreiber and her publisher, Simon & Schuster, be paid to the victim's family.*
>
> *Publishers called the ruling a violation of First Amendment rights of free speech, and an appellate panel reversed the decision.*
>
> *Before teaching at John Jay College, Miss Schreiber taught for many years at the New School for Social Research and at Adelphi College. She specialized in children's speech and wrote a 1956 manual for parents called "Your Child's Speech."*
>
> *Miss Schreiber had no immediate survivors."*

Shirley said, "I know she spent a lot of time and money on that book. She was always worried about Joe Kallinger, always talking about him. That book seemed to bring her a lot of problems."

I replied, "She went through a lot with Kallinger. Every day, she accepted two or three collect telephone calls from him in prison. The terrible thing about the obituary was the ending where they claimed: 'Miss Schreiber had no immediate survivors.' At the memorial service, which her cousin and I prepared, Helen Vogel, the executrix of her will said, 'We are her survivors.'"

"I would appreciate a copy of the obituary. What did Flora actually die of? I knew she had cancer."

"It was reported that she 'died of a heart attack'. She did have cancer, but only a few people knew that. She was afraid of a publisher discovering her illness and then not giving her a contract to write her next book. It was sad at the end. The cancer affected her brain. She became disoriented at John Jay College and someone called me. I took Flora to the doctor and he said that she could no longer teach. She was able to stay in her apartment with assistance from aides and friends. One time she was in the bathtub and couldn't get out. Judith, her neighbor, called me. We let the water drain from the tub and then I climbed into it and lifted Flora. Judith held her as I maneuvered Flora's legs out of the tub."

"Oh, that must have been so sad for you to see Flora deteriorate like that."

"Especially since her whole existence was based on her career as a writer and teacher. But there were some funny moments also. I would write out the checks for her bills, rent, etc. and she would sign them. Well, we ran out of checks and Flora could not remember where she had put them. I searched the apartment. Finally, I had to go to her bank to get new checks. The bank vice-president called Flora to get her permission to give me the checks. Flora said she didn't know who I was. I had a few minutes of anxiety trying to convince the vice-president that I was not trying to steal Flora's money."

"That was a delicate situation, but now you can see the humor in it."

"I finally found Flora's checks in an Indian brass container that was similar to a footstool in her bedroom. I didn't even realize that it opened. When I found the checks Flora said, 'Of course, I put the checks there. I put all my important papers there so no one will steal them.' She would have been a good mystery writer."

"She was funny sometimes. How did you meet Flora?"

"It was serendipity, as Flora liked to say. I never thought about teaching. I had been an actor living in Rome when I met a professor from John Jay College on one of my return trips to New York. He was the director of the Speech and Theatre Department. I had just read a fascinating article in *The New York Times* about the college doing the play "Detective Story" using real detectives since it is the college of criminal justice. The professor asked if I would like to be in a play sometime, because he liked to use professional actors to give the student actors a sense of the professional theatre. When I decided to return to New York to pursue my doctorate in psychology, I agreed to be in the college's fall production of "Spoon River Anthology." After that I was offered a teaching position. At a faculty meeting I met Flora and she gave me her book *Sybil*."

We remarked how certain major events dramatically change the course of a person's life. I didn't tell Ms. Mason at that time how I felt that this event, my meeting her, was now leading me to an important turning point in my life.

I told her that I had the copy of *Sybil* which Flora had inscribed to me and that I'd also send her a copy of Flora's inscription. Fortunately, Flora had not inscribed it until a couple years after giving me the book. By then she knew me better and wrote a touching inscription. It reads:

> Flora Rheta Schreiber
> Jan. 13, 1975
> To Patrick, who is a good friend, a good colleague
> and a great human being. With all my good wishes
> in all possible fulfillment in all things.
> Love, Flora.

I knew that Shirley Mason would recognize Flora's inimitable style and handwriting and hoped that it would bear witness to my friendship with Flora and give credence to everything that I had told her.

The call lasted 19 minutes. I was pleased that Shirley had given me the opportunity to engage her in conversation. I was happy to discover how articulate she was. She appeared to be well adjusted, except for the mild paranoid thinking that I might be a reporter. From my experience doing psychotherapy with police officers I learned to reserve judgment about paranoia. What a naive therapist might think of as paranoia was often reality in the police department. In Shirley's situation, she had to be extremely careful with strangers who might be prying into her life.

During our conversation, I felt a rapport with Shirley. Had she responded to me in a friendly way or was it just wishful thinking? I was convinced that Shirley was Sybil even though she had not confirmed it. I now had a secret, and a great joy, which I could not share with anyone but her. Inherent in my discovery I felt a responsibility to prevent any harm from coming to her.

I wanted to maintain contact with her because I liked her, and also because I wanted to find out if she had been cured of Multiple Personality Disorder. Although I had seen great improvement in many of my patients, I was always cautious about dramatic cures with such extreme disorders. I had learned to be cautious from my sister, who had Schizophrenia and improved over the course of her life with new medications, but was never cured.

Hoping to cultivate a friendship, I asked Shirley during my next telephone call if I could visit her in Lexington, Kentucky. I said, "There is a conference in Lexington that I'd like to attend. I could come to visit you if you would like."

She said, "That would be nice. Although, I don't have too much energy these days."

I replied, "I'd be happy to visit you for just a few hours."

"That would be okay."

I was excited over the prospect of actually seeing her. I had conjured up an image of her and was anxious to see if she matched it. She agreed to a visit on December 17th. I made reservations on American Airlines and planned to stay at the Hyatt Hotel, which was not far from her home on Henry Clay Boulevard. As the time approached, Shirley said that she was not feeling well enough for a face-to-face visit, but that she would like to continue to visit over the telephone. A profound disappointment overtook me as I realized I had rushed the situation and expected more than she was ready to give. The elation I had felt from our initial conversation had evaporated.

Fearing that I had jeopardized any possibility of developing a friendship with Shirley, I thought it best not to impose upon her with any more telephone calls. However, Christmas was approaching and I wanted to convey my good wishes that she have a joyful holiday. I sent her a Christmas card. This could be my final communication with her.

CHAPTER 2

Building Trust

How would I convey my concern for her? How could I let her know how special she was to me? Should I tell her that I admired her courage in persisting in therapy knowing first hand how difficult that process is? How could I reveal my twenty years of thinking about her, when Shirley didn't know anything about me? What could I say to her in our next conversation?

After debating the pros and cons with myself, I decided to put aside my personal disappointment and try to create a bond with Shirley in case she might need my assistance in the future.

I knew I had to call her again. I wanted to gain her trust. That would be paramount if I was going to have a friendship with her. Always concerned about maintaining her anonymity, it seemed that Shirley limited her friendships. Would I be one of the fortunate few to enjoy her friendship?

I wanted to call her on New Year's Day in 1994, but I had a sore throat and fever. Not feeling up to par, I decided against it. In the book *Sybil* Flora had written that Sybil was born on January 20th. I knew that this was not the correct date, but I assumed that it must be close. I decided to call her on January 21, 1994.

After a couple rings Shirley answered, "Hello."

"Hello, Ms. Mason, it's Patrick."

"Oh, how are you? I've been wondering about you."

Hearing her friendly concern, I was greatly relieved. I replied, "I'm okay. I was sick around New Year's, that's why I didn't call sooner."

"I'm sorry to hear that. So many people have been sick here."

"Have you been okay?"

"Oh, I just had a little cold. But it was nice to have visitors for Christmas. Did you go to see your family?"

"Yes, I went to Rochester for Christmas to see my mother and sister. I try to get there every Christmas, since my father died in 1980."

"I bet they were glad to see you."

"I have a big Italian family. My mother always expects me to be there. I try to get home as often as I can because it's hard for my mother taking care of my sister—she has Schizophrenia." I felt that I had to be as open as possible with Shirley. I wanted her to feel free to be herself with me and in turn I wanted to reveal myself completely to her.

"That's so sad. It is a terrible illness. Is she in the hospital?"

"She has been hospitalized several times and had all the treatments, even electroshock therapy when she was first diagnosed. But she has been able to stay at home with my mother. The new drugs have helped keep her out of the hospital, but she still has hallucinations."

"Does she remember what happened during the hallucinations?" Her question was poignant because of her own "lost time" during the periods when one of her alternate personalities took over.

I said, "When she first got sick, she didn't have any insight into her illness and would not remember the times when she hallucinated. She didn't think that there was anything wrong with her. But as the years have gone on and with different medications, she seems to be more aware of her hallucinations."

• • •

It's frightening not to have control over our thoughts. Sometimes we may have unpleasant thoughts, but we can stop them by deliberately focusing on something else. If we're conscious of what's going on in our mind we can do something about it. But when we are not aware of what's transpiring mentally, we're helpless. Shirley Mason knew this from her own experience. When an alternate personality came to the foreground, Shirley retreated into the background and actually blacked out. The alter used Shirley's body and voice, but Shirley had no knowledge of this unusual occurrence. Only after years of therapy did she discover this phenomenon.

• • •

I didn't want Shirley to think that I was only interested in her mental status and previous therapy.

I asked, "Do you have a birthday soon?"

"On January 25th I'll be 71."

"Congratulations. That's an accomplishment these days."

"I never thought I'd live to be this age."

"You sound so alert."

"Oh, I've still got all my marbles, but sometimes I go into the kitchen and I forget what I went in there for."

"Don't worry. I do the same thing at 58."

Not well enough to venture far from her house and her garden, she appreciated our conversations. I was grateful that I could give her some enjoyment and was also grateful for the pleasure she brought me.

Shirley talked about the weather, taking care of her garden, the music she liked, ordinary things that were precious to her in the second half of her life. It was inspiring to know that she had made such a remarkable recovery. Often my patients, knowing that Sybil's painting hangs in my office, ask if she had recovered and maintained her integration. When I tell them that she did, they are encouraged that they too might be able to overcome their neuroses.

Shirley told me how she loved the trees and flowers in her yard in Lexington, Kentucky. I told her of the magnolia trees in Gramercy Park. She told me that hers were different; they were white with a strong perfume.

On February 13th I called Shirley to tell her about the publication of a letter I had written to *The New York Times* in response to an Op-Ed piece about a book written by Harry Kondoleon, who was hospitalized with AIDS.

I said, "The author wrote: 'Psychotherapy for the terminally ill is a little like a pedicure right before having both feet amputated.' Just after reading that article one of my AIDS patients came for his therapy session. He shoved the newspaper into my hands and said, 'What is the purpose of coming for therapy when I'm going to die.' I replied, 'Okay, you tell me why you're coming for therapy and I'll write a letter to *The Times*.' I sat at my computer and wrote what the patient said and then later added my own thoughts to it. Here is part of the letter that I wrote:

> As a therapist I appreciate black humor about the shortcomings of psychotherapy. As a human being, I hope Mr. Kondoleon is jesting. Today, a patient...started his therapy session by commenting on the column:
>
> 'After I read that I wondered why I was coming to therapy. I am going to die, so what is the point?'
>
> I told him that was a good question and asked his reason for coming.
>
> 'I want to learn about myself and grow. I want to live my life as fully as I can. Even if I get sick, I think I would still want to come and talk about dying. That would help me to go through it.'"

Shirley said, "That is a beautiful letter. Connie always said that you can learn so much from the patients. You have to really listen with your mind and with your heart to see what the patient really needs. Therapy gave me a new life."

Although she still had not told me that she was Sybil, she spoke as if she had.

She continued, "I would think that therapy helps those poor people deal with AIDS. It's sad to see such young men and now so many women and babies die from it. I think that you can be an important part of their lives and give them hope."

I thought of the hope Dr. Wilbur had given her. It was a revelation to Shirley when Dr. Wilbur told her that she had a condition that could be treated. Up until that point Shirley thought that there was no help for her.

I said, "I try to be realistic about hope. There have been so many advances in the treatment of AIDS that I do believe the future looks better."

Shirley reminisced, "Connie always believed in giving patients hope. She felt that there was always some improvement that could be made and it didn't do any good to be pessimistic and negative."

"I agree. Some patients have been at death's door, but when they have hope they have come back to life."

She said, "I believe that only God can pick the time for us to go."

Shirley's belief in God now gave her strength to deal with her cancer, which I had not known about at that point.

One winter day, December 9, 1997 at 4:36 p.m., I was speaking with her as a thunder and lightening storm raged in Lexington. She joked about her house being blown away. Suddenly, the line went dead. I tried to call her back but the phone did not ring. I waited a few minutes and tried again with the same result. I waited a half hour before I phoned again. Dead.

At 5:05, I called the Lexington police and told them that I was a psychologist for the New York Police and asked if they would check on Shirley. They were most accommodating and said they would send a police officer to check on her.

At 6:02 p.m., I called her, and the police had just left. She said that she was surprised by a police officer who came to her door. She joked about the neighbors thinking that the police had come to arrest her. She appreciated my concern for her, but made a request: "If anything happens to me and I'm unconscious please do not call the police. They would take me to a hospital. I don't want that. I want to die at home."

I hated thinking about her dying alone. However, I realized that Shirley had accepted her illness and was prepared to die when God called. She wanted to be surrounded by her paintings, books and plants. She wanted to have the beauty which she had created as the backdrop for her departure from this world. I promised her that I would respect her wishes.

After four years of telephone conversations, Shirley's trust in me culminated in her decision to give me the original Sybil paintings. She and Dr. Wilbur had planned to write a book about these paintings. They had hoped to show how children's artwork could provide information which could aid in detecting childhood disorders. However, Dr. Wilbur had a stroke and Shirley wasn't able to complete the project.

The following is an excerpt from a taped phone conversation of January 8, 1998, when we discussed my writing a book about her later years:

Shirley answered the phone, "Hello?"

I said, "Hello, Shirley."

"Hi, Patrick."

"How are you?"

Shirley said, "Well. Just thinking about you."

"Yeah, I've missed talking to you too."

"I was sitting here with all this Sybil stuff. Dee was here this morning and I had her go into the art room closet and haul out these boxes, and put them in here where I've got one on the table and one on the footstool and one on the end table, so I can reach over and take out some and go through it. But it's an awful lot of stuff. Are you sure you want it?"

"Oh, yes. Absolutely. I'm really honored to have it."

"It's every one of the 198 paintings and who did them. And now the pictures are numbered."

"So I'll be able to find it all. That's great."

"Yeah. Now there's 198 of them that's left. I know a few of them deteriorated terribly and so I just destroyed them because they were in chalk and they rubbed and they tore and the paper was thin. But anyway, it's all in there…But I warn you, it's a big thick thing...But I'll send it and you can do what you see best…Have Dee do it up and send it…Then, also with it, I have a few photographs of the paintings…I'll enclose those, and a list of paintings. And then the big book, with the slides in, has somehow eluded me. I can't find it. And I know that it's here…And I looked at the Sybil things, and I looked in Connie's things, and I can't find it, but it's got to be in the house somewhere."

"Eventually you'll find it."

"The last year or so, I could not put things back. I'd get something out, and I couldn't get the drawer shut or open or whatever, and so I've got things stacked…And Dee set out to look for it…Now, there's a complete set of slides numbered 1 through 198 and they're all in order and everything that I find I'll send …I have a projector and screen and all that, but I don't have a way to get that to you."

"No, that's okay. That's too hard."

"But I'll send the essential things, and then, following that, I will send you the paintings—the originals—but I'm going to divide them. I was puzzled about sending that big package, and I think the best thing to do is to sort them by sizes and send them in separate packets, so if anything happens it won't happen to all of them at once."

"Okay!"

I was dumbfounded and didn't know how to express my gratitude for being given Sybil's paintings. They had played such an important part in her therapy and recovery.

Shirley continued about the paintings, "And that will be a little later. I don't know, a few days or a couple weeks at best."

"Whenever you get around to it, that's all right."

"I'm getting at it as quickly as I can…So the thing is, if somebody wanted to do an update that didn't include my identification."

"I would like to do that for the psychological value of it, what you've done."

"I think that would be kind of nice, because I think that people need to know that it can be done."

"It's so helpful for the patients to realize that there's hope."

Shirley agreed, "It was one of the big things that people would write to Connie about—new patients. 'Did she stay well?' 'Did she stay integrated?' But there never was even the slightest indication of sliding back, or any flicker of another person, or anything. It surprised me. I thought, you know, under stress—And there were times. Once I had a very serious automobile accident. Various things that happened could have triggered something and never did. And so it was solid. And I'd like people to know that.

"And the other thing, of course, what interested me the most about doing this book was for people to realize that you can analyze children's drawings and learn something about them in view of children with multiple personalities. I've always been a great advocate of getting problems at an early stage. I think that covers those things, but you can do whatever you want with any of the material as far as I'm concerned…Anything that would help anybody."

I said, "If I could write about your life after the book, *Sybil*."

"Oh, that would be great."

"I would be willing to share any profit with you."

She replied, "No, I'm not asking that. No, I want that to go to scholarships…Not that I'm that flush with money, but that's what this is all about, I've given away most of the *Sybil* money. I don't want to profit from that…You can still do it without my permission…"

"Oh, I wouldn't do anything without your permission."

"You don't absolutely have to. You know, after I'm gone, if you wanted to do something that you hadn't thought of before, it's perfectly all right, just as long as my name is left out. Because that was Connie's wish…" (Unfortunately, about eleven months after this conversation, Shirley's identity was revealed in *The New Yorker* magazine.)

"Okay. I'll talk to my agent and see what form of a book or something like that that we could do."

"That'd be great…I've got a couple of people mad at me because I'm sending these things to you instead of them. A number of people have been vying for it for a long time. And I just didn't give them. It was a selfish thing and it was just not the right time."

"Well, I would try to fulfill your purpose, to educate people, to help other people with it..."

"Well, if you just deal with it, it would, I think, automatically become part of your thinking, and your treatment and so on, and it will be all right. Don't worry about it…Well, it should arrive sometime next week…"

"Okay. I hope you feel better. I just hate when you have that pain."

"Well, it'll be better. Usually tomorrow is better than today."

On the day that the first two packages arrived, I called Shirley. The phone rang for a long time before she answered it.

Shirley said, "I was afraid you'd hang up before I got here." She was breathing heavily.

I asked, "Are you okay? Catch your breath. I have good news."

She said, "I was in the kitchen heating some spaghetti up. I didn't want to leave it on the stove, so I tried to get it off in a hurry."

I said, "Don't worry. I'll always let the phone ring a long time before I hang up. I wanted to tell you that the mailman just came with the packages. I'm opening them right now. I'm so excited."

Shirley said, "The one I sent second really is the important one. It's the one with the most tape on it. It's got the big black book of slides in it and a list of the paintings."

I said, "Everything is in good shape."

"Oh, that's good. I was so afraid they'd throw the box around and burst it open that I put a lot of tape on it. For two or three days, I would get a sponge and a dish of water and the tape and scissors and I'd cut a strip and paste it on, and after a while, I'd go back and paste a couple more," she laughed.

"You did a good job. There's a lot of tape."

"Well it held. That's the main thing. It's hard to know how much tape to put on, the way they handle things. I didn't want it to burst open."

"I'm opening the second box now. Everything is in great shape."

"There are some photographs in there. I put your address inside the box in case it got destroyed."

"I see the white envelope with my name and address. Here are the photographs. They're wonderful."

There was a photograph of her when she was going to Columbia University while undergoing analysis in New York. She posed by her painting which won the college student competition at The National Arts Club on Gramercy Park. What a surprise it will be for the members of the club when I tell them that they gave the award to Sybil! (This photograph appears in the Appendix C.)

There were two "Alpine Brand Tablet, White, Vellum, 2 Ply Bristol, 12 Sheets, 5X7" notebooks. On the front was written "Drawings by Peggy Lou" (one of Sybil's alters). The charcoal drawings were exquisitely detailed heads of African-American men and women. Rebelling against her mother, who told her that she had "lips like a Negro", which was printed next to her self-portrait in the book *Sybil*, Peggy Lou drew *beautiful* African-Americans. Also, there was a drawing of windows, reminding me of Peggy Lou's penchant for breaking glass. (These drawings appear in Appendix A.)

I said, "Thank you so much. I said an extra prayer for their safe arrival."

"That did it."

"You packed everything so well. Here's the black book."

"That's the list of pictures and who did what. And the size and all. It just doesn't have the numbers. I have to give you a list of the numbers. The numbers are on the back of the paintings along with the titles, so you'll be alright eventually, but I want to send you a list with it on there."

"Here are all the slides. Oh, they're wonderful. I can't thank you enough."

Shirley laughed, "Well, you better wait 'til you start going through that stuff before you thank me. I spent hours and hours on that stuff. There's about five times more than anything called out because it's copies of the same things. I have a lot of other copies of the same prints and the same slides. There's a pack of envelopes with brown cardboard at the end of the box. Those are the negatives of the slides of the paintings. There are several of each one and then there's one little print showing what it is. I've got more of those little prints that I'll send you."

I said, "This envelope says 'Sybil Exhibit'. Each envelope contains one or more negatives and one small print of the painting listed. Is that it?"

"Yes. Now that's the only set of negatives there are."

"Okay. I'll treasure these."

"The slides are made from that and also the prints."

"Everything is in such good shape."

"But until I can get you a list with the names and the numbers together, it's not going to make a whole lot of sense. I mean, you won't know which painting is which. But I'll get it to you. Dee only comes twice a week and there's too much to do in a couple hours with the housework and things, there's too much."

"Ok. Well, you just take your time with it."

"But it will get done."

"How are you feeling today?"

"Today was a good day. I got around this morning and I did the dishes and watered the plants. That's a lot for me to do all in one morning. I have a lot of plants all over the house."

"Did the nurse come to change your bandage?"

"Yeah. So far, they've decided not to come twice a day, which pleased me because it's just too much for me."

"But do they think that once a day will be enough?"

"Well, the nurse who was here today thought so."

"Do you change the bandages at night?"

"No. I can't reach them. They are below my knees. The nurse who comes in the middle of the week is the one who wanted them to come twice a day. The one who comes on Mondays and Fridays is the head nurse, so she has the call. So it's up to her, and she'll be here tomorrow. Then I'll know for sure. She said there are several patients who have the same thing. And she said it's just the same problem with all of them. She said they just don't heal. And she said that some are caused by congestive heart failure and some by other reasons but she said they go on month after month. They've got inquiries out in different places to see if anybody else has any ideas or suggestions. They talk to pharmaceutical people to see if any of the salesmen knew of any new products. I've got three or four different things on each leg. Different kinds of spongy-looking stuff, and some cottony-looking stuff. They've got names like 'Soft Sorb' and 'Allevian' and so on. And then they bandage the whole thing afterwards with a tight, rubbery kind of bandage that they use on horses. They've got brown—I don't mind the brown wrapping, but when they use that royal blue, Kentucky Blue, everything is Kentucky Blue here, you know. I said, 'Well, maybe the horses like it, but I don't' (she laughed). One day they ran out of the brown, so they did one in blue and one in brown. Of course, that's the day that my doctor and his wife came for a Christmas visit. They got a big kick out of that. I said that I was making a fashion statement. And she said I looked like a Christmas Day wrapping. They wrap all this with padding so it can absorb all this moisture, and so they're huge. She said that I looked like I was going to play ball—stickball or something. I thought, there are times when I could give someone a kick, but I wouldn't say so."

"You've got to have a sense of humor. So, you look like a hockey player. Well, you never know—that might be your next profession."

Shirley laughed, "Oh, my. Oh, my."

CHAPTER 3

The Invisible Person

Shortly after the book was published, while riding on a bus, Shirley gazed out the window. Suddenly, a bookstore appeared that was filled with the *Sybil* book. Startled, Shirley quickly looked around at the passengers to see if anyone recognized her. Did they know that she was Sybil?

She hurried off the bus and pondered going into the bookstore. She braced herself and entered. Picking up the book she thought that the drawing of a woman's fragmented face was striking, even though it looked nothing like her. The title *Sybil* blazed in orange-red letters with a smaller white subtitle: "The true story of a woman possessed by 16 separate personalities." She was stunned by the realization that this phenomenon had actually happened to her. Silently, she thanked God that now she was well.

She attempted another test of her anonymity. She brought the book to the salesclerk, who merely glanced at Shirley and then rang it up. She knew that she was safe, but that her life from that moment would never be the same. She could never risk revealing her identity because the consequences might be devastating.

"How did you react when the book came out?" I asked.

"It kind of startled me. Eventually, I got over that. But to be places and have people sit around or stand around talking about it—sometimes they'd ask me what I think about it. I'd be very guarded and I wasn't comfortable."

"Was it too soon for you to hear about it?"

"Well, it wasn't that. I didn't want to be identified. I was afraid I'd say something I wasn't supposed to know. I'd go with Connie to conventions where they exhibited my paintings. People would comment on what they thought was the meaning. Sometimes they were right, but sometimes they were wrong. They never knew who I was. They never thought that Sybil would be right under their noses with Dr. Wilbur. They thought I was her assistant. It was interesting to be in the background and hear what they said about me."

Shirley sent me the brochure of an exhibit of Sybil's paintings which were sponsored by Merck Sharp & Dohme at an American Psychiatric Association convention in Chicago. The brochure stated that they were "privileged to sponsor this interpretive exhibit in association with Cornelia Wilbur, M.D [who stated]: 'One of the main purposes served by the use of spontaneous artwork in the therapeutic process is that of unconscious revelation. What was going on under the surface of Sybil's paintings and the drawings. Many times these served to initiate a subject, a fear, or a memory that needed to be dealt with in the healing process of analysis.'"

This exhibit traveled to New Orleans and the Philippines.

• • •

Shirley said, "I had to leave my job and move and everything when the book came out." She took such extreme steps to prevent being identified as Sybil.

During her analysis Shirley had taught art at Falkirk Hospital in Central Valley, New York. The hospital had been founded in 1889 as Dr. McDonald's House; it was known for new approaches in the treatment of mental illness. This tradition was carried on by Dr. Charles Pilgrim, who purchased the hospital in 1920 and retained ownership until it closed in 1988. Unknown to most people at that time, Shirley was also undergoing an innovative treatment—psychoanalysis for Multiple Personality Disorder. After receiving her M.A. in art at Columbia University and her completion of therapy, she taught art at a public school in Memphis, Michigan and later at Rio Grande College in Ohio in 1969 and 1970. Once the book was published, Shirley was financially able to purchase the house on Henry Clay Boulevard in Lexington, Kentucky, where Dr. Wilbur was teaching at the university.

Attempting to erase clues to her identity she said, "I changed and moved so I couldn't be tracked down, but I was anyway."

Surprised to hear this I asked, "What do you mean, you were tracked down?"

"Shortly after the book was published in 1973, this newspaper writer in Minneapolis decided to run down and find out who Sybil was. So he went to some places there [Dodge Center, Minnesota] and he got my name and he doggedly kept at it. Oh, it was just a terrible thing. But anyway he got hold of it and he put an article in the *Minneapolis Diary*. There was a picture of the house where I was born [in Dodge Center]. And he interviewed some people in the town that I went to school with. My fifth grade teacher.

"And the lies. Oh, the whole thing was awful. And you know the way he gathered his information. I had no idea what was going on. One day a woman called me here at the house and she said she wanted to know if this was Shirley Mason. I said, 'Yes.' And she said, 'Well, my name is Shirley A. Mason too, and I'm on Route such-and-such. And they keep getting our mail mixed up. I wondered if you happen to have any of mine? I sent yours on.' So I said, 'No, I haven't had any trouble.' And she said, 'Well, is your middle name Ann?' And I said, 'No.' And she said, 'Well, what is your middle name?'

"Well of course, Ardell is an unusual name and I was stupid

enough to tell her. Because she was a private detective. Next thing I knew, she was out here in the street taking pictures of my house. And they went to the little town where I was born. My birth date was changed in the book, but only by five days. The year and month were right. And so they just looked on either side of it and of course they found my name. And so they put that in the paper. But fortunately there weren't any repercussions except that a few people in Minnesota, who knew me, wrote to Connie. They asked about me and she denied it. She worded it so that what she said was the truth, but, you know, one of those kinds of situations where you mislead people.

"And so nothing came of it except that I was so panicky, because it could have spread. The reporter thought that he was going to make a name for himself by making the identification. And it was just fortunate that the people up there, they're not like they are in some other cities."

I said, "They protected you."

"Yeah. The reporter went to a number of people that I knew, all the years I was growing up. He went to interview them and they wouldn't have anything to do with him. 'No comment. No comment.'"

I asked, "Did he find the boy Danny in the book?"

"He's a friend and we grew up together. We were just an identifiable couple. As kids we were always together. Now he's a professor at the University of Minnesota. He told me that they contacted him and he said, 'Don't you ever call me. Don't you ever mention that name to me. That is none of your business.' He would have nothing to do with it.

"Not like one of the aides when Connie was sick, twenty years after the book was done. She said, 'While I'm working here I'm going to find out who Sybil is, or else.' Well, of course, she never did."

I said, "I remember Flora saying that someone had almost tracked you down."

Shirley told me that she had found out from a neighbor that the reporter, pretending to be the minister from her previous church, called the house next door to her. The reporter said, "She used to be so thin. Is she still thin?" The neighbor said, "No, in fact, she's round."

Shirley said, "Of course, that wasn't true. I wasn't thin, but I've never been round in my life!"

The reporter continued, "I understand she has nine cats." The neighbor said, "She only has three cats."

Shirley angrily said, "She was just so willing to say everything. But the lawyers from the newspapers wouldn't let him use any of that material.

"Then the reporter called me and said, 'We saw when you left the house this morning. We know what you're wearing and who you're with.'

So Shirley devised a plan to elude the reporter. She drove her car to the airport, knowing that he was following her. Unbeknownst to him, Dr. Wilbur also drove her car to the airport to a designated exit there. Shirley parked her car in the airport parking lot and walked into the terminal carrying a small suitcase. Walking around the airport and keeping an eye out for the reporter, she headed to the designated exit. When she did not see him, she darted out the exit and into Dr. Wilbur's car.

"I ducked down in Connie's car and went home with her for a couple of days. It just shook Connie to the core, because she had worked so hard to keep this thing secret and she was worried for me and everything. But we lived through it. So I have just a little bit of an idea what it must be to have the paparazzi on your neck."

I said, "That was so awful. Well, I'm glad you made it through that one. You'll get through anything after that."

"Yeah, that's what we figured. It was a pretty good test for what Connie had done for me. We figured the analysis was a success."

After Shirley died, I went to Minnesota and interviewed Shirley's cousin Patricia Alcott and her childhood friends, Betty Borst Christensen and Wilma Volberding Bode. They spoke of Shirley's reserve and her demure behavior. They remembered her as always being polite and never causing any disturbance. Shirley's behavior was in stark contrast to her mother's extroverted behavior.

Even in her youth, Shirley tried to blend into the background. An example of her timidity was revealed in a conversation during a snow storm. Shirley and I talked about sledding in our childhood.

She said, "I was never that fond of it in the first place. We kids would just go up and down the road. And if you hook on behind a sled going by or something—it's dangerous."

"You had big hills?"

"Yeah, but I wasn't reckless. I was a cautious child. I wasn't about to get hurt. Of course, I never had enough energy, either. I was anemic all those years. I had a little heart trouble, so I'd go out and play, and I couldn't jump up and run. I'd get dizzy. I had to get up slowly. So I was careful. I didn't risk. But the boys—they'd run with their sleds, put them in front of them, and then slam down on them."

"That's scary."

"Yeah. But the snowballs, oh I was deathly afraid of snowballs! One of my classmates lost an eye from a snowball and another one had a severe head injury and had to have spinal surgery. This snowball business is serious. They're like rocks. You rub them hard and get them wet and cold. They're like ice balls. Oh, I used to be scared."

I remembered about her mother's wild sled ride when they lived in the "chicken house." One of Flora's critics claimed that Shirley and her parents never lived in such a place, because he could not locate it. He stated that Flora's description in the book was not true. When I met Professor Daniel Houlihan of Minnesota State University at Mankato, we located the property where the original "chicken house" existed. (See Appendix H.)

In addition to the ordeal of a reporter discovering her identity, Shirley's integration was further tested by another traumatic experience. A lawsuit was brought against the book by a shop in Philadelphia. Shirley had to remain the invisible person and depend on Dr. Wilbur and Flora to settle the suit.

She recalled, "Then I had another scare over losing my house. The lawsuit against the book."

In the beginning of the book *Sybil* dissociates and Peggy Ann emerges and flees from Columbia University to Philadelphia. She goes to a shop and buys pajamas that are "loud and gay." In reality she had bought them from a department store. The editor didn't want Flora to use any real names. So Flora made up the name of the shop. Unfortunately, there was a real shop by the same name which sold flowers. The owner, claiming that people who read *Sybil* came to the shop looking for "gay" pajamas, sued the publisher. The lawsuit blocked the money from sales of the book for a long period of time. This caused distress for Flora, Dr. Wilbur, and Shirley.

Shirley said, "Wasn't that ridiculous? The whole thing was so stupid, but we had to pay them to end it. The pajamas were actually stripes. It was a nuisance suit that would be thrown out of court now. And they held up our money for the longest time. I had purchased this house and I thought I was going to lose it. I didn't buy it until I had the money, and then I had to send back $125,000. I had to get a loan and wait months and months for them to return the money.

I knew that Shirley had not received much money from the television sale of the book. On two nights in 1976, NBC aired the television movie "Sybil." Although it was a huge success, Shirley, Flora, and Dr. Wilbur received less than thirty thousand dollars each. I asked Shirley what she thought about the script written by Stewart Stern, since it was somewhat different from the book.

She replied, "Stewart Stern is a wonderful writer."

I asked, "Were you pleased with the script?"

"Yes, I was, by and large. I was. The writing. The thing is that he had no control, well, not much control, over what was in it, and they insisted on certain things being in there that never happened."

I added, "The boyfriend."

"Yeah. He represented something—a couple of things. This was all right out of my childhood. And it was the scene where I was in the apartment with them and so on. That kind of thing never happened and I didn't like it. And I just hate, at the beginning—Sybil's standing out there in that pond. And nothing like that ever happened. Nothing ever happened when working with children."

"No?" I questioned.

"In fact, I wasn't working with children when any of it happened. That all came after. Well, I hated that.

"And the publisher, when Flora did the book, the publisher insisted there be a romantic interest in it or the book wouldn't sell. And I insisted absolutely not. I said I had friends and I said I was engaged at one time, and so on; but I said nothing happened. I get so worked up over that, well, anyway because it wasn't true. If it isn't dramatic enough for you the way it actually was, leave it alone."

Shirley continued, "And I would not sign permission, you know, for it to be done if they did something like that. And then the same thing came up again when we—and Flora, herself, said, 'Well, there's gotta be some romantic interest.' And I said, "Well, there wasn't, so leave it alone.

"It was not one of my big problems. It wasn't a problem. The problems that I had had nothing to do with sexuality at all. And they kept trying to bring it in. It wasn't a true picture of the patient, or the condition, or what went on. And that would be misleading. One reason it took me so long to get help was that the different ones that I went to for help would try to start right off with sex. And I wasn't the least bit interested. At that time I was too bad off to be interested. And I was extremely immature, because of my childhood. I couldn't grow up. I couldn't get beyond those childhood problems. But boy, Connie was right on the mark."

• • •

Having learned that she was once in dire straits and almost lost her house, I asked in our taped telephone conversation on January 14, 1998 how she was able to maintain her anonymity when she received royalties from the book.

She replied, "I used my company name which is Mason Arts, Inc. all the time. And all the royalty checks, everything, made out to them. And then I sign it that way. Nobody ever has my name on anything. Now some of these papers and slides that I'm sending you—I'll let you know the particulars I think you need to know. I keep Dee informed all the time as we go along so she knows I'm sending you these and why and everything. So she would be the person to contact if I'm no longer around. She'll have charge of Mason Arts and then whatever royalties come into that, she will disburse according to what I asked her to do, rather than putting it in my will what I wanted done with it. And because I trust her completely. She and Don Frei would be your contacts. But I don't see any problems at all with anything. But you might be challenged whether you own these things or not.

"And the ownership of the paintings always remains with the artist. It's all set up for Dee to handle. But if you own them, I guess it would go to you. I'll have to get that worked out. I'll ask my lawyer, Don Frei, about that."

"I hope it isn't too much work for you."

"Well, it's not. It's just that I don't want to leave any loose ends that would cause anybody any trouble."

Unfortunately, there were "loose ends." Shirley died one month later. Her wishes were not carried out. The Sybil paintings which had played such an important part in Shirley's analysis were never sent to me.

• • •

Although I was disappointed over not receiving the paintings, I was comforted knowing that Shirley had a full life after treatment with Dr. Wilbur in New York. She was elated when she discovered that Dr. Wilbur was in New York because she felt that she could engage in meaningful therapy. She could also be invisible among the millions of people in New York City. Often, her odd behavior was not interpreted as bizarre in light of the many other eccentric people in New York. I asked about her analysis with Dr. Wilbur.

Shirley said, "The intensity of it in New York—I went every day."

I said, "And then you were also going to Columbia University?"

"Yeah."

"I don't know how you did both."

"The worst thing was that cross-town bus trip twice every day. I tell you, the way people there rush to get on and off the buses, you gotta watch your footing or you lose your balance."

"That's incredible. The worst thing was the cross-town bus?"

"Yeah, it's very taxing. I lived in the dormitory in Whittier Hall at Columbia. I'd stand out in all kinds of weather over there by the Hudson River waiting for the bus. Of course, the first two or three or four would be full and go tearing right on, and Connie was over on East 78th Street. And then getting back was a different route, and that was another set of problems."

I said, "When that wind blows off the river, you could freeze to death."

She replied, "Oh, it was cold. I didn't miss a session. I was always there. Sometimes I was half frozen to death, and then in the summer, it was all the heat. And all the mob and everybody pushing to get on the bus. Oh!"

I laughed, "That was the worst part of the treatment! That's good—I love that!"

"That was my shock treatment," she added.

• • •

It's a struggle for most people to discover and accept their true identity, even with therapy. Once they have a sense of themselves, then another conflict is presented. They have to reveal their self image to other people. For Shirley it was just the opposite. She had revealed herself to others in bits and pieces of her personality. Then she discovered her identity through the integration of all those bits and pieces, her alters.

One of her alters was Marcia, who painted in grays and blues to express her depression. Peggy expressed anger by painting objects that had been used by her mother to hurt Sybil. Mary painted scenes depicting her longing for love from her family and neighbors. (Shirley sent me a print of Mary's painting called *The Neighbors.*) It took years of therapy, probing and uncovering her emotions, for her to be aware of her complete identity. Once she had been fully integrated, Shirley had to project her new self-image to the world. She knew the dangers of revealing that she was Sybil, so she had to be a newly evolved Shirley. She had to learn how to interact with the world in a new way as one complete identity.

Her art was one way. When she was painting, she could express herself using her name, Shirley Mason. She no longer had to fear revealing her emotions. Another way was as a dedicated art teacher, which sustained her throughout her life. Even after she retired she kept up a correspondence with many of her former students. This provided her with a pleasurable connection to the outside world when she could no longer leave her home due to her advanced cancer.

During her analysis, Shirley made a painting for Flora. It is the one I described in the Introduction. Since Shirley never had a photograph of that painting, I sent her one.

In a letter to me dated January 13, 1997, Shirley wrote:

> Dear Patrick,
>
> I appreciated your beautiful holiday greeting and I thoroughly enjoyed your letter with interesting photos enclosed which came last summer. This letter is my 'delayed reaction.'
>
> So many friends and former students have written to me that I wish I could answer them all—I keep picking away at the stack, but it is slow going and I don't make much headway, I'm afraid.
>
> The painting doesn't look the way I remembered it, but it is mine. My style has changed a great deal since those years. I still enjoy painting when I can—am limited in energy especially, but am full of ideas and enthusiasm anyway.

Only a couple of people know the reason for my limitations but I would like to tell you so you'll understand why I haven't written sooner—or more often—as I have enjoyed your friendship and our phone visits.

About a year and a half ago I found out I had inoperable cancer which had not been bothering me much until then. Later, it spread to lymph glands causing swelling, etc. in my left arm and more recently to my brain causing occasional visual disturbances and a couple of light strokes which caused some weakness in my right arm and some speech problems for a while. The latter has cleared up for now, so I am trying to catch up on things I neglected for several months. The longer I write, the more I scribble! Sorry!

I don't know what next but then one never knows *that* anyway, I guess. I have my home fixed up the way I like it and am happy and contented here. I have everything I need so what else could one ask at my age?

Thank you for the photos and your letter. I know you are busy. I hope you are well. May 1997 be a good year for you. Always, Shirley.

I replied:

January 21, 1997
Dear Miss Mason:

I was so happy to receive your letter today. My heart and prayers are with you. You are very courageous. I thank you for telling me about your cancer. Please let me know what I can do for you. I treasure our friendship and enjoy speaking with you on the phone. If you feel like talking will you please call me collect on my private line. The number is ------------. There is no answering machine on that number and if I am not working I'll answer the phone. My office number is ------------ which has an answering machine. If you would like to leave a message you may call that number.

Your handwriting is beautiful. I got a chuckle out of your modesty over it. You should see how my handwriting deteriorates over the course of a letter. I can't even read it myself. That is why I am typing. When I was in grammar school in Rochester, N.Y., the nuns taught us the Palmer Method of penmanship. I wrote with a straight pen and even think I once received a prize. During the course of a day now I am writing notes, etc., and I do get weary. My assistants still have trouble deciphering it.

Although it is difficult for you to answer all your letters, it must be gratifying to know how many lives you've touched and what an important part you have played in the lives of your students. I received a call the other day from a student I taught at John Jay College fifteen years ago. He saw me on television discussing my book [*Male Sexual Armor*]. He said that the public speaking course he had with me has helped him in his career. That made my day. There were often moments when I wondered if I was getting through to the students and if it meant anything to them.

It is wonderful that you have ideas for future paintings. I think it is important to keep the creative juices flowing even if you are not able to execute the ideas now. I look forward to seeing more of your work.

The fact that you are able to be content in light of your medical problems shows the strength of your spirit. I sometimes get frustrated dealing with the meaningless aspects of my work—the insurance companies. But then I try to remember that it is for the benefit of the patients that I have to deal with the insurance companies. I hope that you have not had any problems with your insurance. Let me know if you have and I will be glad to help you with that. I have learned how to be firm with them and get what one deserves, since they are trying not to pay benefits.

I went to Rochester to see my family for Christmas. My mother is 83 and having memory problems, but she is still able to care for my sister who has Schizophrenia. My sister is taking Clozaril, which has been very helpful in controlling her hallucinations. I have a cousin, Carol Ann, who is a nurse in Rochester and I employ her to look after them. We have to live one day at a time, and thank God for what we have today. I know that you are able to do that.

Your friendship is special to me. Please let me know if we can speak on the phone. My thoughts and best wishes go out to you for 1997.

Fondly,

Patrick

It took several years of shared telephone conversations, beginning in 1993, before Shirley admitted she was Sybil. Now she confided in me. She did it simply and directly. I was struck by the irony of her having brain cancer. Would future research show a link between brain abnormality and Dissociative Identity Disorder as it has with Schizophrenia?

Shirley told me she also revealed her brain cancer to her cousin Naomi. She hoped one day I would meet her. Shirley spoke glowingly of this cousin on her mother's side of the family. After Shirley's death I contacted Naomi and we met when she and her husband Jim were attending a conference in New York City. Immediately, I felt a kinship with them due to our mutual love for Shirley.

Upon their invitation, I visited them in their home. Naomi showed me many items Shirley had sent her. Among them was a letter in which Shirley revealed her brain cancer in 1996. Shirley wrote:

> My writing is so poor, hope you can make it out. I start off quite fairly, but soon deteriorate in form...I've had inoperable cancer for several years without much distress. But last spring it spread to the lymph nodes, with swelling and pain in my left arm, and possibly to my brain more recently. I've had several vision disturbances, some loss of sight, and a couple of light strokes, with weakness in my right arm, during the summer. So writing letters, although high on my priority list, just didn't get written. But I still think of all of you often. I wish you'd convey my love to the girls and all, and tell them I will write. I just don't know when.

In December 1997 Stewart Stern, the screenwriter of the TV movie "Sybil", was coming to New York with his wife Marilee, who was having an exhibit of her art at a Soho gallery. Shirley expressed disappointment at not being well enough to attend. I wondered if she would have risked being discovered as Sybil had she been well enough to come to New York.

She wanted me to go in her place. When she communicated this to Stewart, he was concerned about me preserving Shirley's anonymity. Shirley told Stewart, "If he's never told anybody, he's not going to now. At this stage of my life, it doesn't make that much difference." I told her that I would be pleased to attend the opening.

Shirley said, "Now getting back to the exhibit, Roddy McDowall is going to be there. He's playing Scrooge. I wish I could see him. I got a picture postcard from Roddy—a picture of him as Scrooge. He used them for Christmas cards—in his nightcap, and holding a candle, and you know those piercing eyes, he's got, and he had a long, grey, scraggly hairdo. I told one of my friends that I looked a lot like Scrooge myself. Looked at myself in the mirror, all bent over and everything. They tell me that as long as I have a sense of humor, I'm alright. I'm basically a happy person.

"And Joanne Woodward will be there. Joanne and Roddy were absolutely marvelous to Connie. They wrote to her and sent her pictures. Connie, of course, adored Roddy. She loved him from way back when. And Roddy sent me the nicest note when Connie died. So if it should happen to come into the conversation he knows me as Shirley Mason. He doesn't know I'm Sybil. So if you could tell him I appreciated the note."

The next day, December 16, 1997, I called Shirley.

"Hi, it's Patrick."

"Uh-huh. How are you?"

"Okay, how are you?"

"Oh, I'm not very good right at the moment."

"Pain?"

"I wanted to get some medicine."

"Okay."

"I had kind of a rough day."

"Oh, dear."

"The nurse says it's the cancer spreading. The back problem is the main pain and I take pain pills for that. Makes me drowsy. Oh, I had company this morning and yesterday."

"Wears you out?"

"Well, I'm on my last legs."

"I just wanted to let you know that I went to the gallery. I saw Joanne Woodward.

"That's nice."

"Marilee was lovely, explaining her work. That was very interesting."

"The hardest thing in the world is to explain your work, because those are feelings."

"And I saw Roddy McDowall. He said he had spoken with you.

"Yeah, he's wonderful."

In the past, Shirley had accompanied Dr. Wilbur to see Roddy perform in plays and had spent delightful times with him. She first met him during her analysis with Dr. Wilbur in New York City.

• • •

Toward the end of her life Shirley had to make a decision about revealing her Sybil identity. She told me that Stewart Stern had called her with a request from a television program to do a follow-up on Sybil. He told them that he would contact Sybil.

"He called me," said Shirley. "Flora and Connie were gone. And I'm half-gone. So Stewart didn't know who Sybil was at that time. I told him to give me a couple days and I'll get in touch with Sybil and see what I can do. But they wanted to have her in it to bring it up to date and really show people that there was such a person. It was not Connie's wish that anything should ever go public. She was willing enough to tell people what had happened to Sybil and give them a little rundown about how she had stayed well and was able to teach and do things. That was the extent of it. She wouldn't tell anybody even what state Sybil lived in.

"So I told Stewart no. It's my life and it's too much to face up to. I'm just not able. I may sound alright and everything. But I just couldn't take on something like that."

Although Shirley managed to live on her own since Dr. Wilbur died in 1992, she never quite recovered from taking care of Dr. Wilbur. While maintaining her own home, she had moved into Dr. Wilbur's home for six years. She ran the household: arranging for nurses, paying bills, etc.

• • •

After Shirley died, I asked Naomi why she thought it was important for her to keep the secret of Shirley's identity.

Naomi replied, "Oh, I think it was absolutely. The fact that it was so important validates the character of Shirley, that she was more concerned about her own peace, privacy, happiness and wellness and her family's not being hurt in any way, hounded by anybody, by their reputation being tainted in any way. Her heart was so magnanimous towards the people she loved the most, which was her family."

I informed her, "I know the National Enquirer contacted Flora telling her they would give a huge sum of money to Sybil if she would grant them an interview."

"Oh, she had no desire for any of that. That was not within her realm of desire in any way. She enjoyed her life, and she loved her family. She would not allow this book or this movie to be done until it was promised that her identity would never be revealed."

"She could have gone on television and become famous," I reminded her.

"She was not that kind of person," emphasized Naomi. "I think she was thrilled to be well. She had no need for any notoriety. I think she moved on, was no longer a multiple personality person. She didn't want to dwell on it. She certainly did not want to be seen that way by her friends and relatives. She didn't want to be treated differently because of that."

• • •

In spite of having the added stress of preserving her anonymity, Shirley led a productive life. She continued to paint and sell her paintings in galleries in New York, Kentucky, Florida, and elsewhere under her true name—Shirley Mason. She was an exemplary art teacher who gained respect and friendship from her students, an active member in her church and community, a loving relative to Naomi and her family, a devoted friend to Dr. Wilbur: evidence of her complete recovery.

CHAPTER 4

Life With Her Rescuer

Psychotherapy can be a lonely business. If successful, a therapist and a patient form an intimate bond. The patient reveals intimate details and the therapist processes those events which then become a part of the therapist's life. Shirley understood this process very well. When she told me that she wanted me to have the Sybil paintings, she said they would become a part of my thinking and my work and lead me in the right direction.

Eventually, therapy ends—successfully or unsuccessfully. Often the patient and the therapist never see each other again.

During the course of therapy a patient may reveal her innermost thoughts to the therapist. On the other hand, elements of the therapist's life can only be revealed if they play a part in helping the patient to heal. Everything that the therapist does must be in service to the patient; the interaction must be therapeutic for the patient, not the therapist.

The word therapist can be divided into the words "the" and "rapist." Some may see therapy in that light. They feel that the therapist may "rape" them in the sense of violating their mind; the patient may view the therapist's probing into areas which the patient had blocked with thick walls of denial and repression as a "rape." Ideally, the therapist must recognize when it is therapeutic to persist in exploring a topic and break through the patient's resistance. However, the therapist must also recognize when not to force the patient to reveal what the patient is not ready to reveal. The patient may feel that she is submitting to this probing against her will. The idea of therapy raping, robbing the mind of creativity and spontaneity, is vividly portrayed in Peter Shaffer's play *Equus*.

An element that is important to successful therapy is transference. Transference refers to positive or negative feelings that a patient develops toward her therapist. Shirley developed positive transference to Dr. Wilbur during most of her analysis. Understandably, there were difficult moments when she questioned Dr. Wilbur's motives or developed resistance to Dr. Wilbur's probing.

Counter-transference refers to the therapist's feelings for the patient. Dr. Wilbur's positive feelings for Shirley were manifested in her caring behavior. Her therapeutic technique of mothering Shirley was unorthodox but proved to be effective in facilitating her integration.

During the time of her therapy, Shirley revealed her positive feelings for Dr. Wilbur in a letter:

> Dear Dr. Wilbur, Hi! Hope your trip is proving to be lots of fun and that the evening at Antoine's will be special, too. I've been thinking about you and wondering if you found time for the golf you missed this summer—(an English friend of mine calls golf "a long walk punctuated with disappointments"—I hope you have better luck!) Our little heat wave has turned to 60° weather, so for a few days now we've been energetic again. Louise drove over yesterday and asked Willie and me if we'd like to see the ocean—course we said yes! We went to several places of interest and ended at Jones Marine Beach.
>
> I was to do a painting—she pounces on the paper,

> chews the brush handles, takes side-swaps at the bristles, tramps through the paint on the palette, then, while I'm in the kitchen washing the brushes she leaves four-toe foot prints on the paper. Big help! And she loves the puppet Willie and I are making—eats the paste every time we look away. Sometimes we think we should have named her the "Spotted Demon" or "Flying Atom" (can she leap)—but, of course we know she is the cleverest, cutest, sweetest cat in all New York! And the most pampered, without a doubt. Well, guess I'd better get this in the mail if it's going to get to New Orleans before you do. Hope you have a really enjoyable time in Mexico. Lots of love, Shirley.

Shirley's positive transference to Dr. Wilbur was also evident in her diary entry of November 27, 1956:

> I came home yesterday and 'painted up a storm' to borrow an expression. I did two Philadelphia street scenes, one abstract, one semi-abstract of leaves, and so forth, and two moody ones based on feelings toward historical sights. I felt like painting in large and sweeping strokes, so I used big paper and a sponge and my largest brushes as backgrounds and therefore everything is too big to conveniently carry anywhere considering I am not making a direct route to your office today. But I would like to show you what I have done and I can later---I am still in a painting mood, so thought I would just wait a day or so and put everything together---I did something else too—first of all---this is different but I HAD to paint it---I just loved the dress you were wearing yesterday and the color with your hair made a perfect assemblage for color combination and I did a little portrait of you before I painted anything else as that was very much with me and had to be represented somehow.
>
> While I painted (with lots of help from Capri, of course,) I played the record player---the ballet music I bought the other day and some Stravinsky ones. I got to thinking about music and some ideas occurred---afraid to think much along any one line of it, but did feel it could be talked about today and now that today is here I still feel I could---and in the light of what you said a couple of times lately, I feel I should get at it---immediately, some other thoughts come in, but that is probably distraction. I have

> some feelings of confusion about those papers and that one painting I brought in and did not discuss much---so I am not sure what is what, but anyway I painted freely enough yesterday---I guess more freely than in months---just did it and enjoyed it and was not concerned that the results were not perfection.

• • •

The relationship between Dr. Wilbur and Shirley did not end with the termination of Shirley's analysis; they remained friends for the rest of their lives. They were constant companions living near each other in Lexington, Kentucky; they traveled together to conferences and shared vacations. Shirley had found the person who understood her best and who cared for her most.

Dr. Wilbur first became interested in Shirley as a fascinating patient, then as a lovable person. When Shirley was fully integrated and the treatment ended, they formed a friendship. As Dr. Wilbur explained to Shirley years earlier, she needed their friendship as much as Shirley did. When Dr. Wilbur's husband Keith Brown died, Shirley was her primary companion.

After the book was published and Sybil became famous, Dr. Cornelia Wilbur felt it was her responsibility to protect Shirley's anonymity for Shirley's well-being. Flora Schreiber, the author, was also given this task. It was a price that they both paid for doing spectacular work.

I said, "It was a miracle that you found Dr. Wilbur in New York."

She reflected, "I had started with her about nine years before in Omaha. Then I didn't know where she was. When I learned that Connie was in New York, I moved there and started therapy with her in 1954."

It took about nine months of psychoanalysis before Dr. Wilbur discovered that Shirley was a multiple. She did this without pressuring her to talk about her sexual or aggressive feelings, even though

Shirley did manifest repressed sexuality and overt aggression. She broke a window in Dr. Wilbur's office. When this happened, Dr. Wilbur immediately reassured her that she still cared for her. Then a second personality, Peggy Lou Baldwin, revealed that she was the one who broke the window. Dr. Wilbur "was right on the mark" as Shirley expressed it, in diagnosing Shirley as having Multiple Personality Disorder.

Although some of Shirley's alters were extroverted, such as Peggy, the conscious Shirley was more reserved. There was early evidence of her desire to not be outstanding or obtrusive.

In later years she told me, "Well, I don't want to be a complaining old woman now and I never was one to talk much about how I felt or anything. I was thinking the other day about when I was in college [Minnesota State University at Mankato], I had impacted wisdom teeth and they got infected and I had to have them all out in a relatively short time. When I had the last one out, I was just about done for. The school nurse came to take me back to the dormitory and we had to stand and wait for a cab to come. There was a counter nearby, and the nurse said, 'Why don't you go over and lean on that counter?' and I said, 'Oh, no, I'm alright.' And the nurse just laughed and said, 'You won't sit down because somebody might know that you weren't able to stand up'. And I guess that kind of stayed with me. I don't like people to know I don't feel well or something is difficult. And no matter, pride or what it is, but weakness is what I always thought it was. But I know better as I get older. Some people cover their feelings and some don't."

I asked, "Did you bleed a long time?"

She replied, "With the first one, yeah. Then they gave me vitamin K tablets to chew to help with that. Of course, I had anemia all my life. If the teeth hadn't been infected, he would have waited two months between each one. But they were impacted, they were up above the other teeth and had to be cut out. In one place, they had to crack the jawbone in order to get the root out of it, and it took quite a long time—it took all morning to do one of them. And it kind of wore a person out by the time they got to the fourth one."

"You had all four done at one time?"

"Well, not at one time. Two weeks apart. He wanted to wait two months, but he couldn't. And the last time the nurse said, 'That's the first time I've ever seen you when you weren't smiling.' And I said, 'Well, if I had one more, I wouldn't have been able to do it'."

• • •

It seemed that once Shirley had worked through the damage from the torture inflicted upon her by her mother in her childhood, she was better able to cope with adversity in her adult life.

In *Sybil* there is a gut-wrenching section in which little Sybil's mother filled her urethra with cold water and tied her to the leg of the piano, forbidding her to let go of any of the water while her mother pounded away at the piano. When the little child expelled the water, the mother had a reason to beat her.

In her later life, Shirley had three traumatic car accidents. They might have caused a relapse, or at the very least Posttraumatic Stress Disorder, but she coped with them in a healthy way.

"One was when I first went to West Virginia from New York so that was in the 1960s—'7 or '8, somewhere there. I was in an intersection downtown here and a young man was on his way to a university class and he was late. He ran a red light. He hit me broadside and spun the car around. I had a heavy car, but it spun the car around and a car coming from the other way hit me on the other side and totaled the car."

"What happened to you?"

"Broke my glasses, that's all. Connie would say I was hung with horseshoes. I never got hurt, but it really shakes up the nervous system."

"Oh, the shock of that!"

"Well, I was on my way to the airport to meet Connie in Florida.

So the police came and they tried to lift his car off of mine, but the cable broke and they had to get another tow truck. I was sitting in the police car with a terrible whiplash in my neck, but I was anxious about getting to the airport. I had my little toy poodle with me and she kept growling at the policeman. I said, 'She just never did that before.' But in spite of her bad behavior, the police took me to the airport, because my car was towed away.

"They had called ahead and held the plane. I didn't know that until we got there and it was the most embarrassing thing. I went through the airport and everybody was looking at me. I never saw such a long walk out to the plane. They must have thought, 'who is this important person they've held the plane for?' Oh dear, it was something. I had to change planes in Atlanta and I had such a terrible headache. I wandered through the airport and couldn't find any place to take an aspirin. All they had were fountains and you can't swallow anything turned upside down over a fountain. I finally found a cleaning lady who found a paper cup for me.

"I finally got to Sarasota where I met Connie. The next day we went to the marvelous big Ringling Brothers mansion. All around the balconies, they had huge woven tapestries from way back, like the thirteenth century or something. They were very exotic, wonderful things. So I was going around holding the back of my head with my arm so I could look up at them. Now I always think of that neck pain in connection with those tapestries.

"Another accident was when I was teaching at the university [Rio Grande University] in Ohio. One afternoon the roads were very icy and I wanted to go home, and get home after school. Somebody had called a meeting about the graduation services so I had to attend. And I did. And then when I headed for home, everything was just ice.

"In that part of Ohio, it's very hilly. And I was going down this long hill and started to slide. I was only going twelve miles an hour. And so I lightly pumped the brakes. I kept going and then I slid. It was a double highway and I slid and crossed the median. And there were tractor-trailers coming from the other way and I stopped at the railing and he couldn't and he clipped the back of the car and it flipped it right over the railing and it rolled over a time and a half on the bank. It stopped on its side, halfway down the bank and there I was. And I didn't know whether I should try to open one door and get out and risk it falling on me, or get out the other door and risk rolling with it. And I sat there a while before I thought and figured it out. Finally, I took a chance on the top and went out that way.

"Went on over it. And of course, down in there, nobody could see me. So I had to manage to get up that icy bank and to the highway, and everybody was, you know, traffic. But of course a pickup truck stopped for me and he took me back to the college.

"It didn't cost me anything financially, but it certainly did emotionally. Connie said that she thought if I was ever going to disintegrate again, it would have been under one of those conditions.

"She and I were on the way to Louisville one night, when she was going to give a speech and it was around six o'clock and it turned so it all was ice. And she had a Lincoln Continental, a heavy car, and it started to skid and slide and it went down and over the bank. It stayed right side up. It just went down over the bank. But she let go of the wheel and grabbed me, put her arms around me and hung on to me. I don't know if she was, well, frightened, of course, but I guess she was scared for me or something.

"And of course the car went down there. But you couldn't get it back. You couldn't drive it out and up. Some really burly looking fellows came along and they all got out and pushed us back up the way we'd come down. We went on. Drove on to Louisville. She gave her speech.

"Eventually I stopped driving because of the crazy things other people did. They'd come in the 'out' way. It says 'out' and they're coming in. Or the wrong way on a one-way street. I thought it wasn't worth it as old as I am, so I quit."

Any of these stressful accidents could have triggered a dissociation if Shirley had not maintained the stable integration of all her alters. During each accident she was always in touch with reality. She was completely able to use her cognitive skills to solve the problems. She had sufficient ego strength to accept these dangerous situations without using the defense mechanisms of denial and repression.

Fortunately, most of the second half of Shirley's life was filled with joyful times with Dr. Wilbur. Some of these were connected with their friendship with the actor, Roddy McDowall. While Shirley was going through her analysis in New York, she met Roddy in the elevator in Dr. Wilbur's building.

Shirley said, "We were both in school. I was going to Columbia and he was studying acting. Because we had classes, we had to go early in the morning. I think his appointment was seven, 'cause mine was eight, and he'd be coming down when I'd be going up. And then we got so we'd smile and nod or say something or other. Then after a while we got to talking. Neither of us let on that we were patients."

"Did he know what you were going through?" I asked.

"I don't think he knew that I was going to see Connie. There were a lot of doctors in the building. He didn't know about the Sybil thing. Later Roddy only knew that I was Connie's friend. When he was in a stage play in Louisville or Cincinnati or somewhere nearby, Connie and I would always go and we'd go backstage. So we were always together. He said, 'Oh, isn't that interesting, you know each other.' And there was Coral Brown and her husband, Vincent Price, and others that traveled with him. And this one particular troupe of *Charlie's Aunt*. Connie knew Coral, so it didn't seem funny to anybody. And of course he knew that I took care of Connie and stayed with her and everything, and I went everyplace with her. She talked about me as her friend. Roddy had a group of friends: R.J. Wagner and Natalie Wood."

I interjected, "Oh, I loved Natalie Wood."

"Oh, yeah, she was a doll."

"So sad, huh?"

"Yeah."

Although Shirley had not met Natalie Wood, Robert Wagner, Joanne Woodward or Paul Newman, she kept up with their lives because they were Roddy's friends. She was especially fond of Joanne Woodward because of her portrayal of Dr. Wilbur and of Paul Newman because of his kindness to Dr. Wilbur.

When Dr. Wilbur traveled, she often stayed at Roddy's apartment. Shirley said, "Once Connie stayed at Roddy's and he said, 'You'll have to use the shower.' And Connie said, 'What are these kittens doing in the bathtub?' He said, 'When your neighbor's cat comes over and has her kittens in the tub, what can you do?' They had to stay there until they were big enough to go somewhere else."

Both Shirley and Dr. Wilbur had a great affection for dogs and cats. Shirley had an Airedale when she was a child. She told me in later years she had a Border Collie, "Beautiful, smart. It was a mixed breed. They're usually smarter, stronger, healthier dogs. You know the pure bred are inbred. They have things wrong with them. I had a poodle, pure bred, and she went blind. Connie had poodles. She had three at one time. So her three and my two and her cat—her Siamese cat and my four cats, we had quite a few animals."

Shirley described her house on Henry Clay Boulevard: "I had a lot of room for the animals. I had a large screened-in back porch and much of the year they could be out there. And I had a place fixed for them in the basement. They liked it down there. Occasionally I'd have one of them in the house part, but mostly they'd live that way. And they seemed to be happy. But Connie's Siamese cat was in the house with her. It was something. Roddy had one and so she had to have one. She hadn't got one yet, but she talked about it. She didn't care much for cats, but when she saw this Siamese, that was what she wanted."

Shirley related the story about how they acquired the Siamese cat. She said, "One Thanksgiving Day, Connie and her husband went to visit his mother in Illinois and I went over to her house to take care of the dogs. I went over and took them out in the afternoon and I got home about six o'clock and it was starting to get dark, November. I came up onto the screened porch and my cats had gone in. I had the door fixed so they could go through. They'd all gone in, but there was one cat on the porch. And I thought it was mine and I said, 'Come on, cat, let's get in.' She jumped down and I realized it wasn't my cat. And I looked and it was a Siamese kitten. I said, 'Hey, you don't belong here.' And I opened the door to put her outside and she turned right around and scooted back in. So she came in the house and I didn't put her in with mine; I was afraid she might have something. She was obviously a stray. There is a school across the street from me and people are always dumping stray animals over there. The kids will take them home with them. So we get quite a number of them over the years. I take them and care for them until I can find a home for them. So anyway this was a Siamese. When Connie got back from Illinois, I said, 'I've got something to show you. Come on over.'

Shirley continued: "She came over and I told her that I found a stray cat on my porch Thanksgiving night. I had it in the art room. Connie went in and said, 'Oh, it's a Siamese.' It was a blue-gray, instead of the brown markings, with bright blue eyes. It was a beautiful, beautiful cat. She wanted that cat. And I didn't, because I had enough. So she took it and named it "Tula."

I said, "What in the world is that?"

Shirley replied, "Well, when she went to Siam, now Thailand, she said she was there giving a series of lectures at the university. And she said the people there were so sweet to her and so nice and so considerate. She said she just fell in love with the place. And the name of the university was Tulalongcorntenarret. So that she wanted to name her cat after that. We called her 'Tula' for short. And I'm telling you, she set out to fix up a room for the cat and it was just like outfitting a nursery. We went to the pet shop and she bought a bed for it, all the cushions and everything. She bought a scratching pad and a food dish and water dishes and toys galore and catnip mice and all kinds of things, and a little sweater. So when we took it home, and she bought a litter box and a whole mess of litter and fixed that up for it.

"Then she had the man that does the yard work make some kind of a design thing that—a wood frame that went up level with the windowsill so it would make the windowsill wider and she could sit on it, and covered it all with carpeting. And she had to crawl around on, sharpen her claws and everything. She kept her shut in that room for a while, 'til she got used to the place, and then she'd let her out into the other part of the house and eventually outdoors. And Connie had a high fence all around, but I was afraid—you know—cats will go anywhere, but she never did. She stayed in the yard, but she just kept disappearing. And Connie would call me at night: 'Can't find Tula.' I'd be in bed and she'd call, 'I can't find Tula. Can't find Tula. Can't go to bed 'til I find Tula.' Because Tula slept with her. So did the three poodles. She had a king size bed and she and all three dogs slept in that bed. And sometimes the dogs would get so close to her, she'd have to get up in the night and go around and get in on the other side of the bed. But anyway, I'd have to get up and get dressed and go over and help look for Tula. And usually, she'd be up on the roof. And of course, we'd have to talk her down. All she had to do was walk over to a tree and come down, but she didn't always want to. And mornings, she would want to get out so Connie'd let her out early in the morning, so when I'd go over there about 6:30 and drive in the driveway, there'd be Tula up on the garage roof looking down. And by the time I'd get in the house and open the double-doors to let the cats and dogs out the back, she was down there with them, running with the dogs. And she was something, that cat. Oh, Connie adored her. The cat lived beyond Connie."

I exclaimed, "Isn't that something."

Shirley continued, "She was pretty old and anemic and we had to keep her in the back of the house by herself. She was never terribly social. She didn't like children or other animals. She'd spit at anything that came near her except my dogs. And she and my dog would curl up together in the big chair. I took a picture of them one time and called it 'Love Thy Neighbor and Keep Warm.' When it was winter, in the chair by the fireplace they'd curl up together in the big chair. She was an experience.

"She was lying out on the deck of the pool one day and a windstorm came up and it blew the neighbor's television aerial down. It was a huge one and it crashed through the fence through the top of the tree and down into the pool. And it grazed the side of her head, close to killing her. So she dragged herself in the house and we didn't know what was the matter with her. We could see she had a slit under her eye and we didn't know what happened 'til we went outdoors and saw the thing and it was where she liked to lie down. It just missed her by—but anyway, she spent the whole rest of the day in the hallway, the back hallway, with her head down and her nose and head flat on the floor. I'd never seen a cat lie that way before, curl up and then just put its head down like that. Expect she had quite a headache. When we'd look at her to see if she was alright, her eyes would dance back and forth. There's a word for it, but I can't think of it when their vision whooshes back and forth, back and forth. And so Connie said, 'Well. she's dizzy. Leave her alone 'til she gets better. And of course, she would only eat gourmet cat food. She didn't like just the regular cat food. Connie said, of course, my cat would have to have the gourmet."

I asked her, "Do you have any cats now?"

She replied, "No. I don't have any. I can't take care of them. It's too hard. I can't stoop and I can't lift. And I miss them. And I miss the dogs. There's no way—I had to—after Connie died. I had an all-white cat that lived over at Connie's with me while Connie was sick. But I couldn't see bringing it here and trying to care for it, already having problems with my health. And so a friend of mine that worked for us for many years said that his friend's mother had lost her cat and she wanted so much to have another cat. So I gave her that one. He told me different times how she'd take care of it and how well they got along...how she loved that white cat. It was a beautiful cat. It wasn't terribly friendly to other people. It was alright with me and it was alright with her."

• • •

Even after Dr. Wilbur had a stroke Shirley managed to bring some laughter into her life.

Shirley said, "Connie had a heated swimming pool and she swam night and morning, all the time, year round. Sometimes she didn't feel much like it, but she was out there swimming anyway. And when she got in her eighties, she was pretty slow, and it took her quite a while to get across the pool and all, but she—she needed the exercise, and of course she couldn't walk much."

"Did you swim?" I asked.

"Uh-uh! Well, I don't like water—I'm afraid of water. And I don't like it, and so I would—of course, she couldn't—she didn't want to go out there alone, you know, it wasn't safe. So I would always go out with her. And so she insisted years ago that I learn to swim. She'd show me how to swim, she'd teach me to swim.

"I said oh my cousin tried that years ago and it didn't work. Well, she had a foolproof way. And she tried to teach me to swim, and she just—it was dreadful. I got a head full of water and I accused her of trying to drown me, so she said, 'I'm not going to give up.' But she certainly got disgusted. So I decided that she was so insistent that I thought, well, I've got to do it, and it was awful.

"And so I went to the sporting goods shop and I bought some goggles, so I could get under, and I bought a thing you put in your mouth and the air tube goes up to the top, and I bought some paddles for my feet and I got padded air things to put on my arms. And I was a sight.

"I had all that stuff and I put it on and I went stomping out and I got in the water. And of course, I could stay afloat, you know, and I'd kick around. And she said, 'Well, if you just kick around and you just push yourself' and then she started, and I said, 'Well, don't! Just stay away from me!', and I stayed in the low end of the pool all the time, and I went back and forth. I just didn't like it. And so finally she let me give up on it and I'd sit out there and read, while she swam.

"Of course, in the winter, she had a big plastic bubble that she put over the entire pool. It was a huge bubble, zipped at one end and you'd open it and go in like a door. So I'd go inside there and I'd bundle all up and I'd go in and I'd sit and read there in the steam while she was swimming. She thought I was something and I thought she was something. So it was mutual. I had to help her in and out. Because the thing of it was that I worried so that if she went under or something, because I couldn't swim to get her. And she got in the deep end and I said, 'If you wouldn't go down where it's so deep,' I said, 'so I could get you.' But no she had to.

"So finally, I decided it wasn't safe for her, and so I refused to go anymore. I told her that I'd see to it that somebody was there. So we hired somebody to come, different people at different times who would come because they wanted to swim and others we paid to swim with her. And there were plenty of girls from the sorority house, her sorority, that loved to swim in the pool at the university but it was always so full and crowded. So they liked to come over there and swim. So we got it worked out and so I didn't have to do it anymore. But I just didn't think it was safe for her because she was pretty weak. She couldn't get up the steps out of the pool alone at all. We had to practically lift her. And she's bigger than I am and I just thought it wasn't safe."

• • •

Naomi told me that over the years she and her husband had many visits with Shirley and Dr. Wilbur. She told me that Shirley, along with Dr. Wilbur, had confirmed that "the book *Sybil* was 100% accurate. Shirley was absolutely an integrity-based person, as was Connie. We were with Connie, oh, many times, we stayed in their homes several times in Lexington. She was in our home."

When Shirley first visited Naomi in New Jersey she was in treatment with Dr. Wilbur.

Naomi stated, "I want to validate Shirley's work and her reputation. But my primary reason is to validate that through the process of psychoanalysis, psychotherapy, faith, love, friendship, and family, this woman became well. And she did not go away from her faith. Rather she came back to her faith in an even stronger way. And because my faith, my spiritual faith, my Christian faith, is so important to me, I want to validate the healing power of God in a person's life."

Naomi and her husband, Jim, saw the progression in the interaction between Shirley and Dr. Wilbur.

Naomi said, "Dr. Wilbur was not warm and fuzzy. However, there was a gentleness in her relationship with Shirley. At the beginning their relationship was that of an older woman with a younger woman. Dr. Wilbur was concerned about Shirley; she was in charge of the relationship. But in the last years that we saw them together, I think there was much more of a peer relationship, a good friendship."

Naomi told me about Dr. Wilbur and Shirley traveling to California and stopping at her home. She said, "When they came here, we took them to my husband's mother's and they had coffee in the afternoon. We introduced them to my brother and sister-in-law and their kids."

"How did Shirley act with these strangers?" I asked.

"Very constant. I never saw her in any way not very socially confident. Certainly not overly extroverted. But she always had something to say. Always asked questions, she might say, 'Oh, that reminds me of when my father visited the area.' She was a good conversationalist."

"Did she ever lose track of what you were talking about?" I asked.

"Oh, I don't think so. I think she was very interested in our new business. We talked a lot about the film. They were on their way to do it. I was pleasantly surprised how healthy she was. I remember having the feeling that there are very few people who knew the story. And it was fun for them to be with someone they could relax with."

"After Shirley was integrated, did she and Dr. Wilbur stay in this house?" I asked.

"No, we lived in a different ranch house."

"Did Shirley and Dr. Wilbur share a bedroom?"

"Yes," said her cousin.

Although Shirley and Dr. Wilbur were close, there was no indication that their relationship was sexual.

Jim added, "I think Connie was proud of her success. Connie went out of her way to let me know that Shirley was all right now. And if there was any uncertainty that Shirley had in a particular situation, Connie didn't step in and solve the problem. She said, 'Shirley, you can do that. You can handle that.'"

Although it is unusual for a therapist and a patient to have such a close, continuing relationship after therapy is terminated, Shirley and Dr. Wilbur both thrived from it.

Shirley's devotion to Dr. Wilbur was demonstrated when she accompanied her to New York City for Dr. Wilbur's husband's memorial. Shirley had not returned to New York since the book *Sybil* had been published. She was fearful of returning to the place of her analysis where someone might discover that she was Sybil. But her devotion to Dr. Wilbur outweighed her fear. After the memorial service she returned to Lexington and remained with Dr. Wilbur until her death.

CHAPTER 5

Remembering Flora

During my first conversation with Shirley, I told her the story of getting Flora's obituary into *The New York Times*. I said I persisted because true New Yorkers say that you are not officially dead until you are dead in *The New York Times*.

I sent a copy of Flora's obituary to Shirley. She appreciated it, since neither she nor Dr. Wilbur had been able to attend Flora's funeral. At that time Shirley had the flu and Dr. Wilbur was caring for her.

Shirley and I agreed that the obituary did not capture the quixotic traits of Flora's behavior—her dead seriousness in expressing her opinion in such a way that others might find amusing.

Shirley shared a fond memory of an incident with Flora. When she was living in New York, she and Flora were going somewhere. "It was only a few blocks, so I said we can walk. Flora didn't want to but we couldn't get a cab. We were walking along the side of these buildings on a side street. There weren't any people around, except a man who was obviously schizophrenic. He was just talking up a storm and gesturing and carrying on and he got behind us. She was scared out of her wits. I said never mind he doesn't see us. We're not real to him. He's off somewhere. She said, 'He might rob us.' And she just stood there. I took her by the arm and pulled her forward and eventually she got her feet working. She said, 'How can you be so calm?' She just couldn't quite comprehend how that man could be that out of it."

Usually Flora did not pay attention while walking or crossing streets. She would be so engrossed in her thoughts that she was oblivious to her surroundings. If she were conversing with someone, then her concentration was solely on her words. Whoever was walking with her would have to hang on to her in order to prevent her from walking into the traffic.

During those years, Shirley often visited Flora and her mother in their Gramercy Park apartment. Flora had offered to share that apartment with her mother after her father died. In turn, Flora's mother doted on her. Between her mother and Flossie, the maid, all the chores were magically accomplished.

Shirley recalled, "She couldn't cook anything. When her mother was sick, I went over to their apartment for a couple weeks to cook for her. I slept on the couch. The doctor ordered chicken soup for her, the broth. Flora asked, 'Where do I find a chicken?' I told her to go to the supermarket and buy a fresh chicken that was cut up. She thought it was wonderful that I knew how to cook a chicken. She wanted to help in the kitchen. I was going to fix some macaroni. So she said, 'I'll get it. Where is it?' I told her that it was in the cupboard. She got out a great big pan and started dumping the whole box of macaroni in there. I told her we only needed two cups, because it expands when you cook it. She said, 'How do you know so much?' Lands, I'd lived thirty years, that's how I knew it."

Shirley laughed as she remembered other situations with Flora's mother. She said, "Her mother used up so many sheets. Flora was taking care of that part of it. She'd take the sheets off the bed and put them in the clothes hamper. The next day she'd say she had to get some clean sheets. She was gone for a while and then she came back with some sheets. The next day the same thing. All of a sudden it dawned on me that she was going out and buying sheets. She had been going to Macy's to get clean sheets. She said that the cleaning woman wouldn't be here until next week. I asked her if there was a washer in the building. She said, 'There's something in the basement. The cleaning woman goes down there, but I don't know anything about it.' So I told her to give me some quarters and I took the bedding and went off. I came back with clean sheets. She thought that was marvelous. She said, 'How did you know how to do that?' Good night!"

Flora never ceased to amaze us with her ignorance of every day activities while impressing us with her knowledge of loftier matters.

Shirley recalled, "She was not practical in a number of senses. She was an excellent writer and brilliant at what she did, but everything else was lost to her. I remember when she was down here one time and I showed her old historic houses. She was fascinated with them. Then we said something about my car. And she said, 'I'm sure it cost a lot. Two hundred dollars anyway.' I had a new Mercury Marquis, a big car. She just couldn't get it.

"I took her one time to Transylvania University, the first college built west of the Alleghenies. (It was founded in 1780.) It's very old and the original log structure is still there. She was so fascinated with all that. And we sat in the park, and she said, 'This is just like it was, sitting in Central Park in New York City. I never got a chance to do that again.' And I thought it's too bad to be so busy that you can't stop and look at the park."

I remarked about Flora's work being her life and how she seldom paid much attention to the beauty of nature. Being oblivious to the mechanics of daily living, which occupies hours in most people's lives, she was able to devote most of her time to writing and teaching.

Shirley agreed, "Of course, that's her mother's doing. She waited on her hand and foot. Flora would come home from classes over at John Jay College, she'd come in, take her cape off, toss it over the back of a chair, pull her gloves off, put them on the buffet. Go through the house like that. And her mother would come along behind her and pick it all up and put it where it belonged. Now when she'd get ready to go the next morning, her mother would go to the closet, take out the cape and put it around her shoulders, tell her to take her umbrella and she'd take it. She was wonderful. She would have been a great character in a story or a play."

We reveled over the eccentricities of our dear Flora, whom we truly missed. We agreed that Flora would have made a great comedic actress, because she was dead serious about doing or saying something that unintentionally was humorous. After studying acting in London, she had an audition for a Broadway play. She stepped onto the stage to audition for the show's producers and director. Instead of reading her lines, she announced that she didn't want to be an actress, but instead was going to be a writer. Thus, she made her entrance and exit from the theatre.

"I have to write about her and capture her unique personality," I said. "A lot of people had the wrong impression of her, even at John Jay College. Some of them thought that she was aloof."

"Well, yeah, she gave that impression, but she wasn't if you knew her. She had a sense of humor."

There was also another side of Flora that others did not know. When my mother underwent surgery for stomach cancer, Flora was genuinely concerned because she was aware of my worry. She wrote a heartfelt letter to my mother before she ever met her.

My mother replied:

> Dear Miss Schreiber,
>
> Thank you for your concern during my illness. It was thoughtful of you to write.
>
> Many friends expressed their concern. I feel as though I know you, too, through Pat. And also through your book

> "Sybil," which I enjoyed very much. Am looking forward to reading your latest one.
> Affectionately,
> Josephine Suraci

Flora's friends knew about her humanity but that characteristic was not readily apparent.

I explained to Shirley, "Her appearance was very imperious and stern."

"Well, she was serious about her work and her teaching. She wanted them to learn what they were supposed to be learning. It was her job to do it and she was serious. If she knew something, she really knew it. She'd research something and she hung on to it. And remembered it."

I concurred. When Flora was writing *The Shoemaker*, her assistant Jim and I would drive her to the jail in New Jersey. Flora persuaded the corrections officers to let her interview Joe Kallinger in a private room with no one guarding her. One night Kallinger told Flora that he liked women with big breasts; he would like to cut up a big breast. Flora fit the bill in that department. Despite my warnings she continued to interview him in private because she knew that he would be inhibited talking to her with an officer standing by.

Though Flora was dedicated to accuracy in her writing, she was not so precise in other aspects of her life. Shirley remembered one instance: "When she traveled for the book, she had no idea where she was going. She said they just would buy her a ticket and put her on a plane or train. She got put out one time. She was supposed to be on the radio live, I think it was Larry King. She was supposed to be hooked up by radio from Rochester and they sent her to Albany. She was so mad at them."

I told her about Flora's travel to Rome to see Montedore, the Italian publisher of *Sybil*.

"I gave her the telephone numbers of my friends in Rome. I also asked her to bring back some lamp shades. She found the store.

The shades were packed in two huge boxes, so that they wouldn't get crushed on the plane. Not speaking a word of Italian, she got a taxi driver to carry the boxes up the one hundred and twenty circular stairs to my friend's apartment. Then she managed to get them on her Alitalia flight back to New York. When she delivered them to me, she said, 'That was quite a project.'"

This conversation with Shirley in January, 1998, one month before she died, brought some distraction from her pain.

I said, "Flora gave us a good laugh to start the New Year, my dear. Are you feeling alright now?"

"Yes, I'm feeling okay and I appreciate your calling, Patrick."

Another time, when Shirley and I were discussing Flora, Shirley remembered an incident that was never included in the book, *Sybil.*

"When Flora was writing *Sybil,* I was taking a course in jewelry making and something was said about using a blowtorch—a little tiny blowtorch to melt the metal to fasten the things together. Flora got it twisted around some way and ended up writing that I was sitting on the bed in my dormitory room engraving a blowtorch. I said, 'You wouldn't have a blowtorch anywhere near a bed. I wasn't engraving it, I was using it to melt metal with.' So she left that out of the book. But once she understood something, she could really sink her teeth into it. She was a wonderful writer. Connie and I just marveled so many times how she could take something that was completely foreign to her one day and understand it the next and write beautifully about it the next. She could do that."

I said, "I always loved the beginning of the book. I felt that she really captured the mystery of Multiple Personality Disorder."

"Yeah," she replied, "I think she did. It was beautiful."

I said, "The reader is wondering what is Sybil doing in Philadelphia, she was just in New York? What's going on? And it's the same thing that I imagine you were feeling."

"Yeah. She took you right along with me. The total time we started 'til it was published was eleven years. When Flora's mother died, she had the breakdown and for two years she didn't do anything. And then we didn't write anything until I was well. We wanted to be sure that was accomplished, and that it was going to hold. We didn't want to have anything go wrong after the book was published. Didn't want to have me have a relapse or anything, that would be very bad—for the public as well as me. But nothing went wrong. When I left New York, she was still working on the book. We moved from New York and I was living in West Virginia. Then I was working at Lincoln State Hospital. After that I got a job teaching over at the university in Ohio. I didn't move because it was just across the river.

"When Connie and I lived here in Lexington, Flora would come down here and stay five, six weeks at a time in a motel and work on the book. Connie and I'd meet with her evenings and so on. But we didn't dare have her come to the house or anything. We didn't do anything that anybody could be suspicious about. We always went separately everywhere."

The three women worked diligently to preserve Shirley's anonymity. In 1973, when the book was published, in spite of the curiosity of the public, no one discovered Shirley's identity. They were fearful of devastating repercussions if such a discovery was made.

Shirley said, "I stopped teaching when the book came out. Partly it was because I didn't want to have to face anything if it should come out. And also I felt that I couldn't get up there and effectively teach with the kids sitting there thinking about that."

Unfortunately, in order to ensure that Shirley's identity was not revealed, Dr. Wilbur and Shirley did not attend the screening of the television movie "Sybil." The premiere took place at John Jay College on West 56th Street, which in 1914 had been the headquarters for Twentieth Century Fox. Jim and I escorted Flora to the screening. Joanne Woodward's telegram of congratulations was read to the audience. The full three-and-a-half-hour film was shown.

This was a very poignant moment for Flora. She had planned to have a career in the theatre, but never pursued it. Instead she spent many years teaching and writing books and articles. To have her book transferred to film was a thrill. At the after-party she glowed amidst the praise of her colleagues. This was her Academy Award.

Flora had attained literary success with *Sybil.* She relished her television appearances on the major shows and the media attention. She had a childlike enthusiasm reflected in her Christmas card with a drawing of the Christmas tree in Gramercy Park and signed, "Sybil, Vicky, et al—and Flora Rheta Schreiber."

While Flora's literary career was a success, her romantic life was not. Her first serious relationship occurred when she was thirty-two years old. She fell in love with Eugene O'Neill, Jr. (son of the celebrated playwright). He asked her to marry him in June of 1950. She wrote: "I said I wanted to wait until the fall—after we had the summer together—until after the Adelphi summer session was over." (She was teaching at Adelphi College on Long Island.)

Flora saved a note that Eugene had sent her on Yale Club stationary:

> Flora Darling—Forgive the pencil. But pens at the club are unusable. Take the 1:00 train to Rhinecliff. I shall meet you on the platform there. Buy a one-way ticket only. Your return will be by P'kpsee. I shall keep the "Montana project" in suspension. Reason? My belief that the idea of your vacationing with O'Neill is incalculably preferable, and is in your mind. The effects on me of your reaction to the Montana idea have become just another bit of evidence that you are the one. I love you! G.

In a second note from the Yale Club, Eugene wrote:

> Darling—This is a little later than the other note. It's a raison d'etre only because at this frantic moment it seems important to reiterate what you know I feel for you, and to tell you that The Big Day will be that on which you explicitly communicate something analogous on your part for me. I love you G.

Eugene told Flora they would have a "court wedding" and she could only have one parent present, since he would only have one. He wouldn't invite his father.

Tragedy struck. On July 1, 1951, after returning from Woodstock, New York, Flora wrote in a diary:

> Gene and I briefly had Paradise. It was when he had to put Paradise on a practical footing that he lost heart. It was then that he began those half-audible mutterings..."I can't do this to Flora...Flora will make me the best wife, but...My poor baby...I can't do this to Flora...I'll pull you down...I'll stand in your way... I'll hold you back, stand in the way of your work. When I first asked you to marry me, I had only one thought: Flora is good for me. Now I have dared to reverse the question and ask: am I good for Flora? And the answer is No...I thought there was nothing wrong with me that a summer with you wouldn't cure. But now I know I am far more deeply disturbed than that."
>
> He loved me intensely, sacrificially, and never realized how much I loved him...I was not uninhibited enough to make him realize this fully... I had too much of the professional air about me...all my reflexes made it seem as though the most important thing in the world for me was my work...and it was until I met him...but my love for him effected a revolution in my values...looking back, anything would have been preferable to losing him...but at the time I don't think I made that clear...
>
> He turned to me as a savior for redemption. He put himself on trial and made me judge and jury and witnesses. And he gave us too little time. His leaving me was an act of renunciation. His turning again to Ruth [his previous live-in companion]..."Ruth is better than death."
>
> And then it was suicide.

Eugene O'Neill, Jr. killed himself on September 25, 1950. He was forty years old. Tragically, in 1977 his younger brother, Shane, also committed suicide.

The curse of depression and alcoholism in their family began with their father, Eugene O'Neill, Sr., who had attempted suicide in his youth.

On September 21, 1951, Flora wrote to a friend, Effie Lewis:

> This has been, for me, a long, dim year, for, when, in your letter you asked the question of whether I was married, the answer is that I came very close. For the first time in my life I was in love—with heart and mind and spirit. But, although we had plans down to the wedding announcements, he lost heart at the end and, Effie, took his life. He drank and came from a tragic line. He gave himself 3 months in which "to reform". Poor darling—poor foolish darling—he was afraid the reform could not go on. "I'll be a liability," he said just before the end...I shall tell you his name—Eugene O'Neill, Jr.—and the story of my brief membership in that tragic family is a story I must someday tell you. If you read newspaper stories of Gene's suicide, those stories were false, deeply, incalculably, injuriously false. In the last months of his life I was his constant companion and only I know the story of those months.
>
> The day your letter came I became an assistant professor at Adelphi. My writing is not yet where I want it...my biography of Wm. Schuman is to appear shortly—but not yet the deeper writing. The deeper writing must come now when I can gather my wits and make memory mellow. One cannot cry out one's agony and present it naked to the world.

Although Flora had a love affair in her later years, she never married. She did achieve her desire for "deeper writing" with *Sybil.*

CHAPTER 6

Memories Endure

Once Shirley completed her analysis she was able to look at her past from a different perspective. She did not dwell on the negative but instead recalled the enjoyable times with her parents. She kept mementos from her ancestors, including some from her mother and father. She might have destroyed them in anger had she not resolved her torturous childhood. In fact, she wanted the memory of her family to be perpetuated with a family tree that she gave to Naomi. Shortly before she died, she sent Naomi boxes of artifacts from generations of her family. (See Appendix C.)

Shirley wrote about some of the articles that she treasured and was sending:

> I hope you can read this. It looks so scribbly. I can't seem to get good control of my finger muscles anymore. Oh, well. And my thoughts always run ahead of me. I have been working on some more of the family items and have another little boxful ready to mail. You will end up with a lot of little plastic bags. That's the only way I can think of to keep the items and my notes about them together. I have a

> third box partly filled with some very old sheet music I hope you will enjoy as much as mother and I did.

• • •

Writing about her mother in an affectionate way was an indication of how completely Shirley had recovered.

In *Sybil* Flora wrote:

> Distressed by those who didn't come to her rescue, Sybil nevertheless invested the perpetrator of the tortures with immunity from blame...Almost two decades later, when Hattie, then on her deathbed in Kansas City, remarked, "I really shouldn't have been so cross with you when you were a child," it seemed sinful to Sybil even to recollect that euphemistic crossness.

Her mother died before Shirley resumed therapy with Dr. Wilbur in New York. During Shirley's therapy she was able to finally express her hatred for her mother. That catharsis enabled her to begin to repair the damage caused by her mentally ill mother. During our conversations, Shirley never expressed hatred or vindictiveness toward her. She only related factual or pleasant experiences with her.

Although little Shirley's father was neglectful, he was not as damaging as her mother. He was, however, a contributing factor to the child feeling unsafe, unprotected, and vulnerable. Yet, Shirley was able to reconcile her father's inability to control her mother's psychotic behavior. He never took his wife for psychiatric help. He turned a blind eye to the physical damage to Shirley's larynx, shoulder, and her limbs. He never acknowledged how disturbed Mattie really was.

In spite of this, Shirley wrote fondly about her father:

> "...I am also including in the third box all of my stamp collection for the children. My albums are just about worn out, but I figured the children have their own, so I just took out the pages to send. I will send more later. I don't want to overwhelm them with so many. Dad and I collected for

> nearly eighty years total, so it seems an endless number of stamps. Some much better than others, but I thought I'd just send them all eventually, and you can sort and/or mete them out a few at a time, or however you see best. I just hope they enjoy them as much as I. It is really a learning experience to deal with stamps. I am so glad to have someone to share them with. I did not use regular stamp albums, but rather used photo albums, and used my own system of arrangement. But I don't think that that will matter as long as the stamps are labeled and okay. I did pages by countries, with the oldest stamps first, and added the newer ones at the bottom and following sheets. Some pre-World War I countries no longer exist, of course, but I think the stamps from those places are interesting and some are quite rare..."

Shirley's pride in her heritage was evident. She kept records of her family dating back to the Civil War.

In 1997 Shirley was packing these family documents to send to Naomi. She told me that she found her birth certificate in her mother's scrapbook.

She said, "I was born at 4:30 in the morning and I thought, well that's what's the matter. I got started that way." She was always an early riser.

Shirley traced her family back to "England and Scotland on both sides. They came to America in the late 1700s," she said. "They were born in Cambridge and went to the university, so it was easy to find. They settled in New Jersey and then went by covered wagon to Illinois and Iowa."

As her sight began to fade, Shirley used a magnifying glass that belonged to her grandmother: "She brought it with her from Canada, when she came to the United States to get married, before the Civil War. She was born in the Netherlands, because her parents fled England for religious reasons. Several children were born there and then they immigrated to Canada, and then came down into Minnesota. You can get a lot of information sometimes from war records. You can send in a thing that somebody was in the Civil War, whatever, and when they filled out the papers to go in, they had to put down parents and grandparents—some of those things that then you pick up tidbits that are interesting that you didn't know about other relatives and so on."

She also found pictures of herself and promised to send them to me. But when I received a package of the transparencies of the Sybil paintings, there were no pictures of her.

I called her and said, "I didn't find a picture of you in the package."

"No, I will send the photographs separately. I didn't want to put anything of mine in with things of Sybil's. In case it got lost I didn't want anyone to make any connections."

She later sent me photos of herself when she was younger and going through analysis in New York. (Photographs appear in the Epilogue.) A picture dated 1955 shows Shirley posing with her painting, which won the student competition at The National Arts Club. At that time the members of the club did not know that they were honoring Sybil.

Among her mementos Shirley found her childhood books and dolls. She said, "I have a collection of foreign dolls and I have a big baby doll in a crib that's fifty years old. I even have a doll that belonged to my mother. It's well over a hundred years old. And a storybook she got for her eighth birthday."

On October 2, 1997, Shirley wrote to Naomi:

> "The doll Mama received for Christmas 1890 is now packed and will be on her way to you tomorrow. Hope she makes it okay. I put her in two boxes. It looks a lot bigger than she is. Her name is Rosemary, Christmas gift to Mattie Atkinson, December 25, 1890. Mattie was six years old."

Naomi said, "There is also a Bible that she sent me that belonged to Joseph Smith Atkinson Sr., who was her grandfather and my great-grandfather."

Shirley wrote:

> "Naomi's great-grandfather Atkinson carried his New Testament with him throughout the Civil War. His rank and last name are in the back of the book. He fought under General Ulysses S. Grant and named his first son James Grant Atkinson in honor of General Grant. The previous owner, a friend named Allen gave him the book."

Shirley sent a Bible Story Reader, inscribed "to Shirley Ardell Mason from Grandma Atkinson, 1926" and an 1886 grade-school arithmetic book belonging to Joseph Atkinson. Shirley wryly commented:

> "…a no-nonsense volume. This must have brought great joy to the heart of any child."

Shirley continued:

> "…A picture of my mother, Martha Atkinson Mason; my parents' wedding photo; and my baby picture. I don't know if you want these particularly, but I think the antique frame on my picture is interesting anyway. It needs polishing, but I am not able to do it. Sorry.
>
> I needed to make a correction on something I wrote on the first batch referring to Grandpa Atkinson's Bible from the Civil War. I stated it was given to him by a friend from Burlington, Iowa. It should have been Burlington, Illinois. I realized it right away after Dee mailed the package. It does make a difference, because Grandpa had not yet gone to Iowa, not until after the war. The Oliver Allen who gave him the Bible was an old man who had the Bible for a while, so his name is in the front of it. He gave it to eighteen-year-old Joe to take to the war with him. Joe's name is in the back of the book. I don't know exactly how old the Bible is, but at least 140 years, I think.
>
> This is my birth announcement. Five and three-quarters pounds.
>
> A Christmas card my dad received from his cousin in 1898.
>
> Mother's seventh grade report card, 1897-98. Mother developed rheumatic fever and could not finish the school year, but due to good grades was promoted on condition.

> She was very proud of that. Probably that's how come the card was saved. She went on to school another three years, and wanted very much to be a teacher, but her father made her quit to work in his music store when the older sister Cora got married and left the store.
>
> Thank you for sending me the material. Mother had a copy of this photo at one time, but she hated it and always fussed so much about how awful it was. Finally one day she got really annoyed and burned it in the kitchen range. It's fun to see it again..."

Shirley kept a letter which her mother, Mattie, had written to her own mother. It read:

> Well, we have been having some winter-like weather and the furnace fire going near all of the time. The creamery here is going nice. Got some coal, at $6 a ton. Walter just got two tons to try it. It's good to hold fires so good overnight. I have a fire in the range also. I am fixing navy beans. I've been going some this morning, but I didn't get up very early, as Walter thought I needed rest, so I had breakfast at eight o'clock...I must tell you I nearly broke my neck two times lately. Caught my high heels on the cellar steps, and I fell the last time. I fell on Wednesday, sure got a good hard one. My left leg was next to broke. It is a sight. I fell as I was going down, carrying two window screens. It made me sick all day long. If there's once more it will be three times. Enough! I don't want any more for me. My leg is swollen up...See, they are the slippers...gave me when I was home last, and I took them to a shoe shop to have the heels cut down, and a rubber heel on them. You see, I have to go on. I have to have sure footing.
>
> I baked bread again this week. It sure seems too good to have homemade bread again... Am doing a hard job of home cleaning...I washed two curtains...
>
> Still have many that are dirty, and cleaning cupboards. Had Walter paint the wall back in the cupboard so it looks clean and nice. He is putting the wall plates on the wall for the lights now. They never were on. We sacked more potatoes last night and delivered them. I am doing fine on the beans.
>
> How does this find you all? I hope no one is kicking too

> hard. I started to clean Grampa's bedroom. He was out, so I took the rugs out on the line, shut the heater off, opened his window, and now he is in again, reading. So guess I'll go and shut his window and turn on the heat. We are all fine. Let us know if you aren't. Ha-ha. Could you use some beans if we send you some? Will send by parcel post. Love from Mattie

Mattie's lines: "We are all fine. Let us know if you aren't. Ha-Ha." reveal her warped sense of humor. When I interviewed Shirley's classmates they spoke about Mattie's inappropriate and hysterical behavior.

Shirley's letter to Naomi read:

> "My mother was a very haphazard person. She kept lots of clippings, photos, news items, but not in any kind of order. Some she dated, some she didn't and pasted them in whatever was handy. Nothing here is in any kind of order and is an odd assortment. The real wonder is that any of it got pasted at all. I've tried to sort and label as many of the items as possible."

This is a fitting metaphor for Shirley's childhood. Because of her mother's abuse, Shirley split into various personalities and "labeled" her own alternate personalities (alters) to cope with each new traumatic incident.

In her family tree Shirley wrote that her mother, Martha Alice Atkinson, was born August 17, 1883. Martha's parents were Martha Hageman Peister, born June 19, 1849, in York, New York, died in October, 1932, and Joseph Smith Atkinson Sr., born July 17, 1844, in Jersey City, New Jersey. They married on September 12, 1866. Shirley's mother, Martha (Mattie) married Walter W. Mason on February 17, 1910.

After several miscarriages Mattie gave birth to Shirley Ardell Mason on January 25, 1923. Mattie was forty years old. Five years later she gave birth to Willard Wayne, who died in infancy.

When speaking about her parent's death, Shirley told me, "My mother couldn't make it out of her sixties. She looked like she was eighty. My father lived until eighty. He had pretty good health. He worked very near the last. He had cancer of the bladder and it spread. And he was in pretty bad shape, hard to get around. He suffered a lot but not for a very long time. He remarried (Florence) and so he had someone to look after him in a manner of speaking. She put him in the hospital and went to see him when she could."

Shirley did not think that marriage was a possibility for herself. During her college days there was a young man to whom she was engaged. But she knew that she was not well enough to fully participate in such a commitment. After she discovered that she had Multiple Personality Disorder, and during her treatment, she was able to maintain friendships, mostly with other women, but no romantic relationships. Children were also never a consideration. Giving birth was denied her because her uterus had been so damaged by the abuse from her mother. She found fulfillment and enjoyment in her art, her students, friends, church and, mainly, Dr. Wilbur.

Since Dr. Wilbur died I worried about Shirley living alone.

I said, "At least you have someone come to your house once in a while. When you're alone, like you, it's hard."

She said, "Well, you know, I don't feel alone. I have a lot of friends and people like you. I look forward to your calling. You said you'd call this weekend, and so when the phone rang I thought, 'I bet that's him.' And then I thought, 'Well, now, don't get your hopes up.'"

"Oh. You're sweet."

"I always enjoy talking to you."

"Oh, I do too. It means a lot."

Shirley said, "We certainly hit it off, didn't we?"

I replied, "I really just feel a kinship with you."

She said, "We share a lot of things."

To know that she treasured our friendship as much as I did brought me joy. This conversation took place a month before she died. Although I realized how painful her cancer was, I hadn't imagined her dying so soon; she was so lucid, articulate, and funny. I wish I could pick up the telephone and call her now.

Shirley continued our conversation, "I'm a regular pack rat! I keep everything. I have all kinds of mementos from my grandparents."

Shirley's grandfather, Joseph Smith Atkinson, Sr. was born in Jersey City, New Jersey on July 10, 1844, and married Martha Hageman Peister on September 12, 1866. He had fought in the Civil War.

"I had a couple of Civil War newspapers. I've got *The New York Times* printed during the war. [Shirley sent her cousin *The New York Times* of 1864 stating: "There is much sickness among our troops, the result of fatigue and exposure in an unhealthy climate." She also sent the *New York Evening Express* dated 1863 which stated: "What shall be done with New England? What of the abolitionism?"] On the front page is an article about Lincoln and his strategy about the war. And then on the same page is a derogatory article about Mary Lincoln, of course. And some of the ads for patent medicines would just slay you. And the Lost and Found you won't believe. 'Lost: Ladies white kid gloves, between Presbyterian Church and Third and Hill Street downtown Manhattan.' And the advertisements for maids to go with them to their summer homes, three dollars a month. Well, you know, when I was a youngster, a hundred dollars a month in salary was just remarkable.

"We sold milk. We had a cow. We sold milk, five cents a quart. And milk the cow, strain the milk and cool it, put it in the bucket and carry it half-way across town."

Shirley talked about her childhood chores, such as cooking. She said, "Oh, I've always known how, I guess. I always helped my mother. And, see, I was thirteen when she was disabled [Mattie had a stroke and later died in 1948]. I did all the cooking and and all sorts of ordinary things when I was thirteen on, and took home economics in school. But I liked to eat, so I learned to cook. And I was skinny enough. I could get away with it," She chuckled.

During one conversation she told me she liked spaetzel.

I said, "I love it also but have no idea how to cook it."

She informed me, "I like to cook it a little longer than it says, though, because it's a little lumpy, a little hard. It's thicker than macaroni, so I cook it longer."

"My problem is cooking anything else to put with it."

"There are all kinds of things. You can put just plain canned tomatoes with it, spice it up, and a little butter. Or you could put cheese, just like you would macaroni and cheese. And any kind of flavoring of herbs that you like. Or you can have sour cream and cheese. Or you can have chunks of beef or chicken or turkey—anything that's left over like that, or frozen, just chop it and put it in there with butter, and put it in the oven and you can put a little bit of finely ground cracker crumbs over the top, give it a little crust, with butter. And—or there are different things…Sometimes I add peas. I like peas with pasta. Get these small June peas."

Usually Shirley spoke about her present life revealing lessons learned from her past. While telling me about a friend's child, Shirley voiced her thoughts on child-rearing:

"It bothers me, though, when they put a child in daycare from six-thirty in the morning until six-thirty at night. The child seems to be very well adjusted and everything, and they keep talking about how great the daycare is and all the things he learns, but I'd want more control over my child's learning."

I said, "I think you're right."

"It would bother me. I think a child needs some time to themselves and be alone. They can think and play and be. Not entertained every minute and be with other people all the time. They need companionship; they need to be with other children, but I think two or three hours a day with other children is plenty."

On October 9, 2006, a New York newspaper, *Newsday*, announced a study confirming Shirley's theory. It reported in an article titled, "More Than Just Fun and Games":

> "The American Academy of Pediatrics says what children really need for healthy development is more good, old-fashioned playtime. Numerous studies have shown that unstructured play has many benefits. It can help children become creative, discover their own passions, develop problem-solving skills, relate to others and adjust to school settings, the academy report says...It says enrichment tools and organized activities can be beneficial but should not be viewed as a requirement for raising successful children. Above all, they must be balanced with plenty of free playtime," the report says.

Shirley's concern for children was also manifested in a discussion about Third World countries. She said, "I feel so sorry for the children. There's something over four million children that don't have any parents or home or anything, living on the streets, in all those cities. What kind of citizens are they going to make? What kind of future are they going to give their country? And consequently, ours? We have to deal with those countries.

"They're always having food drives and so on for the people here. They have Habitat for Homes. President Carter and his wife were here...So many of the factories and the stores hire people part time, although they work nearly full time; they call it part time and they don't get any benefits. Something goes wrong, and they have nothing."

Shirley switched the conversation to a lighter note, and said, "Kids hear funny things, you know. One of my friends was teaching her grandchildren the books of the Bible, and she had a number of grandchildren who were about the same age, between five and seven. And she'd drill them, and they'd say them all together. And they'd say a few of them, and something sounded funny in one place, and so finally she stopped them, and had them say them individually, to see who it was—And a little five-year-old was saying, "Genesis, Exodus, Leviticus, Numbers, Detour Around Me.

"He'd probably heard that more than he'd heard Deuteronomy! It's kind of ironic, because that's one book that, probably out of all of them, that people tend to detour around. Especially the old law, the Ten Commandments, and so on. You know, parts of those give people trouble. They don't want to follow things, you know, they get bothered by it. So it kind of amused me from that angle, too."

She continued, "I saw a cute cartoon in the Sunday paper. There's 'The Family Circus.' A little boy drew a picture of a Madonna and the Child. Down below he had a round circle with skinny legs on it and he said, 'I drew the mother and child all right, but I'm having trouble with Round John Virgin.'"

"*Round yon Virgin, Mother and Child* from *Silent Night* often does sound like that," I said.

Shirley's discussion about children lead me to investigate her childhood in Minnesota after she died.

CHAPTER 7

Exploring Shirley's Childhood

Once Shirley had been identified as Sybil, her childhood friends were able to speak about her. So I went to Rochester, Minnesota, to see them.

My objective to gather evidence, which might prove or disprove some of the disputed incidents of Shirley's childhood, lead me to the place of her birth. (See Appendix H.)

On August 5, 1999, I arrived in Rochester, Minnesota, on a fresh sunny day. The next day Dr. Houlihan and I were going to retrace Shirley's steps.

That night I dreamt I was fighting a war in a southern mansion of the Civil War era. There was a wide stairway from the foyer to the upper floor, similar to Tara in "Gone With the Wind." I was not able to climb the stairs. I had to get to the upper floors to warn the people about the war. I had to go up narrow stairs to the left of the main staircase to get to the upper floors. It was a perilous climb and I had to reach a scaffold that was suspended high above the main staircase. I tried not to look down. I finally made it to safety on the second floor. There were three women living there. I told them to hide from the enemy and to stay in the house. I told them another man and I were going out to fight the enemy and we would bring back our injured soldiers, so it was necessary for the women to be there to nurse them. The women agreed to stay and take care of the wounded soldiers.

My interpretation of this dream was that Dr. Houlihan and I were going to investigate the allegations by others who were trying to destroy the authenticity of the case of Sybil. Shirley had told me about tracing her ancestors to the Civil War. This would now be our war. The women represented Wilma Bode, Betty Christensen, and Patricia Alcott, who knew Shirley. They would have to substantiate or discredit the facts which were presented in *Sybil.* The facts which had been attacked were represented in my dream by the wounded soldiers. Although my climbing the narrow staircase was difficult, I did succeed in the dream, which gave me hope.

Dr. Houlihan drove me to Mankato, Minnesota to meet Wilma Bode. She was living in an apartment building which had formerly been a dormitory for Minnesota State University at Mankato. Shirley might have lived in that very building while attending the college.

Wilma was seventy-six and physically failing. Even though she was on oxygen, she was very warm and welcoming. She invited me into her apartment and showed me photographs of Shirley in their school yearbook. They were classmates from kindergarten through high school. She related stories similar to those which Betty Christensen later told me. They both had excellent memories of all their teachers and details about their school years. Wilma, along with Betty, was one of the few children who was allowed to enter Shirley's house.

Wilma said, "We always said her mother was on old witch. She was strict. You could only play in a certain area. You were not allowed to run through the whole house. It looked like a normal house at that time, but we always went in though the back door, through the kitchen into the sun room. We were only allowed to play in that room.

"Shirley was in the upper half of the class. She missed quite a lot of school. Shirley was frail, very frail. I think there was sometimes where she had to go home, too. She'd get sick in school. To me she always appeared like she was anemic. She was always pale. Shirley got along with all of her teachers. Sometimes I think she had a problem concentrating. I don't know if she was daydreaming or her attention was drawn away.

"In Dodge Center High School, we had initiation. They gave you a slip of paper and you had to dress as someone. I had to dress like a blacksmith and Shirley had to dress like a doctor.

"When we had the prom, the theme was *Gone With the Wind.* Betty's husband Hank drew life size pictures of Scarlett O'Hara and Rhett Butler that was put on either side of the stage. They were beautiful. Shirley couldn't go to the prom. Seventh Day Adventist didn't allow dancing. Yet Shirley had a friend who was a tap dancer. He lived next door to her, but he moved away. Shirley did the art work for our yearbook." (Wilma allowed me to take photographs of the yearbook).

Wilma continued, "In Dodge Center High School we put out a newspaper called *Dodger's Digest.* Our class started that. I think that was 1939 because we graduated on May 28th in 1941. Shirley did some art work for the newspaper."

When I asked Wilma about Shirley's mother, she related the following:

"On the corner of Shirley's street, there was a produce station with cream, eggs, and poultry. Betty Christensen's father, Charlie Borst, owned the produce station. He rented a small building from Shirley's father, across the alley from Shirley's house. He had to get water from the outside faucet of Shirley's house. He said her mother was an old crab."

After they graduated from high school Wilma said that Shirley told her they were moving to Omaha, Nebraska, because "her father was going to build churches." Shirley's father sold his hardware store and they moved. That was the last time she saw Shirley. When *Sybil* was published, someone in Dodge Center told Wilma that Sybil was Shirley Mason. Some people had seen Flora, Dr. Wilbur and Shirley in Dodge Center during the time Flora was writing the book. Thus, they knew that Sybil was Shirley Mason and kept it to themselves.

When I asked Wilma if she believed that Shirley had been abused by her mother, she stated she believed that some of what Flora had written did happen. But it was hard for her to believe "that Shirley had that many personalities."

She angrily objected to a particular passage in Flora's book. She exclaimed, "They talked about her uncle and there was a prostitution house in Rochester with the nuns....farfetched...this convent with all the windows...that wasn't even built until the '50's and what nun would ever change clothes and perform prostitution...that was so outrageous...the only place at that time where there was any nuns was in St. Mary's Hospital convent in Rochester!" Wilma claimed that if such an unusual incident occurred she would have heard about it. At that time, she had a friend who was a nun.

Another of Shirley's classmates, Betty Borst Christensen, lives in Rochester, Minnesota. She and her husband, Hank, invited me to their home for lunch on Sunday, August 8, 1999. Betty told me about a peculiarity of Shirley's mother...that she walked Shirley to school every day even though the school was just across the street from their house.

Betty said, "Shirley and I met in kindergarten. We were in first grade together and all through the grades and high school and graduated together in 1941 in Dodge Center at the public school. The main thing I remember are the picnics we had in kindergarten and going to a place called 'Stivers Grove.' The mothers took us out and we made a day of it."

I asked, "Do you remember what Shirley's mother, Mattie, was like?"

She exclaimed, "Oh, I do. Very much!" Betty burst into laughter, "It's hard not to remember. No, I always thought she was an old, old lady from the time I remember her. She wore her hair straight back, gray, a little bun at the base of her neck. She was very protective. She had a high pitched cacophonic laugh. She sort of herded all of us kids around. She didn't want Shirley to be alone with any of the group. So she was with us all the time."

I asked, "Was Mattie a warm person?"

"No, I wouldn't say so, that she was a warm person," replied Betty. "She ruled the roost when she was around. She was a rather thin lady that I remember. Of course, I lived in the neighborhood too. Not in the early grades, but when we were about eleven, twelve. Then I lived in the neighborhood about a block away from her for a while. Then we bought a house right across the street from her when I was going into high school. The house that I lived in was torn down and there's a new home there."

"Would you play games?"

"Oh, yes. Kickball."

"Did Shirley participate?"

"Yes, uh huh. She'd participate. She seemed to enjoy it too. But then when her mother'd come around she'd sort of withdraw. Shirley was a very nice little girl but like I say very withdrawn at times. She was a very quiet little gal. We were a bunch of rowdies," she laughed. "And the girls were tomboys. We included Shirley with everything, but we weren't real friendly. She wasn't our best friend or anything like that because she wasn't allowed to be.

"When I was in junior high Shirley's father worked at the local hardware store. In grammar school, her mother also brought her home for lunch. Even when she was in high school. The school was across the street."

Betty told me, "Shirley's mother never came over to visit. But she would come over and look in the windows. My brother had the bedroom up above our living room. She'd come over and peek in the windows if we had company or when Hank came over to visit. My brother would swear up and down that he was going to throw a bucket of water on top of her head.

"Mrs. Mason relieved herself in a neighbor's yard. My parents never said anything to her. When you live in a small town and you have a lot of these characters around, and people accept them. We just thought they were really strange. They were just a little different. And everybody had some comment about it, but we let them go their merry way.

"Mrs. Mason had her own characteristics. We just knew she was different and could see how she protected Shirley.

"Mrs. Mason would walk Shirley to high school, which was just across the street. I thought it was pretty strange. No one's mother walked them to high school. I saw her mother come to meet Shirley for lunch and walk her home. We didn't have a cafeteria. Then her mother would walk her back to school and meet her after school."

Betty had fond memories of Shirley drawing in the fifth grade:

"Shirley signed some pictures 'SAM' for Shirley Ardell Mason." (In *Sybil*, Flora changed 'SAM' to 'SID,' one of Sybil's male personalities, an anagram for Sybil Isabel Dorsett.)

Shirley's fourth cousin, Patricia Alcott, who now lives in Rochester, Minnesota, gave me some background information about the environment in which they grew up.

Patricia said, "Shirley's father, Walter Mason, was my great grandfather's second cousin. The Masons and my family, the Nortons and Sorensons, each had relatively small families, so we were closer than most second, third, and fourth cousins would normally be. I still have a silk baby dress that the Masons gave to my mother when I was born. I was raised by my maternal grandmother in rural Dodge Center. Both families belonged to the Seventh Day Adventist Church and often shared a 'Sabbath' dinner after church services."

Patricia continued, "The religion was naught but doom, gloom, and darkness. Their belief was that the world would soon be coming to its end and Jesus would return and take the faithful to Heaven. This belief lead to very little planning for the future—no need to save for a college education for me, because Jesus would come long before that time. However stifling this religion was, it had a strong grip on all of us, especially a child of three or four, who was taught to be terrified of the apocalypse. I was told that everything that was of the imagination was of the devil. This included reading any fiction, fantasizing, or pretending. I soon came to believe that everything about me was evil, because I lived in a world of total fantasy. The fantasy was necessary to survive the grimness of every day life. Fortunately for me, my step-father was a non-believer, so I did not have to go to the Adventist private school, because he would not pay for it. In public school, the world came alive for me—I learned to read and was encouraged to draw and paint pictures and dance. Because I was in public school, we had ready access to the library, where I reveled in both fiction and biographies of the great composers and artists. I also learned to sneak books home with me and hide them in my room—as a result I read *Gone With the Wind* when I was nine and many other lovely works of fiction and poetry."

Fiction was forbidden in their Seventh Day Adventist Church. Shirley corroborated this in her diary in March, 1956:

> When I was a youngster, I was not allowed to read or listen to fairy tales or any stories that were not 'the truth' nor was I allowed to 'make up' stories. I liked to write things I imagined about as much as I enjoyed drawing things that were not 'true', or actually seen but were made up. I wrote a lot of animal stories and stories about children who had pets and so forth. I wrote quite a lot of poetry. So my father found some of my stories and did not approve and said I should not make up things and although he had done the same thing when he was a child and had liked to write and draw and had expressed a love for music, (his folks discouraged him---his father, that is) he did not think it would lead to anything good for me to write made-up things. It would be better to draw, if I did anything. Then Mother got peeved over something one day and made me promise never to write stories again---a promise under threat, of course, so I promised and I always felt I had to keep the promise but I was not honest enough or else I was not strong enough to give up the stories and keep the promise all the way. So I

> devised a way to create the stories without 'writing it down'. I cut words out of newspapers and I cut out some of the letters if the letters were large as in headlines and so forth. Then I would take some of them to school (grades three and four after Grandma's death) and paste the words on sheets of heavier paper from magazines or whatever I could get hold of that was not plain and good for drawing. The youngsters liked the stories I had and used to pass the papers around and read them. And the teacher would sometimes ask me to tell a story in our story hour and I would make up a story. I loved this. At home when I played with my paper dolls. I would hide the letters under the dolls. I had saved a large collection of match boxes (blue but with gray ends to the box which then stacked in rows showing only the gray ends of rows and rows of boxes). Thence Peggy [an alter she was now aware of] screamed about the rows of gray boxes. And I would put the letters and the words I had cut out into these boxes, put paper dolls on top of the letters and then label the boxes so I would know what was really in each but Mother would be fooled. I labeled them with doll's names for Mother's eyes but they were alphabetical for me for my letters and words. The 'As' would be labeled Anna or Alice or Arlene and the 'Bs' would read Barbara or Beverly or Bonnie. I would not risk pasting these letters and words into sentences and then into stories (I always dreamed of going on into 'real' books with them) at home nor would I get as many magazines and newspapers as I wanted, so I would play with the letters only when Mother was not at home and I would lay the words out on the rug and form the story I wanted and still be able to pick up and hide it all quickly when she came. And I still would have the letters to use another time---saved paper! I guess this explains why Peggy has been so frightened and all but screamed at someone not to walk on those words and pointed to the floor and when she got so excited when someone knocked one day and she was afraid they would come in and get the words.)

Patricia continued our conversation, "And as a child, I had a good bit of spunk. Or maybe just nastiness. I would just steam after church on the way home and rave after church. They had what they called 'Special Music'. Well, I have almost perfect pitch. There was nothing special about it, I'll tell you. I would just rant and rave. They would shush me. You are not to speak badly about church members. They are doing that for God and you leave them alone. I just thought God must be totally offended.

"You were told not to doubt or question. If you did, that means the devil has a pretty good grip on you. The Catholic Church was called 'The Whore of Babylon'. That was the end of us. We knew that they were the ones who were going to come for us Adventists because we would insist on keeping Saturday holy, and they wouldn't have it.

"The Adventists had big representational wall drawings of huge, scary dragons that represented the Catholic Church. And that's what was going to do us in. At the end of the world, Catholics would come and try to kill us all. If we were lucky, we would clear the mountains and they wouldn't find us until after Jesus came. And the next day, I went outside and looked all over and you know what I didn't see? Mountains. I remember that sinking feeling—'this is it'. As a three year-old, I'm doomed. I couldn't ask an adult, because to have questioned that you're as good as cooked. Right there. And I know that Shirley grew up with that. We all did. I was close to forty when I left the Church. It had a strong grip."

I asked Patricia about Shirley's mother.

"Her mother was strange, stern, raucous. Someone to stay away from. Mattie had a shrill voice and ridiculed Shirley. Mattie repeated things. They came to Rochester for my birthday party in the park. There was a zoo, and they had a bear. Mattie said, 'Get the Kodak, get the Kodak' over and over again. She liked to take pictures.

"When the book *Sybil* came out, it upset the town. The people didn't want to believe it. My mother asked me if Mattie ever abused me. She was worried. But I don't remember anything bad happening to me.

"Mattie played the piano too loudly, bombastically, venting anger. She was harsh. Shirley's father, Walter, stood in shaded corners with his head down. The men in our family were not assertive. The ladies ran things.

"Shirley and I drew together. She helped me. She had a lot of toys and dolls. She would let me look, but I couldn't touch. Shirley read to me. She was very demure and dressed plainly. I remember her wearing full skirts that covered her body, nothing revealing. A blouse and a cardigan sweater. Her hair was severe in a kind of page-boy with a little ribbon. In contrast, Mattie wore vivid colors.

"Sometimes I ate at her house. Mattie served Franco-American spaghetti from a can. I liked it. It was different for me. I remember their silverware had plastic or cellulite handles in primary colors.

"When Shirley moved away, she wrote to my mother. She sent greeting cards with her artwork."

Shirley made a painting for Patricia's mother. (See Appendix G.)

• • •

D. W. Winnicott, the psychiatrist, coined the phrase "good enough mother" to explain the requirements for healthy child rearing. He stated one did not need the "perfect" mother to develop normally, but one did need a "good enough mother." This mother would lovingly provide the child with the basic necessities of life and allow the child to grow and develop as an individual. The psychologist Carl Rogers included "unconditional love" as an important factor to the healthy development of the child. He stated that the primary caretaker, who is usually the mother, must be able to love the child unconditionally. When the child misbehaves the caretaker should let the child know that she does not approve of this negative behavior, but that she still loves the child.

Shirley's mother was grossly deficient in these necessary qualities. As a child, Shirley came to view Mattie as sometimes the "good mother" and sometimes the "bad mother." This mechanism of "splitting" contributed to the development of each of Shirley's alternate personalities.

Shirley's lifelong search for her good mother ended when she met Dr. Wilbur. Since Dr. Wilbur never had any children of her own, she mothered Shirley. She provided the love that Shirley lacked in childhood. She could not erase the damage Shirley had suffered as a child, but she did help Shirley blossom as an adult.

CHAPTER 8

Shirley Loves New York

During the time Shirley was in therapy with Dr. Wilbur in New York City, she wrote to her in her diary, April 3, 1956:

> "I have buildings on my mind---very insistent images of the---a city. This city---I want to paint---I feel like I belong to this city and I don't want to go away. I have never felt just like this before even when I felt O'k. It is a new sort of feeling---it is all mixed up with you and the city and the way you looked when you said 'We will work it out and you will be well'. I could tell by the way you looked that you meant it. That feeling and the buildings are all one kind of category---can't explain it---I just want to paint. I am going to try."

The following day, April 4th, Shirley wrote:

> "After I wrote that yesterday, I got the paints and brushes and paper out. Then it occurred to me that I could not watercolor without any water. (It didn't get turned on again until evening). So I decided that I would oil paint on the horse picture I have been trying for weeks to get done.

> It is for a wedding gift. For some reason (Well, because I felt better) it clicked O'k, and I painted and painted and painted and enjoyed it so much that I didn't notice the time nor worry about doing anything else around the house---just had fun for a change. Next thing I knew it was 6:00 and I was starved. Just occurred to me that many times---especially in the past few months---it would have been a sort of 'last straw' kind of feeling to have discovered the water turned off just when I wanted so much to watercolor---I get so frustrated when my plans (no matter how trivial or how temporary they may have been at the time I made them) were changed in any way.
>
> Oops! I got a whole flood of memories of something---will digress a minute to tell you---when I was a youngster, I would get so engrossed in everything that I played that it was almost more like work than play---but it meant a lot to me and I took it all so seriously---then Mother would suddenly announce we were going here or there with a 'Come on now. Mother is in a hurry.' Everything had to be laid aside immediately (if not sooner!!) and I had to go with her---I still can recall---although I hadn't for a long time---how this got to be an awful worry for me---two worries---every time I started to lay out my paper dolls or dress my 'real' (as I called the) dolls or build a town or draw a picture, I would get anxious for fear I could not get it done before she interrupted me---and it became very important for me to finish everything---the second worry was after I was interrupted and had to leave my play---got more and more uneasy the longer we were gone---just remembered something long since forgotten---I got to the place where I worried a lot about the house burning or blowing down when we were gone (don't remember ever worrying about it when we were home) and destroying my play things so that I never could finish what I was doing and I would never have the dolls again and so forth and so forth. I tried to tell Mother these things but she said it was silly 'because it was just toys and if I were grown up I would really have things to worry about'. She worried a lot. Dad used to tell her not to worry all the time---I heard a lot of talk about Mother worrying."

Dr. Wilbur interpreted these passages as Shirley expressing her anger toward her mother. Shirley always wrote "Mother" with a capital M, signifying her dominant position. Shirley's desire that something dreadful would happen to her mother is symbolized by her wish that the house would burn down. Shirley expressed how the city itself played a part in her therapy and evoked memories from her past which aided in her recovery.

While Shirley was undergoing analysis, she continued to paint. In January, 1956, she had written in her diary about obstacles in her creative path:

> "There are certain times of day (toward evening and after supper) I don't mind too much ---and at time even enjoy --- housework ---It's O'K and there is a sense of accomplishment about some of it sometimes. But early in the morning and otherwise best parts of a day, while its raining on a rainy day or in the full sunlight of a sunny one, etc. I want overwhelmingly to paint or sketch or write or make whatever current project I am interested in (paper mache, greeting card, sewing, clay modeling, wood carving, wire bending in mobiles), I've been so anxious to create ever since we've got the fireplace wall painted, etc.
>
> A very cryptic feeling ---remark just went through my thoughts --- I'll stick it in as free association, 'sometimes I even feel like I like to read books'. Some ways it almost seems compulsive (not just sure of the extent of the meaning of that word) for me to do all the (was going to say 'other things first' but different words flashed through so I'll use them) 'important' household duties first ---Mother would approve --- in fact, insisted that they come first 'where they belong' then 'frivolous things like art and your everlasting books can be enjoyed with peace of mind that your work was well done first'!
>
> I guess that was her neurosis. It doesn't have to stay with me and aid mine, does it? It's just that some days (if I'm tired or am worried with or without the cause being apparent, etc.) I keep hearing her constant stream of admonitions and orders in the back of my mind, but I feel condemned if I don't and damned if I do. If I don't follow and do work first, I can't paint with ease and freedom --- if I do work first, I'm too tired (and also mad because I had to obey the injunction) to paint.

> I'd say to Mother something to the effect 'see this picture' (or doll dress I'd made, etc.) or 'Look at the cat'. Mother would say, 'Oh, look at the cat! I can't look at the cat. I've got work to do ---who do you think would get things done and meals ready on time if I stood around looking at the cat?' She said that a thousand times, or maybe even a million times years ago and it keeps running through my head and interferes with what I'm trying to do. It even interferes when I try to paint."

In spite of her mother's admonitions, she found freedom in New York and on May 17, 1964, Shirley Ardell Mason had an opening of her watercolors at the Lynn Kottler Galleries at 3 East 65th Street in New York City. A review by H.G.L. read:

> "A large show of watercolors by Shirley A. Mason currently is being shown at the Lynn Kottler Galleries. Subject matter is varied but there is an emphasis on landscapes. Stormy Point Cove is a seaport scene with a wonderful dreamy quality about it. Gulley, on the other hand is strongly influenced by Japanese prints and has the clean lines so characteristic of that media. In contrast, Philadelphia, is bright with the red brick so typical of its old houses. Burned Forest shows that Miss Mason can take the twisted dead trunks of trees and even in their desolation make of them things of stark beauty. In other landscapes, Mountain Caverns and Sagebrush her earth tones and slightly softened outlines evoke an appreciation for natural beauty. This is an extremely interesting show and reflects the hard work of a dedicated artist."

Shirley was thrilled not only by her first show in New York, but also because Dr. Wilbur, Flora, Naomi, and Jim attended. Many of her paintings were sold that night and the exhibit was deemed a success. It ran until May 30, 1964.

Her resume read: "Shirley A. Mason—Dodge Center High School, Minnesota, graduated in 1941—Mankato State Teachers College, Minnesota, received her Bachelor degree in 1949, took courses at the University of Omaha, Nebraska, 1947 and received her Master of Arts degree from Columbia Teachers College, New York City. She had a one-man show at the time of graduation. She also was commissioned to do murals for the Horace Mann grammar school English Department. And murals for the children's infirmary at the Mankato College while she was a senior in that institution."

Shirley taught Art and English at Omaha Junior Academy, Nebraska from 1945 until 1947. She taught at the Kansas City Junior Academy, Missouri from 1947 until 1949. At the Porter Hospital in Denver, Colorado she taught Occupational Therapy, Art & Ceramics from 1949 until 1951. Moving to Michigan in 1951, she taught at the Jackson Protestant Parochial School and the Memphis Public schools until 1954.

While living in New York and undergoing her treatment with Dr. Wilbur, Shirley gave private art lessons and taught Art Therapy at the Falkirk Hospital in Central Valley, New York, from 1960 until 1963.

During a conversation with me in 1997, Shirley mentioned that she wished she could come to New York on December 15th for an art opening at the Phyllis Kind Gallery in Soho. Since Shirley was not well enough to travel, she wanted me to go in her place. It was especially important to her because the artist was Marilee Stern, the wife of Stewart Stern, who wrote the screenplay "Sybil."

She avidly followed Marilee's career. After the opening I sent her the review in *The New York Times* which said:

> "Well-known as a ballet dancer (she was discovered by George Balanchine), ballet teacher and choreographer, Ms. Stern turned to art as an aid in the psychotherapy, which followed a diagnosis in 1989 of dissociative identity disorder (DID), as multiple-personality disorder is now called."

Like Marilee, Shirley's paintings had also played an important part in overcoming DID in her own therapy.

On the day of the opening I telephoned Shirley:

"I'll bundle up tonight," I said, "I'm going to write you a report on the evening."

"Well, that would be great!" she exclaimed. "I'd like to know what people think about her work."

"Okay, I'll listen to their comments. Then I'll write you a report about the event."

"Tell Marilee I'm sorry that I couldn't come. I should get word to her, but it's so hard for me to do anything. I can't send a telegram easily because I don't use credit cards anymore. And so I can't just call up and order something."

"Okay, I'll tell her that I'm bringing her personal greetings from you."

"I'd appreciate it."

"Are you feeling better now?"

"A little."

"You sound a little stronger."

"Well I had just taken my medicine a few minutes before you called. It takes about ten or fifteen minutes to take hold and lasts for a couple of hours, so maybe I'll make it through the dinner hour."

"Oh, I hope so. I wish you were here for the party but I'll write you all about it. Okay?"

"I would appreciate that if you have the time."

"Oh, I will. But I'm going to call you Monday afternoon anyway."

"Are you sure you're not running up terrible phone bills?"

"Don't you worry."

"Well, I do. Phoning is very expensive."

"No, that's all right. I'll call you."

"Well, I'd love it, if you're sure."

I went to the gallery with my friends Carroll Baker and Marianne Strong.

Joanne Woodward and Roddy McDowall, who were friends of Marilee and Stewart Stern, were also there. Paul Newman had not yet arrived, so Carroll jokingly asked Joanne if he were home making the spaghetti sauce. Fortunately, he was not and did arrive later.

Some of Marilee's paintings were on graph paper; the tiny squares of the paper cast the figures in a stunning relief. Marilee's friends from the New York City Ballet came to congratulate her.

Unable to wait for a letter to reach Shirley, I called her the next day. She and Joanne Woodward had never met or spoken on the phone. I was anxious to tell her what Joanne said.

I related, "I saw Joanne Woodward, and Paul Newman came later."

"Oh, they're great friends of Stewart."

"Joanne asked me what you thought of her portrayal of Dr. Wilbur. Isn't that something? After all these years, she never knew what your reaction was. So I told her that you had told me that you thought she was marvelous. That she captured the spirit of Dr. Wilbur."

Shirley said, "Joanne has been directing."

"Isn't that wonderful."

"She was great to Connie. She called her and she wrote to her. Her letters are beautiful."

"Paul Newman came later. He was very polite and introduced himself. Of course, I knew who he was. They have been married a long time."

"I'm so glad because she really put a lot aside for his career. She had a great start as a young woman. She knew what happened to marriages when you weren't right there. And she was going to fight for that marriage. And she was good to his youngsters."

I replied, "I reminded Joanne about the night she had her picture taken with Flora during the shooting of "Sybil." Joanne said, 'Oh, those were the good old days.' Paul Newman was having such a good time that she had to drag him out of the gallery; they had to catch a plane that night. Marilee was lovely, explaining her work to us."

Since Shirley took such an interest in Marilee's art, a few days later, as a favor to her, I took Marilee and Stewart to lunch at The National Arts Club on Gramercy Park. Since they had never been there, it was a thrill for them, especially when I told them that Shirley had won the college student's art competition in 1955. I have a photograph of Shirley and her painting taken at the club.

(Photograph appears in Appendix C.) I introduced Marilee, praising her work, to Aldon James, the president of the club.

When I spoke with Shirley about it she said, "That's wonderful. She needs the encouragement and help. She's had a rough ten or twelve years. It's been generally hard for her. To give up one profession and try another is very difficult. I'm so glad you did that."

I replied, "You're very welcome. Marilee said she had a wonderful experience in New York. If it didn't go any farther than this, she would be satisfied with what she has accomplished."

I continued, "When I was at the gallery, I also gave your regards to Roddy McDowall. I told him that you said that he had written you a lovely letter when Connie passed away. He's loving playing the part of Scrooge."

"Oh, he'd make a wonderful Scrooge. He's got a regular rubber face. Once Roddy called and asked me how I was getting around. I said I try but things are either too high or too low and they are out of reach. He said that was the story of his life. He has such a wit."

"One year at Easter he sent Connie a card. There was a great big bunny rabbit and he was sitting on the bunny's lap. And the bunny had his arms around Roddy. He wrote, 'You think I need therapy, maybe? Well honey, you ought to talk with this rabbit for a little while.' Connie got the biggest kick out of it. I have several of his photographs—he took double exposures. "Take One," "Take Two," and so on. I think he has five all together. I don't have the last one, but they're gorgeous. I loaned one to my nurse who brought me the recent *People* magazine with his photography. He's got an imagination. I got tickled at his photo of Carol Burnett pulling the dog's tail. Carol said, 'Don't write letters.'"

I said, "People would write letters to complain about her pulling the dog's tail, too."

"Oh, sure, at the least little bit of anything."

"I have a friend here who teaches at a public high school and do the students complain."

Shirley added, "I loved New York way back when I lived there. I taught in Central Valley, but I didn't teach in New York City. I wouldn't do it. I taught art classes at a private school. That was perfectly safe. But I wasn't going to go in those public schools. It was too much stress and strain and too everything. And no money for art supplies."

"Do you ever miss New York?"

"In some ways. Sometimes. It was home to me for a long time. I didn't ever quite get used to the rush of so many people and so much rudeness, but I appreciated all the places there were to go. Stores and museums and the planetarium. And I went. A lot of people say they need to be where they can go to plays and so on, but they never go. I went all the time. And every Christmas for years I'd go to the Rockefeller Center to the Music Hall."

I asked, "The Rockettes?"

"Yeah. And they had other entertainment too. And then they always had a new movie. Some of them were just spectacular. "Auntie Mame" came out there. And I just love that thing. With Rosalind Russell. There were a number of them. There was "No Time for Sergeants." That was another one I saw. And of course, "The Sound of Music." They are all so vivid in my mind because I enjoyed them so much. Some friends and I would go. Two or three of us who were left at the dormitory when everybody went home for Christmas. And we'd go, so there'd just be a few people there, for the very early morning showing and it was great. Didn't have crowds or anything."

"I've done that too."

"And their Easter one too. It's spectacular. I didn't get there every year, but they had beautiful shows."

"That stage is so incredible."

"I know. I was from a small town and the first time I saw the orchestra come up out of the floor—"

"Did you think you were hallucinating?" I joked.

"I didn't know what was happening. I thought it was marvelous. It was wonderful. But I thought what if it fell?"

Shirley had remained mentally stable so that I was able to make light of serious psychological problems such as hallucinations—the black humor that I would normally reserve for colleagues.

I continued, "Now they don't show movies there anymore."

"Oh, no, I didn't know that. Why?"

"They can't afford to run the Music Hall for the price of a movie ticket. So the Rockettes only perform a couple times a year and then singers give concerts. The last movie I saw there was "Gone With The Wind." It was a benefit. They restored the film. At that time I had my boyfriend Tony from Mississippi, so we had to go."

"It must have been fun."

"Yeah. And some people came dressed in period costumes.

"Oh my."

"And they had the original costumes on display. It was wonderful."

I could speak frankly with Shirley about my boyfriends because I knew she was so accepting. Somehow she reconciled her knowledge of the world, including homosexuality, with the precepts of the Seventh Day Adventist religion.

We talked about the demise of the old beautiful movie theaters, of the enormous expense of running them.

Shirley said, "We have a couple of very old theaters here in town and they restore them every twenty years or so. They try to keep them going but people just don't go. They have all the original lighting and the fixtures. So many really wonderful things have gone with the years that, I think, held people and held their interest and held families together."

"It was a more humane way of living."

"And now it's just everybody for himself and the dollar."

"Everything is so impersonal."

"And rapid," Shirley added.

"That's why I'm glad I live on Gramercy Park."

"It's quieter down there. Oh, I enjoyed that picture of the park you sent me. You know when I stayed with Flora I would take my little poodle and go walking around that park. Of course, I couldn't get in. They kept the gate locked. Of course, the people that lived in the area could get in there but Flora didn't have a key."

"I don't think she ever went into the park."

"I don't think so, but I took her one time to Central Park. She had ridden through it but she's never been in it. So I said, 'Why don't we go over to the park and sit and visit?' Because my apartment was small. So we took Connie's poodle and we went over there. We just sat on a bench and watched the world go by. Oh, she thought it was wonderful and she said, 'We'll have to do that again sometime.'"

I thought of Shirley's fondness for Central Park and how she portrayed it in the painting that I have (which appears in the Introduction.) She spoke about the other wonders of New York.

"I used to go on the Staten Island Ferry. My girlfriend and I. We'd go down there around midnight in the summer when it was so hot and the apartments were so hot. We lived in a fourth floor walk-up under the roof."

The building still stands on East 78th Street. It is only one block away from the luxurious high rise buildings of the wealthy on East 79th Street. These signs of opulence meant nothing to Shirley. She was content living with her cat Capri in her modest apartment.

She wrote to Dr. Wilbur about Capri in her diary, November, 1956:

> "Mary [an alter Shirley is now aware of] also cried one night when hot chocolate was made for her. Mary was holding Capri who was watching every move made at the stove. Mary began to cry and said she could not stand to have something nice when the kitty was hungry, so it was said that, of course, the kitty would have some food of her own from the refrigerator and Mary was O'k again. I've digressed quite a way here but as long as I have gone this far, I'll go a little farther and remark about Capri---she reacts to Mary by being quiet and letting Mary hold her and pet her---I was Mary the day you brought Capri in here, then she reacts

> to Peggy [another alter Shirley is now aware of] by being excited and racing around and jumping onto Peggy. Peggy rather roughly handles Capri and says 'Nice little cat' and holds her a bit too tightly, but Capri never scratches (more than I can say for the way she treats me when I am being nice to her!) And she acts concerned when 'anyone' feels sad or cries, rubs against my face and doesn't purr at all. I know animals are sensitive to human feelings but Capri just seems to change with the personality---maybe she is multiple too! "

Shirley continued her conversation about New York with me, "Oh, never cool there. We'd go downtown and go across to Staten Island. And the hot dogs were great. That was a big enough boat that I felt safe. And it was a regular thing. I never heard of any of them going down and they had lifeboats and those round things."

"Life preservers."

"Yeah, and so we weren't afraid. And to see the Statue of Liberty lit up at night was just...we never tired of it."

• • •

During another telephone conversation, Shirley told me what she was cooking, so I asked her if she cooked when she was living in New York.

"Sure. I had a roommate much of the time and shared an apartment. She didn't like to cook and I did. And I don't like particularly cleaning and she loved to get down and scrub the floor and clean the fireplace and defrost the refrigerator. She was such an active gal. And I said, 'Well, you do that and I'll do the cooking and the reading.' When she was cleaning, I'd read to her. She was a non-reader. She was working for her doctorate and she got it. But I wrote most of the papers and…tests and everything. Well, I composed them and she wrote them, you know what I mean."

"Would you read her schoolbooks to her?"

"Yeah, and everything else. She didn't know beans about books. And I'd read her things—I'd start with simple things, like *Papa Was a*

Preacher or *Kneepants*, or something like that, the kind of thing that Russell Baker writes. Of course, he wasn't around then. But anyway, you know, I got her used to it, and then I'd go into heavier things. I'd read A.J. Cronin and so on. I loved to read and I liked sharing things that I liked. I got to read whenever I wanted to. So it worked out fine. Charles Dickens' great-granddaughter, Monica Dickens' books were popular at that time. *One Pair of Hands*, *Two Pair of Feet*, and something of the moon. They're hilarious."

Although Shirley was enjoying reminiscing, I detected a tension in her voice.

"How are you feeling today?" I asked.

"Oh, I'm not very good right at the moment. The nurse said it's the cancer spreading. The back problem is the main pain and I take pain pills for that. They've given me something else to take for that. Makes me tired, drowsy. I had company this morning and company yesterday."

"That wears you out too," I said.

"Well, I'm on my last legs," she laughed.

"We keep going though."

"Yeah, we don't have any choice. I'm a little uncomfortable. There are times when I'm all right. During the night I don't have much pain because I'm not moving around. The next morning I have to get going again. There are certain times of the day when the medicine begins to wear off and it's pretty uncomfortable and so I just start taking it a little sooner. The nurses said that's the thing to do."

• • •

Just before New Year's Eve, I called Shirley and she asked, "What are you going to do in New York for New Year's?"

"I'm going to a party two blocks from my apartment."

"You shouldn't have any trouble getting home afterwards!"

"I should be able to walk home, the two blocks."

"That's good."

"So are you going to celebrate?" I asked.

"No, not if I sit home."

"You won't be drinking a bottle of champagne?" I joked.

She laughed, "No, I'm afraid not. I'm light-headed enough. The pain medicine makes a person drowsy, you know, and I have to be careful and I have to eat plenty with it, otherwise—So I think that's all I can handle."

Shirley asked me, "Did you get either of my boxes yet?"

"I didn't get anything yet."

"What are they doing with them?"

"Oh, they take forever here. The Post Office does."

"Three or four days is all it ought to take. I send things to Arizona. They get there the third day."

"New York now is like a Third World country. That's why I said to take your time. Because we know. But everybody at the Post Office knows me, thank God, the letter carriers and everybody who comes here."

"You'll probably get the second one first."

"Right. So you sound good today."

"Yeah, I'm doing pretty well. I'd like to be rid of the pain for a while, but it lessens considerably with medication. It just won't let go entirely, and it's very wearing you know, very wearing. And it's not as bad sitting down, but I want to do things. And I get up and I want to do this or do that, and it just hurts. And sometimes just simple things. All I want to do is water a few plants. I've got a little brass thing to water with and just to lift that little thing it hurts, to reach out to where the plant is. And doing the dishes, reaching over the sink. The dishwasher, of course, is under the cabinet and I can't get down there. I lean over the sink and just to reach over and turn the faucet on and off hurts. It's just a little further than I can comfortably reach. And I've got a light switch that's under the cupboard for a fluorescent light over the sink. It's just a few inches beyond where it's comfortable to put it on and off. And just little things like that.

It makes me think what it must be like for the handicapped, always. It's always with them. Well, anyway, but I can't complain. It was a good week and things went well."

Shirley continued, "And the nurses are so good to me. They always want to do something for me. I get so tickled. Carol will say to me, 'Now, if anything comes up this afternoon or this evening, if you need anything at all, you call the office and tell them to page me.' I said, 'All right.' And then Terry comes the next day and she says, 'Now, if you need anything at all, you call the office and tell them to page me.' And I thought I'm going to have some trouble on my hands if I ever page one of them. The rest of them are going to-"

I interjected, "Be jealous. They all want to take care of you. That's nice. There are some patients they dread to go and see, you know? They've told you?"

"Yes. There are some of them, they just sit there and won't do a thing for themselves. They said, 'You go in and do all kinds of things for them and you know very well when you go back the next time everything's just like you left it, just like it was. And some of them are just—and then there are others that are a lot of fun.'

"They've got one that just drives everybody up the wall. Fourteen years ago, when she was twenty-something, she was in an automobile accident and had a serious head injury, and she has no short-term memory. She can remember other things, but from one minute to the next is not with her. And she will call the office and want something, you know, but she will call seven and eight times between eight in the morning and noon, and she'll want to know about her medicine. The other day they paged Carol when she was here. So she called to see what the office—you have to do everything through the office—she called the office. Well, it was Patty. She said, 'What is it, Patty?' She said, 'Well now, Patty, I was there this morning. Yeah, I was there, and I fixed all your medicine of the day. You're all taken care of for today. Now you have called the office five times this morning and it's only ten o'clock.' And she said, 'Now you make a note that you have been taken care of for today.'

I said, "That's good!"

Shirley said, "She had the patience of a saint. And of course you know not a thing they can do about it. For fourteen years she's been like this. I said, 'Does she live alone?' She said, 'Yes, but she goes off riding on her bicycle and forgets where she lives.' And so on, the short-term—but she said she'll go back to where she used to live instead of where she lives, and that kind of thing. And I said she doesn't have anybody? 'Well, she's got a mother, but she says they don't get along very well and she won't accept anything from her mother. Her mother's perfectly willing to help her and wants her to live with her so she can look after her, but she says she won't do it. So she said, 'Oh, it takes so much time, you have to explain everything all over again, everything all over again.'"

• • •

Short-term memory loss was certainly not one of Shirley's problems. I was struck by her keen memory when she asked me about my shopping bags. I had mentioned months ago that I had unopened mail stored in shopping bags. She kept track of everything I told her and was concerned about my work and well being. She also kept up with current events. I told her about the impending visit of President Clinton to New York and how we were already alerted to gridlock.

I said, "His trial with Paula Jones comes up soon. They're going to talk about his penis. I just hope that they don't show us pictures."

"I heard on the news this morning that he wouldn't allow her picture to be taken in the White House."

"Right, so they're going to meet at his lawyer's office."

Shirley replied, "This whole thing is the biggest—"

I interjected, "She has identifying characteristics of his penis."

"Yeah, but that doesn't necessarily mean that they were there then or that they're still there. There are things that can be corrected. I tell you, this is such a farce. I'll bet some of the foreigners think that we are crazy. My friend has a two year-old grandson and she said she'd like to see him become President one day. I thought to myself, let's reach for something respectable, like Supreme Court Justice, or something with a little dignity to it."

I told her, "A reporter called me to give a diagnosis of a man in power and his sexual activity. I knew it would be directed towards Clinton so I declined. He found another psychologist who said he's a sex addict and needs treatment. It is unethical to give a diagnosis of someone you haven't examined."

Shirley agreed, "How can people do things like that? But, you know, the thing that kind of boggles my mind is, what woman would find him sexually attractive? No appeal at all. And I don't care for him one bit, never have. I was willing to give him a chance, and I don't know if all this is true or not, but I can't see what difference it makes anyway."

"What?"

She answered, "All the sex business. It has nothing to do with running the country. After all, you can go way back as far as Harding and all that kind of thing going on—illegitimate daughter and so on. The press didn't report it. They just covered it up the same way with Kennedy. I don't think that he can even match Kennedy but you know what? What difference does any of it make? We got through Kennedy without it having to be known, so why can't we get through this one?"

"They can't do anything about the sexual activity. That's up to his wife and his daughter to deal with. Nobody else should be concerned with that."

Shirley said, "Well, I like his wife. I feel sorry for her. She's had something to battle ever since he went in office. But she's up to it, seems to be, anyway."

I said, "Yeah, she said she's going to go on the *Today Show*, so we shall see."

Shirley said, "Well, she could hardly do anything else, I guess. I mean, than defend him."

I said, "Yeah, otherwise it makes him look guilty if she doesn't.

But these psychologists that say anything just to get their names in the newspaper. They're so irresponsible and that weakens the credibility of the field."

Shirley said, "Oh, yeah, they say something stupid and everybody will say, 'Oh, that's psychology for you."

• • •

On January 29, 1998, I finally received the boxes Shirley sent. I called her:

"I got a wonderful present today. I got your photographs!"

Shirley commented, "Oh yeah. Oh, they're old. I told you they are old."

"Oh, yes, but so pretty. You were so pretty."

She chuckled, "Everybody tells me I haven't changed a bit except the color of my hair, but I don't know. Well, anyway, that's what I used to look like."

"Such graceful hands. I can see them holding the painting. They're really beautiful."

Shirley replied, "Well, thank you."

"And the painting at The National Arts Club!" (It is shown in Appendix C.)

"Yeah, that was when I first went to New York."

I asked, "How did you get in the exhibit there?"

"Invitation. Received an invitation from them."

"They must have seen your work."

"Yeah. I had had an exhibit, a student exhibit at Columbia, and I guess that's where they picked it up. I don't know—I kept getting—I had invitations. By the time I went to New York, I had exhibited in twenty-eight different states. It can come from anywhere."

I interjected, "What an honor. Did you go to the Club?"

"Yeah, at that time."

"Did they have a reception?"

"Oh yes. Everything. That was a long time ago."

"Yeah. The picture here had the date on it. The picture says 'June '55.'"

"Yeah, well that's when the exhibit was. I went there the fall of '54. The exhibits were over that year."

"Oh, well, that's wonderful. What an honor!"

Shirley admitted, "I remember being pleased about it, because I was just starting out, and wasn't seeking anything. I just responded when I got an invitation, and that's how it was."

"And that's the painting that you're holding in the photograph?"

"Yeah."

I said, "I love the style. I love the work. It's so emotional."

Shirley described, "That deep, bright blue sky. I've got that painting in my studio. For many years it was my favorite. I've got others I like better now, but I've kept it for sentimental reasons."

"I love the style of your painting."

"The first place I had that shown was in Bloomfield Hills, outdoor art exhibit, it was outside Detroit, a section of Detroit. And they had an outdoor exhibit every year, and I had a couple of things in it that time. And that was one of them. That was the first time that one was exhibited. But it went into a lot of exhibits."

I continued, "The movement, too, I love that. And then all these other paintings there, in the other photograph. You're with all the paintings." (This photo is in Appendix C.)

Shirley said, "It's harder to tell what those are. They were all very early ones. They don't look like my work. Or, I don't now paint that way."

"Well, I can see how the work has evolved."

"Yeah, things change over time."

I said, "They're little traces of the Sybil paintings, huh? But just more refined and sophisticated."

She said, "Well, after I was fused into one personality, the whole thing changed. All the work since then has changed."

"And all the work is different from that. Yeah, I'd love to see those photographs too."

"I'll send you some slides sometime, when you get through with all the junk you've got."

"Yep, I went through it. But you see, what I could do probably with all the Sybil paintings is give a talk on them at The National Arts Club and have the slides projected there. They have a projector there. They have programs there."

"But you wouldn't use my name."

"No, no. We would always say 'Sybil' and the different personalities, Peggy, whoever painted them. And that would be great when the book comes out, to do something like that in conjunction with the book."

"Yeah, it would promote it."

"Yeah, oh, that would be just wonderful there."

"Well, if you want to do it, it's fine with me."

"I wish you could be there, but you'll be there in spirit. And I'll take pictures of it and everything. I should get some nice color pictures of the interior of the club, because that stained glass there is so beautiful."

Shirley recalled, "They didn't have color photos yet in any amount when I had them taken there. I had some color film, but the colors weren't very good at that stage. It was another ten years before they were really good. And of course the trouble with color film, in twenty or thirty years it turns gray and brown. That's what happened with those Sybil prints, slides, because they're in the dark. But those that are printed, they will hold it better. The photographs won't, but the others…That's one reason for keeping the originals. I had thought of destroying the originals, and then my attorney told me that was not a wise idea."

I added, "Better to make the reproductions from the originals?"

"Yeah, He said he didn't think I ought to destroy the originals. I ought to keep those."

"I'm so glad you did."

"Well, Dee is gone on a vacation. They went for a week or so. So that delayed my getting those pictures to you, but once she gets back, we'll get them sorted and done up."

"Okay. Don't worry."

Shirley died a week later and the pictures were never sent to me, but I will have a slide show of them at The National Arts Club when this book is published.

• • •

When Shirley was living in New York, Naomi was living in Ridgewood, New Jersey. She contacted Shirley.

Naomi told me, "I was hesitant to call her. I felt that since she was a distant relative—my father's first cousin—maybe she wouldn't even know me."

[Naomi's father Virgil, born on May 23,1901, was the son of James Roland Reed, who married Betsy Jane, called "Jennie." Jennie was the sister of Shirley's mother, Martha Alice, called "Mattie." Mattie's other siblings were James Grant Ruphcno, Hannah, Joseph Smith, Cora, called "Coke," Roy Peister, William Townlcy, Nell Tobin and Mary Viola, called "May." In 1926 Virgil Reed married Mabel Ellenborg Goodman, called "Ellen," born August 3, 1901 and gave birth to Naomi on May 23, 1938. They also had a son. Virgil died April 11, 1952 and Mabel died March 6, 1962.]

"I was told that she was involved with Columbia University and she was an artist. I pictured her as being someone very important who probably would hardly know who I was. And so I called her, and much to my surprise, Shirley said instantly, 'Oh! So good to hear from you! I have pictures of you when you were a little girl. You were the cutest little girl. I loved Virgil [Naomi's father]. I would just love to see you.'"

Naomi invited Shirley to come to New Jersey to have dinner with her and her family. She told Shirley that Jim worked in the city and could meet her at the Port Authority Bus Terminal.

Shirley replied, "Okay, I'll be wearing a brown fur coat with a flower in the lapel."

Jim found a plain, frail woman in a well-worn brown fur coat.

When Shirley walked into the house, Naomi remembers thinking that she looked so old. "I was twenty-four and she looked sixty to me, although she was forty. She was anything but a contemporary young person. She looked plain, her hair was non-descript, she was very thin, extremely thin. She brought gifts for the kids, who were around two and three years of age. They were friendly kids and they put their arms around her. Shirley opened up gifts that she had made for them. She had made a doll and doll's clothes. She brought art supplies.

"When they drew pictures, Shirley would say, 'Oh, this is so advanced. These are very bright children.' And she'd point out all the idiosyncrasies that only an art teacher would know. Shirley would say, 'This is a sign of a very happy child. This is how you know this is a happy child,' because of this, this, and this.'"

Jim told me about going to an exhibit of Shirley's paintings at the Lunn Kottler Galleries in New York City. He said, "We met Connie Wilbur and Flora Schreiber at the gallery. Shirley sold some paintings, which they took as a sign of success."

Naomi talked about visiting with Shirley in Central Park.

She said, "The kids played in Central Park and they were so impressed because we had always heard of Central Park as being this terrible place, and here all of a sudden is this gorgeous place. After one of those visits, we went to her apartment. It was a walk-up. It felt like it was six floors high. I remember thinking, 'How do you get all your stuff up here? I can't believe it.' And the staircase and the hallway were extremely grim and meager. Narrow, dark, and small."

Jim added, "Shirley's apartment had lots of books. It was the place of an intellectual. The apartment reminded me of an intellectual who didn't care much about looks or appearance, but books and art were important to her. She had art supplies everywhere."

I asked Naomi and Jim if they had ever observed any unusual behavior from Shirley.

Jim said, "Only on the telephone. She was a different personality, a different person."

Naomi concurred, "A couple of times when I called her in New York, Shirley was louder and very much in charge. I felt that she was hyper and loud and very dogmatic. I thought, 'What is this?' I never suspected alcohol because there was no slurred speech. I didn't know what it was."

As the preparation for the book *Sybil* approached, Shirley brought Flora Schreiber and Dr. Cornelia Wilbur to Naomi's house.

Naomi said, "They spent the whole day discussing Shirley's therapy and the book which they were writing. Shirley told me that she was not willing to consent to the book unless I agreed with it."

Jim said, "Flora was pretty nervous about the whole thing."

Naomi added, "Shirley, at that point, had really attached herself to our family so strongly. Connie took the lead and just painstakingly went through what they'd been through in the past years of therapy. Multiple Personality was not something that was easily diagnosed or treated. It had been the result of a very abusive past for Shirley. She was part of my family line and she was so attached to our children. She was protective of the children. She was concerned about doing any harm to them with the book.

"I didn't have any fear for myself or the children. I did feel if it could help someone that they should do it. I said, 'If this is really pioneering work and this can help other people, I think you should do it, so it's certainly fine with me.' And I remember Shirley speaking up, very determined, saying, 'I will agree only if Naomi says it's okay and if there is a commitment to keep my identity secret and Naomi's identity secret.'"

During this period Shirley wrote to her stepmother, Florence, about her visit with Naomi and about her work as an art therapist at Falkirk Hospital and as a salesgirl for little girls' clothes at a shop in Manhattan.

On February 3, 1963 she wrote:

> "I had a novel, but most rewarding experience on Wed. this week, a few days ago, I got a phone call (as I've said before this seems to be my year for phone calls!) from a girl who said, you probably don't remember or know who I am, but my name is Naomi and I am Virgil Reed's daughter...Well, I had never seen anything but pictures of her, but I knew very well who she was...Virgil was my cousin but since my parents were 40 when I was born, my cousins naturally were all grown by then...but I remember the fun we used to have when cousin Virgil came to visit us when I was a small girl...he was a great cut-up (as were all of the Atkinson side of the family... his mother, Jane, was my mother's sister) and he paid attention to me which I never forgot...some people tend to slight the children and don't seem to see them in a family gathering. But not Virgil. Well, here his daughter is married and has two darling children, 4½ and 3 and another on the way in May...due on Naomi's birthday and she in turn was born on her father's birthday. They wanted me to come over to New Jersey for dinner Wednesday evening so I agreed to meet a 6'2" blond with a green hat and a black overcoat at window 27 in the bus authority bldg. at 5. Had no trouble spotting each other...he had already bought me a ticket that morning and we had a pleasant 50 minute bus ride out to Ridgewood N.J. Turns out he is from St. Cloud Minnesota where my aunt Thirza Walkley lived for so many years...we had lots to talk about and a good old mid-western accent sounded fine to my ears after this New York stuff...The children were perfectly adorable and so well behaved. I had taken them some little gifts I hid in various zipper pockets of a bag that appeared empty when it wasn't at all and it became the 'Magic bag' and I was immediately the 'Magic lady.'
>
> I awoke at 5 this a.m. and concerned and not a little anxious about what will happen to me when Dr. Wilbur quits Falkirk Hospital Feb. 15th (I HOPE to continue with increased hours and go by bus for more pay, but I may get tossed out on my ear when she goes. All depends on the paranoid trend of the owner-doctor!)
>
> There is a new psychiatric clinic for adolescents opening just two blocks from me. I am going to stop by and see if they need an art teacher or therapist or something

part-time. Some of my anxiety comes from that, too, as I always get tense when interviewing for a new job...normal I guess. Dr. W. told me to set my fees high...$10.00 an hour for work with an individual and $5.00 an hour each if in a group. Sounds high to me, but she said they value you as you value yourself, so...guess that I am supposed to value myself!

Things are still rather slow at the shop due to cold weather and after-Christmas lull, but notice a pick-up lately. I sold some things but could do better if some of these young mothers would only have more girls and not so many boy babies!! I enjoy having the shop to go to at times and with Falkirk other days I am not home much and still not too much routine with sameness day in and day out. I like that alright so long as I know what comes next!

I have just finished reading a book called, 'Great Religions of the World' sent to me for Christmas by a Methodist friend. The book discusses major religions and how they got started and what they believe from ancient times down to the present...including Mormons and even a rather long section of Adventists and Millerites. It presented Mrs. White in a very favorable light which pleased me as I know many people will read a popular book like this and see that in it, who would never touch an Adventist piece of literature. It is good to know we are recognized and so well presented. I was pleased.

Naomi and Jim had the children each say a little prayer at the table before the blessing was said by Jim, and then they prayed again when they went to bed...he kneeling with the boy in his room and she by the girl's crib in her room. I don't know the denomination but she was raised a Methodist and I suspect since he is from Minnesota he is Lutheran, but I did not ask...told them what I was and they both nodded so know they have some knowledge about us, anyway.

Write again when you get time...always glad to hear, of course. Love as always, Shirley."

This letter was written after Shirley had been in analysis with Dr. Wilbur for nine years. Despite working various jobs which enabled her to live in Manhattan, she found time to produce enough paintings for an exhibit the following year.

CHAPTER 9

The Patient Takes Care of the Therapist

In the beginning of their relationship, Shirley was the patient and Dr. Wilbur was her therapist. After the successful completion of Shirley's therapy, their relationship evolved into a loving friendship.

Eventually they both moved to Lexington, Kentucky when Dr. Wilbur accepted a position at the University of Kentucky. At that time, Shirley was financially able to buy her first home on Henry Clay Boulevard.

In addition to painting and teaching, Shirley assisted Dr. Wilbur with the many tedious administrative duties required to maintain her practice. She provided an environment in which Dr. Wilbur could practice psychiatry without being troubled by unpleasant administrative tasks.

Shirley said, "Connie's husband, an attorney, did the taxes. But I'd help her get everything together. I've always been organized. I hate to hunt for stuff and shuffle through papers and look for things. I have to take care of it in the first place and then I don't have that hassle. But, oh, Connie was terrible about it. She could never find—oh, when tax time would come, we'd all go crazy. She'd get her monthly bank statements, you know, and she'd be short two or three. We'd start looking for them in the drawers of the secretary and then we'd look in the drawers of the desk in the office. And then we'd look in the stacks of stuff in the family room or on the edges of the bookcase where everything was stacked. And they wouldn't be in any of those places. Then we'd look in the box in the little cedar room where she kept her safe and the records. They weren't in any of those places. So then she'd have to call the bank and have them do another one for her."

In later years Dr. Wilbur suffered an incapacitating stroke that reversed their initial roles—Shirley became her caretaker. Although this was a highly unusual position for a former patient to assume, Shirley did just that without hesitation. Her love for Dr. Wilbur enabled her to accomplish the Herculean task of managing Dr. Wilbur's treatment in her own home.

Since Dr. Wilbur's husband's death in the 1970's, there was never any question in Shirley's mind about who would assume the duty of taking care of Dr. Wilbur. Shirley was the one whom Dr. Wilbur wanted by her side. She didn't want to go to a nursing home so Shirley carried out her wishes.

Shirley temporarily left her own home on Henry Clay Boulevard and moved into Dr. Wilbur's home on Bristol Road. She drove back and forth in order to maintain the basic necessities at her own house.

Shirley performed various jobs for Dr. Wilbur. "The phone would ring. She'd answer it and then she'd tell them to wait a minute. She'd come out where I was and say, 'In what capacity do I know So-and-So? You know, relative, friend, former patient, who?' And I'd give her a little rundown and it's just like she never heard of them. And I'd tell her what I think is pertinent, and then she goes back and talks to them."

I empathized, "That must have been hard for you."

"Yeah. Hard to see it. Of course, her reasoning went with it. She was so unreasonable about a lot of things. But she was all right with me."

"Would she listen to you?"

"Yeah. Oh, she always listened to me. And she relied on me a hundred percent and she didn't argue with me and she didn't complain ever, about anything. But everybody else, she just couldn't get along. Argumentative. She liked a good fight."

I offered, "Sometimes stroke patients do that with everyone."

Shirley emphasized, "Well, she said she'd trust me with anything. She told me that years ago. And she did. I had power of attorney for a long time. I wrote all her checks and paid her bills and deposited her money and all those things, and everything from her stocks and bonds and all that, I took care of for years.

I said, "It was a full-time job for you."

"I spent anywhere from six to eight hours a day doing book work and so forth. Usually it would be at night, because I did housework in the daytime. We had a cleaning lady come once in a while, but we had to let the maid go because she [Connie] couldn't get along with her. I did the cooking. And of course, she had this terrible tremor, so she couldn't feed herself. So I guess about three years that I fed her. It was—oh, I was busy."

"Did you have a break, ever go on vacation?" I asked.

"Oh, no. I couldn't leave her. It was all right. I had people to help, you know. I had a yard man that did errands and go to the drugstore. Once, she got so bad at the end, after the stroke and so on, we had nurse's aides around the clock. When she got real bad we had the nurses because she had the I.V. and everything."

Shirley continued, "But we kept her there at home. I had promised her that I wouldn't put her in a nursing home and that I'd stay with her. And I took care of everything and watched what everybody did and kept track of the schedule so there'd be sure to be somebody there and everything. And it was—I can see now that it was a lot. At that time, all I saw was, that I was just busy every minute."

"For three years?" I repeated.

"Yeah. Well, it was more than that. I was over there six years, but

I wasn't that busy. But the later years I was, because she had fifty years of medical files in those file cabinets. She had eight big cabinets upstairs and a couple downstairs she brought from her office and I had to through all of those."

"What did you do with them?"

"The ones that were more than six years old, you could destroy. I had to go through them carefully—I had to find that out, first place and second place. I had to do it extremely carefully, because if somebody gets hold of some of this material—she had a number of professional people that didn't want it known that—she had, oh, people that were murderers, and so on, that never confessed, and things, you know, that could do a lot of damage. And so I destroyed them. The others, I kept. There were celebrities and so on. I was going to be sure nobody put anything together. I had lined up six wastebaskets. And I would tear the records and I would put some of each one in each basket. Then I would bag them in separate bags. The yardman would take them to dumpsters in different parts of town. If it was very sensitive material he would burn it in the pit in the back yard. And I could trust him. He'd been there about twenty years, helping, doing yard work and things. And, a very intelligent person. He had a college education. He did yard work because that's what he wanted to do, but he could do anything. I was probably too fussy, but I didn't take any chances."

Shirley continued, "I hired Teresa. I've known her for twenty years. She helped me at Dr. Wilbur's. She's very reliable. There were times when she would stay forty-eight hours straight because they couldn't get anybody. And we had a nursing service, but you couldn't rely on them. They couldn't get anybody sometimes. And I couldn't be alone with her because I couldn't do everything. I did the cooking and I could feed her—she couldn't feed herself. But I couldn't lift her. I couldn't get her from the bed to the wheelchair or anything."

Shirley said, "She [Connie] had a lot of letters to answer all the time. So I had Dee—Dee was her secretary—and I would just dictate the letters when I had a chance and she'd take them off the dictaphone machine and type them. Oh, she was a life-saver in that respect because I could no longer type—arthritis in my fingers."

I said, "I don't know how you did all that."

"Well, I wonder sometimes myself."

"When you look back now, wasn't it incredible how you could go through that?"

She said, "Yeah, of course, I was so sick then. I had a lot of trouble with my back." Unknown to most people Shirley had breast cancer which was spreading to other parts of her body. The cancer did not deter Shirley in her pursuit of the best care for Dr. Wilbur, who grew progressively weaker. She and Shirley devised a system of communication.

Shirley related, "She didn't have much strength, but she would squeeze my hand. That's the way she answered my questions. She'd squeeze my hand if the answer was 'yes' and I asked her things, you know. I asked her if she was in pain, and she said, 'Yes.' And I said, 'Is it your back? Your stomach? Your head?' And she squeezed my hand. I said, 'Do you have a headache?' And she squeezed it again. And I said, 'Do you want me to have the nurse get something for it?' And she squeezed my hand. But of course, when she got so weak, she could barely squeeze, and it took a long time for her to do it."

I said, "To respond. It took time to register, huh?"

Shirley said, "Earlier than that, weeks before that, when I'd ask her something or tell her something, and it would be a long time before she said anything. And then she'd answer me and she said, 'I hear the words, but I have to process them.'"

"Did Connie die at home?" I asked.

"I kept her—oh, yes, I was with her. And I knew she was going when I went to bed that night. I told the nurse to call me when the end—after a while I got a feeling I should go, and so I got up and went in and I said, 'Should I get dressed now?' and she said, 'I think so. I was just going to call you.' So I was there with her. Yeah. She knew it."

I asked, "Connie knew?"

Shirley replied, "Yeah. She was, I guess, only semi-conscious, but she would squeeze my hand.

Dr. Wilbur died in Shirley's arms.

Afterwards, Shirley moved back into her own home.

"I was so tired. Worn out. I didn't want to see anybody or go anywhere or do anything. I just wanted to come home and sit here. Some of my friends were worried about me, but they said however they understood. They said it was a terrible strain. They didn't see how I did all that. But, you know, you do. You don't have a choice. If you care about somebody, you do it. You don't think about it. But it still takes a lot out of you."

When Shirley told me this, it was difficult for me to accept that she had inoperable brain cancer and was close to death herself. Although the pain in her voice was audible, we continued to have interesting conversations. I hoped that our talks diverted her attention from her pain, at least temporarily. Sometimes she even laughed.

Her mobility became very limited. She now slept in a big easy chair with a footstool. She actually found it comfortable when she didn't roll over on her side. As long as she stayed perfectly still, the pain was bearable. She used a cane to walk from her living room to the kitchen. Often she needed help with normal daily activities.

• • •

Over the years, Naomi and Jim visited Shirley and Dr. Wilbur many times. They witnessed the different stages of their relationship.

Naomi told me that Shirley and Dr. Wilbur had confirmed that Flora's book *Sybil* "was 100% accurate."

Years prior to my contacting Shirley, Naomi received a letter from her. It confirmed what Shirley told me about taking care of Dr. Wilbur. The letter read:

> "Dr. Wilbur's memory was bad. Bad memory, bad judgment. I lived with her for six years. She was in a wheelchair

> for two years. During the day, I went through her papers. There were famous people, sensitive material, people kept writing to her—had to answer letters on multiple personality. Fifty years of records. I've lost her—left it to God."

Becoming a patient of Dr. Wilbur was the pivotal moment in Shirley's life. Her successful treatment provided her with a second chance at life as a whole person. In later years Shirley became the pivotal person in Dr. Wilbur's life. She was her primary companion and caregiver.

Shirley had spent thirty-eight years with Dr. Wilbur—longer than the time she had spent with her mother. Shirley was thirty-one when she began treatment with Dr. Wilbur in New York on October 18, 1954. From that time until Dr. Wilbur died in 1992, their lives were intertwined.

CHAPTER 10

A Life Fulfilled

A thank you note from Shirley illustrated her appreciation of nature and its soothing powers. She often sought nature's solace when dealing with the hardships in her life. Nature had the ability to evoke joy as she moved towards finding peace. The note read:

> "Dear Patrick,
>
> The magnificent bouquet of flowers you sent have arrived at the end of what had been a particularly stressful day—could not have been better timed nor more appreciated! I just can't tell you what it meant—the joy—the hope it inspired. Thank you so very much.
>
> Also enjoyed the long letter you sent earlier—glad all is well with you—you do sound very busy—I plan to answer that letter one day (soon, I hope) as I want to comment on a couple of things you said.
>
> Thank you again!
> Sincerely, Shirley"

Flowers and other wonders of nature were gifts that Shirley treasured. Her friends were also treasured. They appreciated her kindness to them and they in turn expressed their love for her.

She shared an example of a friend's thoughtfulness during a telephone conversation; we'd been discussing some severe storms that had hit Lexington.

Shirley said, "We're not prepared for them very well. And of course the utility lines are above ground here and there are so many trees. Trees go down with the ice and take the lines down. One spring we had five days with no electricity. It was about 40 degrees which is cold if you don't have any heat in the house. So Roberta [Shirley's helpful friend] came. I stayed that way overnight—I sat here all bundled up. The house was so cold. And she called me and I said well they'll have it on before too long. She said, 'No, they won't. It's all over town.' And the next thing I know she came over. Roberta said, 'I called all the motels and I found one with a vacancy. Pack your bags. I'm taking you to a motel.' So she did. I stayed there four days and she looked after things here at the house and when the electricity came on she put the heat up and got the house warm and came and got me and brought me home to a warm house. She checked on me. She came two or three times a day and brought me food. They didn't serve meals at the motel, didn't have room service or anything. It's the best we could do. So many of the big hotels were in town and that's where the electricity was off. This was out on the edge of town. So it was a good place to stay."

Shirley's account brought back a personal memory of staying in a motel in Kentucky and I told her about it: "Once I was in Louisville for the Kentucky Derby and I stayed in a motel that had once been a jail. The rooms were actually jail cells." I described the experience as being "great fun."

She laughed, "Yeah, as long as you have your freedom."

Her freedom from mental illness enabled her to produce her art, which was a great source of fulfillment. She sent me a print of a painting done by Mary, one of her alters, called *The Neighbors* and a print of *The Family* that had been painted by Sybil.

She said, "A few of my other originals were in chalk or on thin paper. And thirty-five or forty years of handling them—they just disintegrated. There are a few that I didn't keep, but I have one hundred and eighty-nine or something. They'll be coming one of these days. We got a lithographer in Cincinnati to do those. We took the original to him and he did the lithograph from that. We just had two of the paintings done. "The Neighbors" and "The Family." I've got two to five thousand of each.

I exclaimed, "You have?!"

She laughed, "Oh, you'll know it when you get them. Connie sold quite a few. We made quite a bit of money. That is what I was thinking you could use for scholarship money. The first five hundred are numbered and after that they become less valuable. They are not all numbered. I was not able to do that. I numbered the ones we sold and kept records and everything, but all that got to be too much with Connie to take care of.

"If you have lithographs made you want a lithographer that you can trust, that will destroy the plates afterward. They showed Connie the broken plates. You don't want them selling some on the side or selling them to a foreign country or any number of things to make money on the side. You want to be sure you have a market for the prints before you get them made. You can try it out with the prints of the two paintings that you will have."

Although Shirley died before the paintings and the prints were sent to me, she believed that her wishes would be carried out and that we would be funding scholarships for needy art students with the proceeds from sales of her work. This idea pleased her immensely.

Our conversation on February 5, 1998, a few weeks before she died, was about the difficulty of being an artist.

Shirley said, "I used to wonder sometimes why I had to be an artist. There were two or three other things I was too. But in every case it was what I considered a minority thing to be. I thought, 'Why do I have to be interested in those things? Can't get anywhere with it. You can't convince anybody of anything.

"That was when I was real young, in college and so on. I felt like it was inferior. I wasn't in the mathematics department or this or that. I majored also in English and Literature and so forth. But none of this was like being in sports or something important. Ha."

I agreed, "Right. Art wasn't considered that important, huh?"

Shirley said, "I don't know whether it was or not, but to me it wasn't because they didn't have art galleries and exhibits. They couldn't get money for the art departments and they always had them in the basement of the schools and all this kind of thing. And everybody else was... So I thought, 'Well, why couldn't I have been something important?' Anyway I got over it, but I never forgot the feeling, because I ran into it with my students. Some of them felt like art was the stepchild to everything else."

I asked, "Did you ever feel tortured when you painted?"

She responded quickly, "No, I enjoyed it. It was my life. I couldn't do without it. And everything turned on it and all my thoughts and all that."

This was very different from the time she was painting during her analysis. In her diary, she wrote:

> *May 16, 1956.*
>
> "I am worried about art now---can't finish my circus piece I felt so strong with---I wondered when that feeling left and I realize it was when I got the offer from the gallery and came home all excited and pleased (I was pleased) and thought that poster paint (as in circus pictures!)was something 'that could hang with oils' as far as medium was concerned. I lost something to fear. My anxiety is too much for me today---I can't even do my Central Park pieces---I feel very unworthy and unequal to the task of painting---I remember your saying on a few occasions that I should just go ahead and paint for myself and not for any purpose---that is the best---ISN'T IT? In fact it is just about the ONLY thing I can do---I am struggling so much (Yes, all

> these months) with that horse painting I am doing. I just sink inside every time I think of it---but do you see me getting right down to work on it and getting it done and out of the way for once and all? No, here I sit typing---then find a dozen other things to do."

I continued our conversation, "Van Gogh's suffering is apparent in his paintings. Since his paintings were not accepted in his lifetime, I think that added to his suffering."

Shirley agreed, "Oh, yes, I think he did. His mind was so mixed up that I think that his suffering came from other things as well. It's all mixed together. His work is strong, magnetic. I'm fascinated by him. Roberta was telling me the other day that her little granddaughter, who is in the second grade, is fascinated by Van Gogh. She was poking around the library and she found a book of some of his things and she brought it home for Roberta to read it to her. Roberta wanted me to tell her some things that she could tell the child. And I said, 'I can do a little better than that. I have a number of very fine Van Gogh prints I'll give you. They're unmatted. Just frame them for her room.' Oh, she was delighted. They were the ones of the sunflowers. And for a second grader that's very unusual."

Shirley continued, "She draws a lot. I imagine she's artistic. Roberta is. And Roberta loves the modern paintings that I have that don't have any subject matter. I had one, sort of a fantasy thing, that I called *Blue Motion*. I had it hanging over the piano and when she'd come, she'd always sit where she could look at it. She said, 'Oh, it just makes me feel so happy and relaxed. It's just beautiful.' She kept saying it and saying it until finally I gave it to her."

I said, "Isn't it wonderful that she would react that way to it?"

Shirley said, "From an uneducated lady you wouldn't think that… It's got to be innate or it wouldn't have been there with her. Oh well, she thinks I'm wonderful anyway."

"Well, you are."

Shirley laughed, "She's a great gal and we're really very fond of each other. And we're both Scrabble players. We're a lot alike. She loves poetry. One of her sons writes poetry, very nice verses."

"You will inspire these children through her."

"I encourage them. I give them books and they love them. The little girl loves books. I've given her dozens of books over the years. Her grandmother reads to her. She said the child takes such good care of her books."

I interjected, "You've just reminded me. I know two young men who have just published a children's book called *Snow Inside The House*. It's written by Sean Diviny and illustrated by Joe Rocco. I'm going to the book signing and I'll buy one for you. If you want to pass it on to Roberta, I'll send you another one."

Shirley stated, "Oh, one would be just fine. I can share it with her."

I said, "I want you to see the drawings. They're unusual and the story is so original."

"Great. That'd be fine."

When I bought the book for Shirley I told the author, Sean, and the illustrator, Joe, that it was for an artist, without revealing Shirley's identity. So the inscription and drawing for Shirley were apropos for an artist.

I continued our conversation about art: "When you talk about that stepchild feeling—I think it has to do with the value that society places on art."

"Yeah, well that's what I'm talking about."

I added, "Some people don't value it, right?"

Shirley murmured, "My dad would look at things I did and he would say, "Well, it's nice, but I don't understand it.' Or he would tell people, 'She studies art. She's going to be an art teacher. The teacher says that she's real good.' He didn't know, because he didn't understand that kind of art. He was very realistic. His drawings were ducks with every feather in place and that sort of thing. Beautiful. Pen and ink drawings and pencil drawings. But he didn't understand things that had a slant, that weren't realistic. They were what I would call more artistic than realistic."

"Some people are tied down to the realistic, concrete and it's very hard for them to transcend."

"Well, it's what they were taught."

"When you were teaching, did you get satisfaction from that?"

"Oh, yes."

Shirley kept up a correspondence with many of her former art students. When she was homebound it was her window to the world. Since she could no longer take care of her garden, I often sent her floral arrangements. On January 24, 1998, the day before her birthday and a month before she died, I sent her flowers.

Shirley exclaimed, "Patrick, Patrick, Patrick! You are something else!"

"Did you get it?"

"Oh yes. I'm telling you there are no words for it. It is the most beautiful. Those lilies are just heavenly and those coral colored daises and the white roses. I don't know if I ever saw anything so beautiful in my life. The lilies are pink striped with little dots in them. My favorite lily. I just love them. It's just so beautiful. You shouldn't do those things."

"Well, it brings a little cheer into your life and it's your birthday!"

"I would like so much to get my paper and pastels out and do a drawing of those lilies. I thought when Dee got back I'd have her get the supplies out and I'd get a board across the chair and see if I could do it. I thought if I could get a decent drawing of the design of the lilies the way I see them in my mind, then I could send it to you."

I said, "Oh great! I'd love that."

She said, "I don't know if I can manage it. I love to draw flowers. I'll use pastels because I'm too shaky to paint anything."

I said, "You can do that?"

She replied, "I have a little trouble with the colors. Navy and purple and brown all look alike. I did one of what I thought were white magnolias, but they were cream-colored. It gave them a richness so it was alright. It's been a number of months since I did anything at all, but I just yearn to do it. It's so relaxing and I just love to do anything. There are little squirrels I'd like to do in pencil."

I said, "That's a wonderful talent to have. That's good therapy for you, too."

She said, "Yeah, it is. If I can work at all. I'm shaky."

I said, "Well, whatever you can do, that's alright. It could be a shaky squirrel or a shaky lily. That's fine, too. Gives it a little twist, a little originality to it."

She said, "Yeah, just call it 'Modern Art.'"

I said, "Right. Some of the things they have here in the galleries! I really can't relate to them."

Shirley said, "I have that trouble with some things, too. And then they give you a long lingo about it. You don't know if it's the truth and you are too stupid to be grasping it or if it's just hocus-pocus. One time, my girlfriend and I, we just absolutely collapsed laughing. And I know it was terrible because the people around us went to giggling. It was the Museum of Modern Art."

I exclaimed, "Here in New York?"

"Yes! They had a huge painting. It was like six feet by five feet or something. A big, huge painting with a little narrow silver frame on it. And the whole thing was black, and in the center, there was a little white dot. The name of it was 'White Dot on Black'. And it just struck us funny. And we just hooted right out loud. But honestly! That's one museum I didn't care for. They had things, I just didn't care for that museum."

I said, "They do have some really weird things in there. One year, it was wonderful when they had the whole museum filled with Picasso's work."

She said, "Well, that'd be different. Well, that I would like to see."

• • •

Shirley painted because her artistic nature sought this medium. While she was living a modest life as an artist, I was observing the other extreme—that of a "superstar" artist, Andy Warhol. Long before I knew about Shirley, I was acting in a play that had been written by Warhol's screenwriter, so I was invited into the inner circle. Not fully a participant, I was merely an observer to this American phenomenon. I was amazed at how unassuming and selfless Warhol could be, showing great interest in other people. Yet, he could also draw all the media and television cameras to him. When I was at the New York Film Festival honoring a French film, when Warhol entered, all the attention turned to him.

In 1964 he captured the art world with his silk screen of the Campbell's Soup Can. I was at the "factory" when reporters from *Time* magazine came to see this famous work of art. I overheard one of them remarking to his colleagues: "What is all the fuss!!! There isn't even a naked girl in the painting." So much for the appreciation and popularity of art in the 1960s!

Flora met Andy Warhol at my birthday party. Carroll Baker was acting in "Warhol's Bad." Our birthdays are three days apart so Warhol gave us a joint birthday party where he gave me a lithograph of the Electric Chair. Flora spent most of the time sitting on a sofa deep in conversation with a huge, fierce man. At the end of the party she told me that he wanted to take her home. I informed her that he had just been released from prison after serving his sentence for murder. I took her home.

Although Shirley was greatly amused by the esoteric paintings at the Museum of Modern Art, she liked Warhol because he painted "recognizable objects."

Her paintings evolved out of the different periods of her life and each had significant meaning and offered important insights into her world. Some had readily recognizable objects, but others required deeper analysis.

• • •

I said, "I'm so glad that you like the floral arrangement. I want to bring a little cheer into your life. It's your birthday."

"It will be a conversation piece for two weeks. It is just so gorgeous. I know they came from you but I thank God for them too." She gave a hearty laugh, which was so good to hear.

"Yes, He made them. Will anyone come over tomorrow? Your birthday is tomorrow, isn't it?"

"Yes. A few people said they'd stop by."

"Do people from the church still come?"

"Occasionally. I don't encourage much company. It's just too hard for me. I can visit on the phone, but it's difficult for me to have people come. The way I look. The way I feel. I mean I'm not comfortable with people seeing me this way. They know this and they respect it. They call. I get phone calls from a lot of people."

"You know they all love you."

"I get friendship cards and 'I'm thinking of you' cards. Things that I appreciate very much and I can handle that. But the visits are something else at this stage. I received a beautiful three-generation picture from my cousin Naomi and her daughter and the little girl. Dee brought me a loaf of homemade pumpkin bread which I love. I got a stack of birthday cards and notes, so I opened things today. I decided to do it today."

"We'll celebrate today and tomorrow. You get two days. You deserve two days."

"Well, I think that 75 years deserves two days."

I blurted, "I can't imagine being that old."

"I can't either."

"Did you ever think you'd make it?"

"No, never. I never thought I'd live beyond 50. Never planned to when I was young. I figured 50 was the cutoff date. But I don't feel that old, I mean, you know, I can't do much of anything. 75 is what I considered old or what I thought old age was. But it's not what I feel."

"In your mind you still feel younger?"

"Yeah, it's kind of as if I could get up and go if this would just clear up. That kind of thing. Of course, I know better, but it's...."

Shirley exemplified the conundrum of aging. The younger person trapped in the body of the older version of that person. The mind may think and feel as if it were 25, but the body has the ravages of 75 years. Even though the mind may think in a manner appropriate to the younger age—other people may react unsympathetically to youthful behavior coming from a 75 year-old body.

I offered, "You do very well being limited in your movement."

"That's what the nurse said. The doctor keeps saying he's amazed that I can move around at all. From the condition that my back is in. It hurts every step when I'm up. When I'm sitting down, then it doesn't hurt so much. Sometimes it does, but other times it doesn't. But moving around always hurts. So I limit it, but it's boring. I have to do something. I get up and move around at least to look out the windows and see what my neighbors are up to." She chuckled.

I laughed, "That will keep you occupied. So, are you going dancing for your birthday?"

"I think so. I never did in my whole life, but I think it's time I started," she laughed.

A simple thing—dancing—that so many of us take for granted was denied to Shirley. The religion of her youth forbade it. She didn't express regret or resentment, but accepted it as one of the things in life she did not experience. Now, even if she wanted to dance, she was physically unable to do so. Instead she used humor to reflect on the vagaries of life.

She added, "Thank you for calling. I do appreciate the calls."

"I know and I appreciate them too. Take care. Bye."

"I will. Bye."

Shirley's sense of decorum and manners never left her, even when it proved discomforting. One day I called her and she said she was not able to talk then and asked me to call later.

I called an hour later and said, "Hello, it's Patrick, Can you talk now?"

She apologized, "I'm sorry. I'll tell you what happened. I was supposed to take my medicine about 3:00 and I always have to eat when I take that. So about 2:30 I went to the kitchen to start fixing lunch, and got the food going, and the phone rang. It was my doctor and he wanted to know if he could come by in about fifteen minutes. I said, 'Well, if you want to.' So I turned off the stove and everything and hoped he wouldn't stay so long I couldn't take the medicine. I was starting to hurt. So he came in about ten minutes. He had his wife with him. I had never met her before. I met his first wife, but not this one. She's about half his age and a very vivacious, lovely woman. They brought me a Christmas plant and they just got set down when you called. So I thought they weren't going to stay very long, so that's why I asked you to call later. Otherwise, I wouldn't have been so rude."

"Oh no, no. I'm glad you had company."

"Then after they left, I got two phone calls and I thought, 'Boy, the phone's going to be busy when you call.' So at the same time as I got my lunch, I talked on the phone and ate at the same time. And I thought for anybody in my position, I certainly live a hectic life."

We both laughed at the paradox. I kidded, "You're running around."

"I tried to be quiet for the last ten years."

"You sound good."

She said, "I'm tired, but I'm all right. Once I get the medicine and it takes effect, I feel better. When it begins to wear off, I get to hurting. I just get really very tired with it and not good for anything. But I've got my second wind now. So how are you doing?"

"I'm getting ready to visit my family for Christmas. I'll come back to New York Sunday night."

"That sounds nice."

"Will you have anyone there on Christmas?"

"Oh, yes. Two or three people have called and said they were going to come by and of course the nurse will be here. There's always something going on."

"That's good. Keeps you busy."

"Some days it's almost too much. It's wearing to try to keep up with things, but I do enjoy people."

"When you feel tired just say, 'I'm tired now.' People understand."

"I guess it shows. Sometimes they say, 'You're getting tired. I'll leave.'"

• • •

A couple weeks before Christmas, I sent her a Christmas arrangement. She sent me a Christmas card dated December 15, 1997. Printed on the card was:

> "Season's Greetings. Wishing you a beautiful holiday season and a Happy New Year."

Inside Shirley wrote:

> "The precious little red & green sleigh with bold runners arrived filled with gorgeous greenery and red and white flowers. A real holiday treat. Thank you ever so much!! Fondly, Shirley."

On Christmas I called her. She exclaimed, "The flowers are absolutely beautiful!"

"Still?"

"Oh my, yes. I put them where it's cool at night and then I put fresh water in them in the mornings and bring them in here. I take real good care of my plants. Everybody admires that little sleigh. It's the cutest thing. It's got one of those new kind of ribbons, bows and it has some wire kind of stuff woven into it. It's just gorgeous, a big plaid. And there's some holly with a white edge on it. It's a gorgeous piece. I thank you so much for it."

"You're welcome. I just hope you enjoy the holiday."

"I think I will, if I can live through it."

I said, "You're doing well with the medicine. You keep track of it?"

"Yeah, if I don't have too much joy."

I joked, "If you don't drink too much."

She laughed, "Oh, no."

"Do you drink at all?"

"No. I don't. I did at one time for a little while. I had drinks a few times with Connie. Then I got thinking about it and I thought, 'Well, you know, I've got troubles enough. I don't need to become an alcoholic because I liked it. So I guess I'll just skip this particular thing. I like it too much.'"

"You didn't want to develop another problem."

Shirley continued, "So I told Connie that and she didn't argue with me. She would drink, but when she got older she stopped. She had this tremor and glaucoma. Caffeine and alcohol are not good for that. So we both cut out coffee."

I admitted, "I drink coffee in the morning. That's what I'm addicted to."

"I was too, but I got over it. You know, things change when you get older and symptoms in older people are different from symptoms of the same thing in a younger person. And you have to be kind of alert to what you're doing."

• • •

On December 28, 1997, I called Shirley again to inquire about her health.

She said, "I've had one visitor after another. I'm adjusting to it."

"I just got back from visiting my family in Rochester."

Shirley inquired, "How's your mother?"

"She did well for the first Christmas since my sister died. We visited relatives so it kept her busy. But it wore me out."

"Yeah, anything out of the ordinary. Visiting is hard. Keep up your spirits. I wish I could show you a photograph I got. I think you'd get a smile out of it."

"What is it?"

"The youngest member of my family, my cousin Naomi's granddaughter. It's a picture of her when she was not quite a year old and she's bald-headed. She's wearing a white dress that goes all the way to the floor, sitting in a little rocker and she's holding a doll that is bald-headed. Looks just like her. It's just a scream seeing her with the bald-headed doll!"

Shirley's interest in her extended family and friends brought her sustenance. She always maintained a social network, even during the time she suffered from Multiple Personality Disorder. Shirley was often embarrassed when people related an incident in which she was a participant but didn't remember. But this did not deter her pursuit of relationships with family and friends. MPD/DID could have set the stage for her to isolate, but she did not isolate.

Shirley even kept in touch with her friends from Mankato College. There were twelve girls who lived on the same floor in the dormitory.

She said, "We were bunched together, all twelve of us. For fifty-three years now we've kept in touch. I had a round robin letter. Everybody writes a letter and takes out the one from the time before and sends it on and it comes about three times a year. So all these years, all these people and their children and now their grandchildren. We have a reunion every year and it's usually in Minnesota. That's where most of them live. They had it all written up in the alumni paper. Most of them sent me birthday cards this year."

I said, "Isn't that something?"

Shirley replied, "No matter where we were, one of the girls said on her card, 'Old friends are the best, aren't they?'"

I asked, "When was the last time you went?"

She said, "Oh dear, twelve, fifteen years ago, I think."

I said, "You have a great correspondence going with them."

She replied, "Yes, I used to have really a lively one with a lot of people, but they live in so many different places. So many of my students keep in touch with me. But it just got so that I couldn't keep up with it anymore. I hear from so many people that I hardly ever get a chance to write to. But I appreciate hearing from them."

I said, "They know your situation and so they can still keep in touch with you even if they don't hear from you."

She replied, "Well, they just figured I was busy because they knew I did a lot of things. I traveled and so on. But they didn't know I wasn't well. I haven't told anybody that. It's not necessary."

I said, "You don't want people asking you all the time?"

She said, "Well, there's that, but it's not me. Inside I'm what I always was and it's not necessary to know all these other things. And besides, we're interested in other things and it doesn't center around sickness."

Shirley didn't want to burden other people with her cancer. If her friends were busy, she found other activities to occupy her time. When she was alone, she enjoyed watching television and listening to the radio. She enjoyed choosing what she wanted—a simple pleasure that was denied to her during her youth.

During the period of her analysis, on February 19, 1966, Shirley wrote in her diary:

> "I was permitted to hear radio programs if Mama liked them also. Otherwise, 'We can't be bothered with nonsense.' I was permitted the indulgence (considered such because it was not really 'necessary') of two of the children's programs, 'Skippy' and 'Jack Armstrong' --- (Oh boy, I loved neither). Skippy was such a kid and the other was so evident it was not interesting. But he did have a smart dog and when the dog had a puppy from heaven the network (radio network, that is) had a contest: Just Send In One Kellogg's Box Top (as if we had any other kind...) Well, back to the dog---they couldn't think of a name for her puppy either so there was a contest. The winner's name and phone number

appeared on the corn flakes boxes a month later. Mother almost wrote to the winning kid to ask him if he really won. Then just when I thought she was going to, she announced she wouldn't waste a two cent stamp to prove something she already knew. It was a put-up job."

Referring to the second radio show, "Jack Armstrong," she wrote:

"Then tragedy struck! Just as Judy married Jerry and was all set to be happy ever after, Jan was told John was dead! So, of course, Judy and Jerry had to move in with Jane and the housekeeper to help care for the poor fatherless twins so Jane could go out and work hard in an office to support said kiddies. Mama felt awful --- and I guess she did --- after all she did believe all that crap and the sadder and the more wretched the individual in the story, the more she 'felt' for them. And days like that were no fun for me either ---she would be so irritable and she would go around sort of daydreaming and developing headaches and be so 'tired out' --- I wonder why? I know people react to stories in books or plays and movies, etc., but she over reacted to the 'awful' (her term) events and didn't follow the story very well and seemed to miss completely anything humorous or 'light'. Well, to get on with the story---later---much later---the poor twins needed a father and Jane had to decide from the many ardent admirers as to whom she would marry (a good spot for a contest but no one needed any box tops at the station, I guess) and finally she married a fellow whom it seemed to me took over and bossed the kids and ran everything. But Mother thought he was perfect---just the reforming influence that was needed before it was too late and the children were delinquent. The guy's name was Donald North. Mother and I never got over disputing one way or another about him until the program went off the air.

So when one day I was sitting beside you and (what seemed like) all out of the blue you said to me, 'Oh, by the way, does the name North mean anything to you?' I got all flustered and almost went that-a-way and I got so worked up and I didn't know why---Remember I said to you there was a Donald North and Mother liked him but I hated him only I can't remember who or what or something ---it doesn't seem real. You said it was all right. It was just that you had found out that it was the name of a police detective in Precinct 24 that I had talked with. But I could not shake the feeling. It disturbed me for a long, long time. I could not place Donald North. I remembered reading the names of Mr. and Mrs. North in the radio and TV listings as detectives in serials but this could not be it. For I didn't listen and I did not have a TV. I knew another family named North that I remembered who 'really' existed but for several weeks I could not get hold of that Donald North business. Then one day I asked myself why I thought of twins every time I thought of that name. And 'POP' Jack and Jill fell into place (or down hill). So you see how much power there was behind those old radio programs Mother and I so lovingly endured together as a family not all there.

Then there was a program 'Hymns of All Churches' that was broadcast every weekday morning---this we had to hear because it was one of the few 'good' programs on the radio that justified Christian people having a radio that was otherwise a waste of time. The hymns made Mother think of her dear, sweet, patient mama and her wonderful musical father who led the choir for so many years (always this wording and just this kind of sentence---with all the heart rendering sighs and wistful glances---I wonder why she clung to her father's 'status' so much---I think I see some reasons but it is aside from this so we will leave it for now). I did not like this program for it made me feel dead---funeral music---sad---and somehow made me feel guilty as if I ought to be doing more religiously or something. I don't know what but it often made me feel sick enough I had to go lie down and many of those times I lost out just before or just as the program began but usually (if not a number of other things pressing in) came to when 'Its High Noon in New York, and Time for Kate Smith!' with 'When The Moon Comes Over the Mountain' and so forth. 11:00 where we were and I could not see why. And every spring and every fall our programs got changed as to time. This caused a real upheaval in our household. Mother had just gotten things going smoothly on the old schedule when the time changed and we had to hear things at a different time (in those days it made more change than now) and I can still see the strained position and the stressed look when she would stand in the door and look at the paper the night of the 'time change' hoping yet fearing what she would see in the new listing---Would Ma Perkins come right at dinner time?! (Save us from that fate). Sometimes she would sigh with relief. She could hear all of her programs and still have meals at the exact time she had always considered they had to be eaten. But sometimes something was changed and she would get so peeved she would threaten again to write in (where ever that was) and tell them 'a thing or two'. It is a wonder she did not go there herself---good thing New York WAS 'way off'. They were lucky. I remember how angry she got when one of her favorites got set for 3:45 at the time the school made a new plan to begin at 8:45 and dismiss at 3:45 daily. It was so distressing to her to try to listen to the program in the sun parlour which was on the back of the house, and watch the kids coming out of school at the same time from the front of the house, the latter seen only from the living room windows and she could not miss either. It just occurs to me what you meant when you said once that my mother was a very compulsive person. I agreed as I thought of some examples such as her washing and boiling things so much and so forth but I just realized that what I have been telling makes it look as if it invaded several other areas too. Well, I never did find out about the time situation until I was in 9th grade and we studied it in Math. But the teacher was such a crab. She scared the wits out of me (so that's where they went!) and I could not get it straight so I took the book home and showed my Dad. He was busy so we just went over it briefly and he said let Mother help---Mother tried! She could not see why they had to change the time in the first place. After all, they had never hea[r]d of Day-Light-Saving Time when she was a youngster. (Dad intervened with something about the boon to farmers but he got no where, of course). 'After all (head erect, brows raised, and shoulders stiff) we raised plenty of good corn in Illinois then and I guess we could do it now without changing all the radio programs twice a year.' Who wanted to refute such an intelligent argument? I have always thought (or at least for years and years) that I would like very much to have seen my mother on a witness stand---I always day-dreamed it one way---she would get the lawyers and the judge so mixed up that they would not know where they were and that would just show people how impossible it was

> to get Mother to help me. I guess I did not know how significant that day-dream was. No one seemed to show up to help me and no one even seemed to see a need for it---after all, I was no 'orphan' (Mother's term for...ah...well) but I had a loving mother and father who did everything for me. Yes they did. The thing about it is I never did find out about that time business. So in the 6-weeks test I got it wrong. This made mother mad because they asked such foolishness. (Anything newer than when she was a youngster). And she did not blame me (sometimes she didn't!) for not bothering with it (only I did bother with, by and for it) and Dad said that if the school taught it it was necessary to learn it. But they should TEACH it and not expect the parents to do it---that is what teachers were paid for---I ran into that time stuff in Geometry class in college---then last summer I let you tell me how long it would actually take me to come home from Detroit---.
>
> Sometimes, though, I think it is rather remarkable that I ever learned much of anything, all things considered."

• • •

During one of our conversations in 1997, Shirley told me about one TV program she especially enjoyed watching: "I watch those Brit-coms—the British comedies on Saturday night. They come on at 9 to 11. Sometimes I'm too tired to watch more than one or two. But sometimes I take a nap before they come on. I like the one called 'Keeping up Appearances.' I think it's a scream."

"What's it about?"

She said, "This gal tries to make out she is somebody. Her name is 'Hyacinth Bucket' but she pronounces it 'Bouquet'. She has sisters: 'Daisy', 'Rose', and 'Violet'. Of course, one of them is rich and has a swimming pool, and the other one's very poor and has a slob for a husband, so she's always pushing them out the door. Her husband, Richard, is a long-suffering guy. He makes all these faces and everything behind her back. She's always doing something to impress people and it's so ridiculous it's very funny. Everybody calls her 'That Bucket Woman.' She's a marvelous actress."

Shirley didn't need to venture far from her home to be entertained. She appreciated the things that were available with her limited mobility.

• • •

Shirley found a way to live the second half of her life in keeping with Carl Jung's theory by placing emphasis on the "cultural" aspect of living. She was not defeated by her physical illness as she had not been defeated by her mental illness in her youth. She used her formidable intelligence to cope with the disability of multiple personalities and later with the debilitating aspects of cancer. She was able to analyze her state of being and to fight to correct her deficiencies. The strength that enabled her to persist in psychoanalysis, to overcome multiple personalities, now gave her the fortitude to carry on with the medical treatments to fight her cancer.

On January 25, 1998, I called Shirley to wish her a Happy 75th Birthday. Although in pain, she had been going through pictures to find the one of her posing with her painting at The National Arts Club. In 1955 she won the college student's art competition. At that time no one at the club knew that she was suffering from Multiple Personality Disorder and would be called "Sybil" in the 1973 book. She said, "I've been sorting through to get the picture for you. I will mail it tomorrow. Got to get it out, get myself around to get cardboard and an envelope and so forth. Everything is such an effort. I want to do things and it helps me to have something to do, but it's just so painful. It just gets kind of wearing. I get tired of it. At night I dream that I'm hurting. I get awake and I want to do something for it and I can't. But otherwise, going along fine. Everything's pretty good. I just made out my grocery list for tomorrow and wrote the check to go with it. I paid the phone bill."

These photographs of Shirley at The National Arts Club appear in Appendix C. It was Shirley's final present to me.

CHAPTER 11

The Paintings of Peggy, Marcia, Mary, Vanessa, and Sybil

In January, 1956, while undergoing analysis, Shirley wrote in her diary about her childhood painting:

> Grandma kept her writing tablet in a drawer and she let me use sheet after sheet of the paper for drawing. I was careful not to waste any and would draw small objects on every square inch of it on both sides. It was one of the most wonderful times I can remember---sitting there drawing and telling her all about my pictures. At home, I was forbidden to touch anything on the study desk or in Dad's office; and never, never was I to touch what Mother termed 'perfectly good paper' for just scribbling. She let me have scraps of paper, old envelopes that I could open and draw on the inside, or paper sacks (I never did like the seams in them.) And when Mother would come upstairs, (usually quietly to see if I were behaving myself) and find me drawing on the writing paper, she would be very stern and yank me by the arm down off the organ stool (turned up to its height for me to reach the desk) and tell Grandma that she should not

> let me waste paper that way. (I always felt very guilty and also ashamed that I had in some way 'wronged' Grandma.) Grandma would change the subject and another time when we were alone let me draw some more. (A friend once said, I worried on several occasions, when, as Peggy, she gave me paper and said I could draw---she said I kept asking repeatedly if she was sure it was all right to use all the good paper--- I seemed especially worried the other day about the colored sheets. I think that was due to the fact that I was taking each one out of a tablet like I had done at Grandma's). I used to draw people all the time, whole families with lots of children. I always drew the same sort of an arrangement with the oldest child a boy (big brother) and on down, each a head smaller than the previous one. I can remember Mother saying many times that she got so blamed tired of seeing drawings of families, families, families all the time. (I wonder if this is why I was surprised the other day when I was told that the person who was watching liked what I was drawing.)
>
> My early drawings always followed a similar set-up to this. Sometimes many more children, but almost always a boy, then a girl, then a boy, etc. The baby set on the floor. I learned to put one child behind another, to save space.

The following chapters contain paintings of Sybil and the alternate personalities Peggy, Marcia, Mary, and Vanessa. Each painted in her own style. My interpretations are based on my notes and knowledge of Shirley's history.

CHAPTER 12

Peggy's Paintings

Peggy was the first alternate personality to appear in Dr. Wilbur's office. Shirley had already been in therapy for three months. She described herself as having black hair in a Dutch haircut. She was the repository of the anger Shirley was not allowed to experience. Shirley remembered from the age of 2½ being told that anger was a sin. She had to repress it or God would punish her. She especially could not feel or express anger toward her mother. She learned that not only would God punish her, but that her mother would torture her. The nuances and reasons for anger produced two Peggy personalities. Peggy Lou Baldwin expressed anger directly by smashing glass. Peggy Ann Baldwin was more tactful. They were both fighters. They did things together, including painting.

Although there were restrictions placed upon Shirley's range of emotions, both Peggy Ann and Peggy Lou were free to express these forbidden feelings in their paintings. In the beginning they only used black and white because they felt they were not even allowed to express their feelings with color. As therapy progressed, Dr. Wilbur gave them permission to use other colors. Their drawings became more colorful and more complete. Later, they used violent reds, yellows and greens. As they made progress in therapy and their anger began to dissipate, they used warmer and softer colors.

1. Stemware. 2. *Glass Horse.* 3. *Glass Fish.* Black pencil drawings on white paper. Examples of Shirley's mother's devotion to cleaning her crystal. She demanded that it be spotless. Shirley was forced to clean the crystal until it was shining. In *Sybil*, the child Sybil was wrongfully accused of breaking the crystal pickle dish and punished. From then on, she associated crystal with danger. When her mother used crystal as a weapon to hurt her, Peggy would emerge to absorb Shirley's anger and use it in detailed drawings of crystal glasses, a horse, bowls, and a fish.

4. Self Away From Church. Tempera. Presents a lone childlike figure in the foreground. The figure is in profile bent over looking at the ground. Far away in the background is the church. Peggy is distanced from the church and its congregation. She often expressed feeling disconnected from the people around her.

5. *Christmas Tree.* Crayon drawing. Peggy's attempt to make a drawing with a joyful content, but she did it in black crayon against white paper. Christmas was unpleasant because Shirley would receive a great many toys and games which her mother would put away. Her mother told her that she could play with them some other time. However, Shirley's mother would give them away to "some poor family who didn't have anything for themselves". Shirley's family's fundamentalist religion did not permit them to celebrate Christmas in the usual Christian way.

6. Alone. Black crayon. Depicts her obstacles in the form of mountains. There is an ocean giving some sense of the life force which enabled Shirley to attempt to overcome the obstacles. She is the solitary figure sitting at the top. Her bravery was expressed by Peggy telling Dr. Wilbur, "I am all alone in the world, but I am still on top." This tiny figure is looking towards the horizon and the future.

7. *Trapped.* Black pencil drawing. An elaborate maze completely enclosed without any exit. It articulates Peggy's inner state. She often felt there was no way out of her horrendous situation except to die and be with her beloved grandmother in heaven.

8. Daddy's Car. Black, gray and white tempera. A painting of the front of her father's car. The ominous object with headlights like frightful eyes and a grill like the vicious mouth of her mother, conveys Shirley's hatred of the car, because of what transpired in it. When she was twelve, she and her mother sat in the car waiting for her father. Having severe cramps, Peggy complained to her mother, who told her to get out and walk around to ease the pain. Peggy became angry at her mother's insensitivity, which only intensified her pain. She got out and walked to the front of the car. She stood in front of the car painfully menstruating and displaced her hatred for her mother on to the car. When Peggy talked about this incident in therapy, abreacting her pain, the symptoms disappeared.

9. Red Moon (Peggy's First Color). Abstract tempera of gray and black. A mountain with a splash of red at the top denoting the moon. Peggy was elated when she brought this painting to Dr. Wilbur. Then, inexplicably, Peggy became anxious. Dr. Wilbur asked her if she was anxious because she had put red in the painting. Peggy realized that the red was the source of her anxiety. Dr. Wilbur assured her that it was permissible for her to use colors when she painted.

10. *Rage Around A Door.* Tempera. Shows Peggy's freedom to use color. She expresses her rage toward her mother in the form of a door blocking her escape. The reddish-brown strokes signify the beginnings of Peggy's anger, exploding into bold red lines which slash across the black lines of depression. Peggy's rage bubbled up in this artistic outlet.

11. Hills In Rage. Watercolor. This painting continues Peggy's discharge of anger and rage toward her mother. Shirley had repressed these emotions, but Peggy was able to blast through that defense mechanism. She painted broad strokes of violent red and brilliant yellow set in relief by black and gray heavy rocks. The impenetrability of the rocks is her mother's black mood and fierce stance. Peggy's frustration surges through the motion of the reds and yellows. The dark green sky above is the ever-present danger of Shirley's hovering mother. There is a lighter shade of green higher up—the moon shedding some light of hope in the distant future. This catharsis caused Shirley to feel peaceful. When she brought the painting to her next session, Dr. Wilbur stated that the frustration within her had been painted out.

12. *Endlessness of People on Streets.* Tempera and pencil. It was started by Peggy and finished by Sybil. Subdued red and blue buildings swaying, leaning and threatening to fall on Peggy and Sybil. Mattie often said, "What will people think. Mustn't let anyone see." And then she pulled down the shades and abused Shirley. Thus, the windows in the painting have shades that no one can see through. The rows and rows of people always in the distance ready to criticize Shirley as her mother had, Shirley felt that she had to keep a distance from people for her own safety.

13. Trees. Oil. A painting revealing the struggle within Peggy. The writhing trees of rage are contained by definite shapes and outlined forms. However, there are eyes in the trees watching Peggy and limbs reaching out to grasp her—shades of her mother. The placid mountains and sky of the environment are overwhelmed by the dominant trees reaching out of the painting.

14. Under the Elevated. Watercolor. Elevated train tracks in New York City. During the analysis Peggy painted this structure to illustrate her feelings about being under her mother's control when she was a child. She painted the tracks from below looking up. The wide black lines are depressive and foreboding. As if something might come crashing down on her—her mother's wrath. As Peggy looks up through the tracks she catches glimpses of a pink, yellow, and blue sky, signs of hope. If she can survive the onslaught of her mother there is hope in the future.

15. Mama on the Street Corner. Tempera. Muted colored buildings and streets with a black figure, her mother. There are no other people. The stark loneliness is penetrating. There is no way out for mother. The streets hem her in. It represents the death of her cruel mother. Peggy was able to express her hatred for what Shirley's mother had done to her.

16. Grandma's Rocker. Abstract. A painting of Shirley's grandmother's rocker. Peggy and Shirley had fond memories of sitting in grandmother's lap in her rocking chair. In the painting, brown covers the red as her grandmother's love would diminish the anger. The blue covers the green as grandmother's love would cover the anxiety. Peggy and Shirley felt that their grandmother had truly loved them. Peggy wrote, "Where is my home?" She was searching for the grandmother who loved her, but she had died.

17. Clowns and Little Clowns with the subtitle *Church Grandpa Shouting.* Watercolor and tempera. Her grandfather's behavior in church embarrassed Shirley. He would shout, "Amen!" and preach to anyone around him. Since Shirley was not allowed to feel anger, Peggy dealt with the anger in a sarcastic way. Peggy is in the red clown suit in front of grandfather. She is the main target of his shouting. Grandfather is the large clown figure monopolizing the scene. Peggy felt that others ridiculed her because of grandfather's behavior, so she attempted to withdraw from him.

18. Illusions. Tempera. Various shades of blue trees and grass. The peaceful scene is intruded upon by black edges of tree trunks alerting the observer to the three white heads floating among the trees. They are various attitudes of grandfather: sarcastic, mocking and sardonic.

19. Church With People. Watercolor and ink pen. At the top stands the preacher in the pulpit with his arms outstretched over the congregation. Tiny black lines represent the people in the pews. Peggy's anger is the red blotch covering the people whom she perceives as hostile towards her because of her grandfather's domineering behavior. The minister is not touched by the red anger, showing that Peggy does not direct her anger towards him. Shirley had maintained a belief in the Seventh Day Adventist religion, which was beneficial at various times in her life. The doctrine that it is a sin to take one's own life saved Shirley's life when some of the alternates were determined to commit suicide.

20. *Big Rooster and Little Chicken.* Crayon. The big rooster fills most of the canvas. He is in warm colors of purple and pink, looking over the little chicken. He is the idealized strong and protective father who Peggy would have wanted. She is the little chicken looking up towards her father for guidance and safety. The little chicken is also in warm purple and pink colors—a direct offshoot of her idealized father.

21. Family I. Burnt sienna crayon. Gives a warm glow to the mother holding the baby with the father looking on. This was Peggy's wish fulfillment of the perfect family. The mother and father are enveloping and protecting the child. The expression on their faces shows their love for the child. However, we only see the back of the head of the child, signifying Shirley's lack of her own identity.

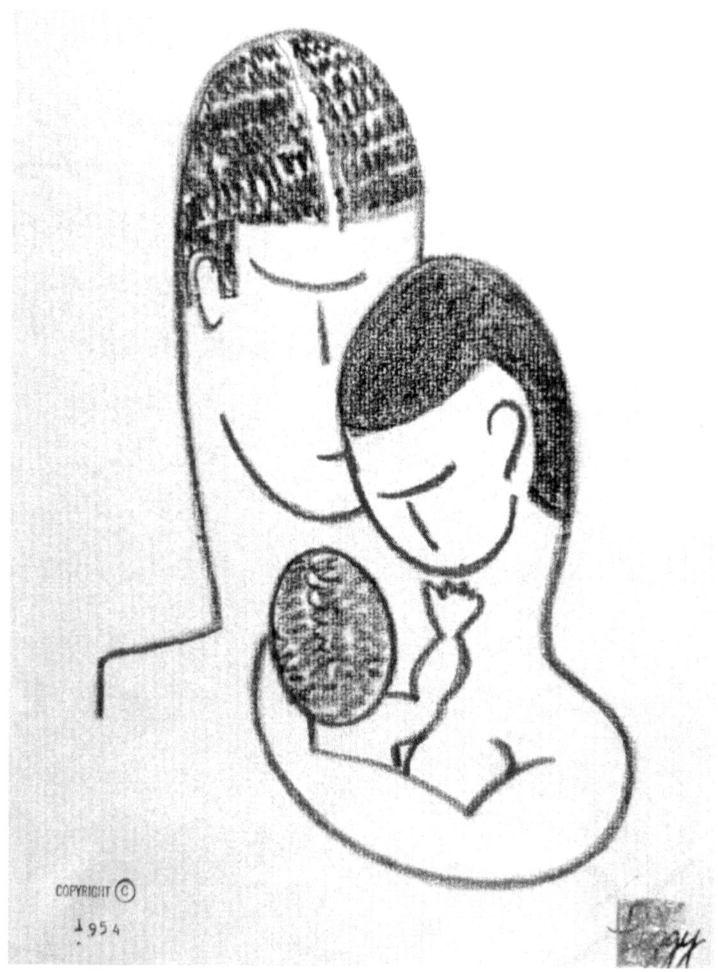

22. *Family III.* Blue crayon. Gives a peaceful aura to the father and mother caressing the baby. It is another portrayal of Peggy's idealized family. The baby reaches up to touch the mother's face as both parents look serenely and lovingly at the child. Again, we only see the back of the head of the child and not an identifiable face.

23. Northern Central Park. Watercolor on which Peggy wrote "trees and rocks solid forever—unfeeling. I'm on a rock & I can't get up nor down."

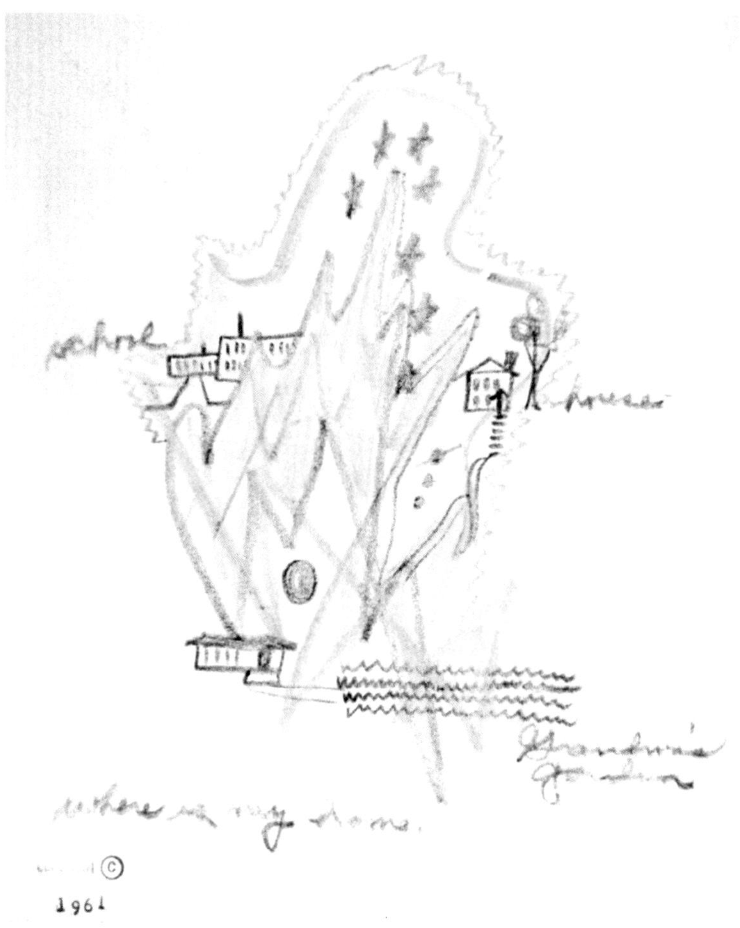

24. Grandma's Garden. Crayon. Peggy wrote, "Where is my home?" She labeled her "house" which was directly across the street from her "school." She wrote: "Grandma's Garden" at the bottom of the painting. As a child this was the extent of her universe. She longed for a home, where she could feel safe.

25. Survivor. Watercolor. A world of buildings, steps, trees and grass swirling around Peggy's head. The body is missing because she did not have a sense of identity as a whole person. The haphazard arrangement caused Peggy to say, "The world is all mixed up and I am alone in it." When she asked Dr. Wilbur if the world could ever be set right, Dr. Wilbur assured her that in time her world would not be so mixed up.

26. *Behind the 7 Ball.* Tempera. A painting which has contradictory symbols. The lucky number 7 is overshadowed by the huge ball, evoking the expression "behind the 8 ball." The red rage is contained by a band of white. The ever-present depression is a ball of gray with black specks here and there. Despite the bad luck of being behind the ball there is hope in the spectacular blue circle enveloping the symbols.

27. Tree Form in Wind. Tempera. Shows the ultimate feeling of aloneness. The barren tree is reaching for something, someone. Peggy often stated that she couldn't find a place in the world. Beautiful blues and whites of the sky and land make her aloneness more poignant. The emptiness of her existence was exacerbated by her inability to trust anyone. Once she engaged in therapy with Dr. Wilbur, she was able to trust her and then extrapolate to the rest of the world.

28. Faces. Tempera. A stylized construction of movement. The various elements are balanced and cheerful. The black shape in the form of a boot heralds the movement containing the white faces emerging from the black background. As the various alternates appear, Peggy said, "I am not quite so afraid of everything anymore." The orange is milder than the red of her previous rage. The yellow is a sunnier and happier color, replacing her former muddy greens and purples.

29. *Fantasy City Without People.* Tempera on matte board. Draws the observer into a city of free form swaying buildings. The background of benign yellow sets the buildings in a relief of battling colors of reddish-purples and deep blues conveying the inner struggle which Peggy fought. There is not a soul in sight—Peggy's feeling of isolation.

30. Tree. Tempera. A desolate tree with no vegetation, no sky, dead branches reaching up and outward toward nothing. The bark is withered. Black and pale shades of purple of the tree and the ground stand in stark contrast to the white background. Peggy expresses her loneliness and hopelessness again in this painting.

31. Purple Sun and Rays. Crayon drawing. Peggy drew this after one of her sessions with Dr. Wilbur. Peggy felt that the radiant purple sun and rose-violet rays signified her changing anger into hope that Shirley could be cured. If this were possible then all the personalities could be integrated and have a happy future. There is an explosion of joy in this abstract.

32. Green Sun. Crayon. Depicting a period of discouragement and loneliness. She felt it was taking too long to get well. She portrayed a city along a river with boats in very low tones passing away from the observer. Peggy said, "New York Harbor at dawn, fog in the distance, all away from me. I'm the green and purple sun."

33. The Red Boat. Tempera. A red boat sailing majestically through the deep, blue sea with three smaller black boats in the background. Peggy's painting shows her turning the red rage against her mother into a sparkling red boat in which she could sail away from the depressing elements in her life, represented by the three black boats in the background.

CHAPTER 13

Marcia's Paintings

Marcia was sad and depressed. She felt that people ridiculed her. She had no one to help her and she felt alone and trapped. This was evident in the low-toned colors she used: gray, pale blue, and dusty rose. She outlined in heavy, dark brush strokes giving a sense of doom to her paintings. Her fear and anxiety found an outlet in painting rooms without doors and streets with no exits. When Dr. Wilbur interpreted these paintings as Marcia's feeling of being trapped, the depression and anxiety were alleviated.

Her paintings were small, tight scenes of walls and shrubbery because Shirley would not give her any good paper. Marcia had to make do with the scraps left over from Shirley's paintings.

As therapy progressed, Marcia painted light blue flowers instead of dark blue ones, which she had previously painted. Now she painted green leaves instead of black ones. Her self-portrait in the form of a bird exhibited her spirit soaring, escaping from her misery portrayed in the red eyes of the bird.

34. Parents. Chalk. A drawing of two figures—mother and father, with chalk white faces and black bodies. This family portrait does not include her. Its funereal tone is symptomatic of her suicidal impulses. Marcia said, "There is no love." She thought that it was her fault that her family did not love her. She felt that since she was not worthy of love, she might as well kill herself.

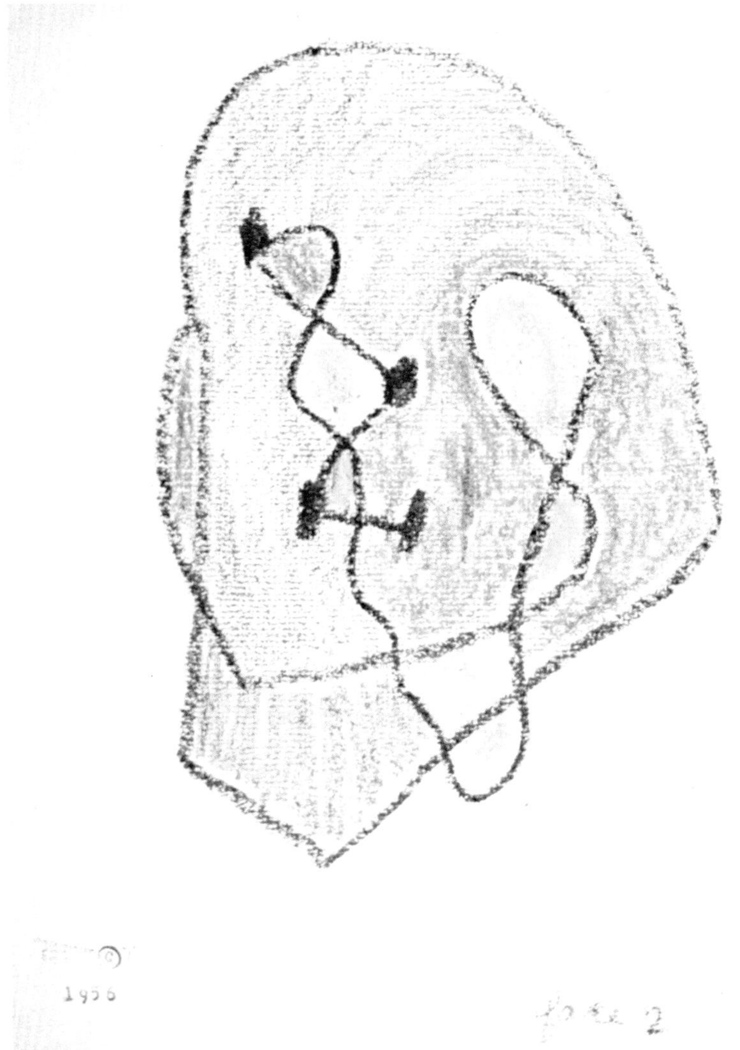

35. Face and Ear. Crayon. An abstract presenting Marcia's fear of her mother's presence hovering over her. Her mother's spying eyes and listening ear ready to criticize and punish Shirley are twisted and deformed. Mattie's behavior was just as deviant. Marcia wrote on the painting: "She was always listening."

36. Depression. Tempera. In shades of purple and black, the Marcia figure has a pale white face and arms with long black hair. She is frozen in a position of helplessness. Marcia would stand inertly and feel blank. She said she was even afraid to move her eyeballs because of the pain. Sometimes she would hug a wall and remain motionless for long periods of time. She was so depressed that movement was not possible. This painting was done following the period in which Marcia was almost totally incapable of doing anything. It shows severe depression. Her body would become very still, and movement would be difficult. She said everything seemed to be a kind of purple color or blue-gray-red as used in the painting. Colors are low, muted, showing a depressive stupor.

37. Depths Below the Clouds. Black crayon. It illustrates various stages of depression. Marcia experienced her life with a cloud over her, blocking out sunlight, preventing it from penetrating her depression. The various shades of gray descend to black in the depths of her being. She told Dr. Wilbur about her feelings of loss, futility, desolation and aloneness. Marcia said, "The real feeling is in the center." Shades of the same feeling surround it in varying degrees of intensity.

38. River Walls. Watercolor in low tones of grays, blues and purples with touches of black. The black, representing depression, is not so prominent. The scene almost has a pleasant aura, except for the walls encasing the scene. Marcia said, “I am still closed in. There are still walls around me.”

39. The Clown. Crayon drawing. Projects Mattie's sarcasm onto the face of a clown. Marcia was aware of Mattie putting on one face for people while hiding behind the face of a clown. She often denigrated them behind their backs.

40. *Rough Seas of Life.* Tempera. Waves and sky crashing around the earth. The large white sailboat in the center represents Marcia with the smaller sailboats in the distance representing the other personalities. Marcia saw her life as a perilous journey trying to avoid crashing into the rocks.

41. Abstract in Purple. Watercolor. The red stains in the center are Marcia's rage which is repressed by the heavy purple and black strokes causing depression. The heaviness is characteristic of Marcia's inability to move when she was depressed. She felt closed in and unable to scc thc importance of anything. She said that everything seemed to be dark purple hills closing in around her. She was sinking into depression and hated the sensation, but was unable to prevent her decline into it.

42. Reaching. Watercolor. Fiercely writhing trees. In the trees are spying eyes and devouring mouths. These are symbols of the way Marcia felt about the destructive mother. The trees overpower the earth and the sky. There is no escaping them.

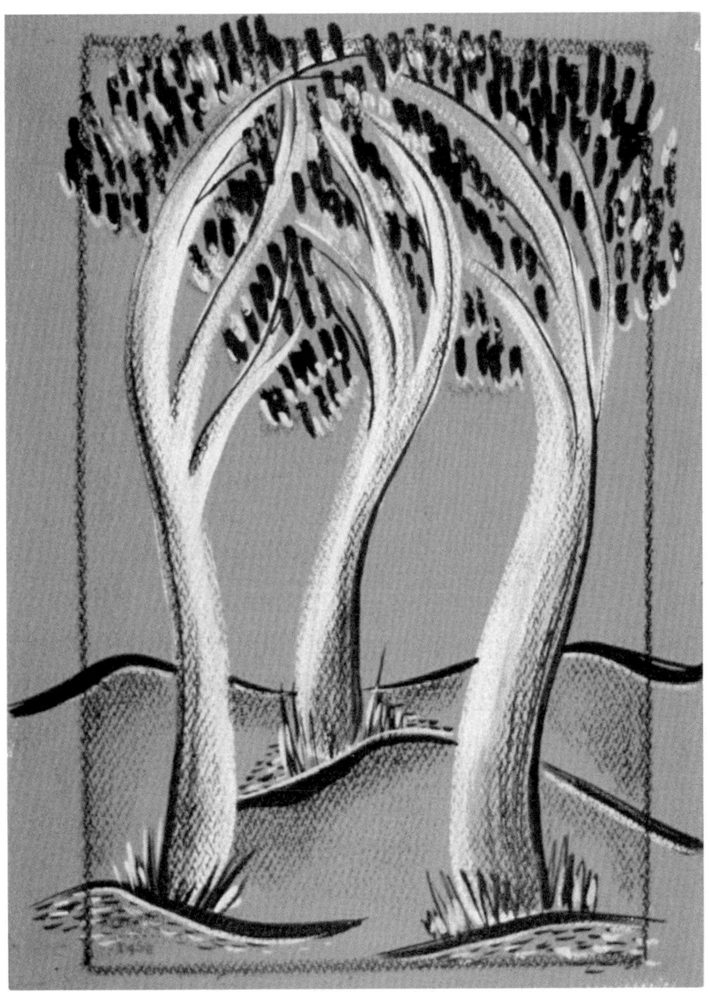

43. Orange Trees. Pastel. It was done late in Shirley's analysis. Marcia felt freer to use color and blooming trees. This is a sign of the life force arising within Marcia. The trees are stylized and interlocking. Marcia still needed to have control over her emotions. The black lines attest to her need to feel that she could contain her feelings. However, signs of hope appear in the light oranges peeking through the dark leaves.

44. The Rock. Watercolor. Sketched by Marcia and painted by Vanessa. Although Shirley loved the scenery in Arizona, the huge rock is threatening to topple over and crush everything. It is the mother figure looming over the child. The somber colors of brown, gray, and deep blue give a grave tone to the painting. It is a lonely vista.

45. Mamma. Chalk. An impression of Sybil's mother. The blob-like figure is sitting with her back to the observer. The skin tones are red, signifying the torture inflicted on Sybil

46. Alone on the Family Tree. Watercolor. A lone bird perched on a leafless tree. It is Marcia not connected to anyone else in the family. Behind the tree is a brick wall preventing escape. There is a tiny bit of green shrubbery at the foot of the tree, suggesting some foundation to the personality which might blossom.

47. Park Trees. Watercolor. Marcia painted it after a session with Dr. Wilbur, where she revealed her suicidal thoughts. Dr. Wilbur suggested that she paint out her feelings as Peggy had been doing. Marcia drew in pencil, stark, barren trees twisting and turning upward toward nothingness. She painted in deep purple, olive-green, and black purging her lonely and depressed life. Her sense of futility and hopelessness wash over the painting.

48. Blue Boats. Watercolor. Stylized blue sailboats crowding the canvas. Marcia said that the boats represented the present. They are so large and demanding that she claimed to be unable to access the past. She used denial to block out horrific memories of mother torturing her.

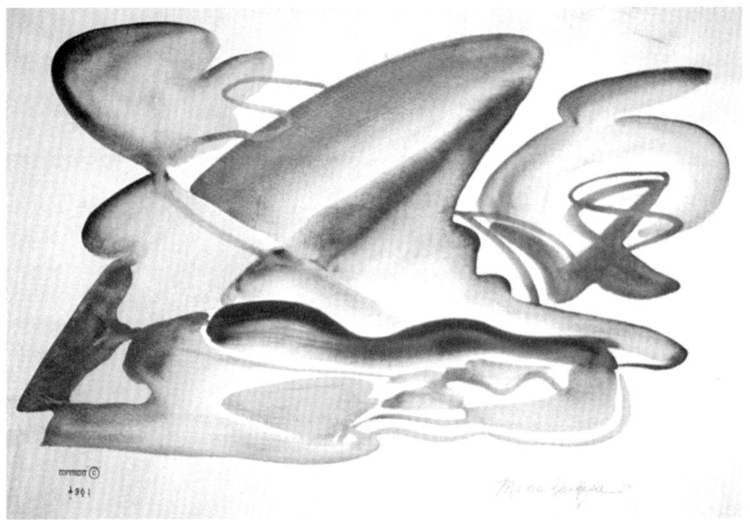

49. Hills. Watercolor. An abstract outlined by Marcia and finished by Vanessa. The icy blues and grays produce a bleak atmosphere. The desolate scene has no vegetation, people, or any living creature. The shapes and forms compel the eye to search through the hills and the sky, but lead nowhere.

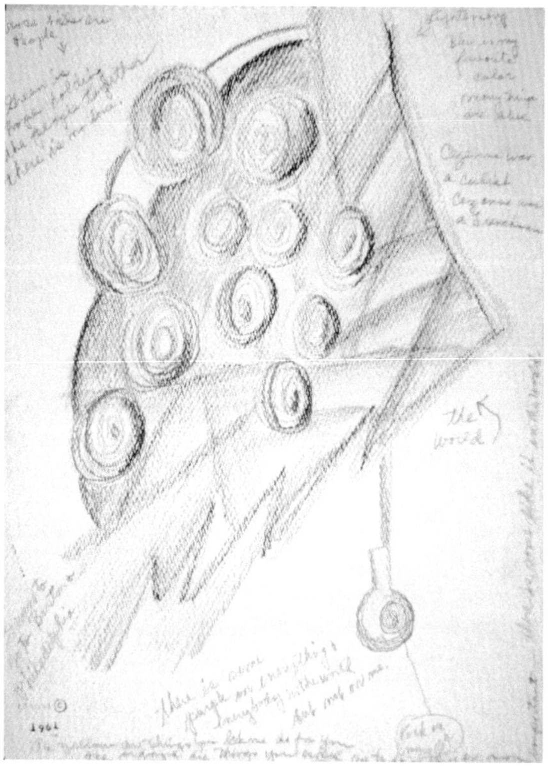

50. *The World.* Casein. An abstract with red circles representing different aspects of Sybil. In the extreme top left corner Marcia wrote: "Rose balls are people. Green is hope holding the people together. There is no love." In the upper right-hand corner Marcia wrote: "Lightening [she drew an arrow pointing to the adjacent vertical red line in the painting]. Blue is my favorite color. Many things are blue. Cezanne was a cubist. Cezanne was a Frenchman." In the lower left section, Marcia wrote: "I want to go to Boston & Philadelphia." At the bottom center of the painting, Marcia wrote: "There is some purple in everything & everybody in the world, but not on me." Along the bottom and right-hand edges of the painting, Marcia wrote: "The yellow are things you let me do for you. Ask me to do."

51. Caught in the Web. Watercolor. A painting of arresting black strokes. This is the outward representation of the inner feelings of Marcia. What is worse than being caught in a spider's web where the spider is the avenging mother inflicting pain on a blameless child?

52. *Homeward Flight.* Watercolor and India ink. A black bird in a somber and barren scene. Marcia shared the feeling with Mary that their loss over grandmother was inconsolable. Feelings of emptiness come across vividly.

53. *Self Portrait.* Tempera. Soft blue-greens of a bird blending into the blue-green background. Marcia felt a lack of distinction between herself and the world. Marcia's lack of confidence and assertiveness are exposed in the hesitant flight of the bird. The bird's eye is red from sobbing. She often said that no one cared about her. The bird embodies her desire to flee and escape.

CHAPTER 14

Mary's Paintings

Mary is described in *Sybil* as "a maternal little-old-lady type, plump, thoughtful and contemplative." Mary was the alter who loved romantic poetry and art. She dreamed of having the ideal loving family patterned after the love she received from her grandmother. Her grandmother's love contributed somewhat to the shaky foundation of Shirley's personality. It was a thin foundation, but one upon which she could build ego strength through her therapy with Dr. Wilbur.

Mary emerged when Shirley was ten. One day, she began to menstruate with a great deal of pain. Not knowing that Sybil had her period two months earlier, she thought that she was dying. From then on, she was especially sensitive to pain, physical and psychic.

Shirley's psychoanalysis began in September 1954 in New York City with Dr. Wilbur. On June 15, 1955, Mary appeared in Dr. Wilbur's office. Mary asserted that she was the one who kept Sybil's home going. She affirmed that she was the one who helped Sybil to accomplish practical tasks. She managed the apartment, making renovations and cleaning it. In her spare time, she wrote poetry and painted.

In her diary in May, 1956, Shirley wrote:

> I was so alone---I can feel it now and would explain it more as desolate than anything else, because it was not only the aloneness but a kind of useless, meaningless, futile kind of feeling that the word desolate connotes for me. (Like the poster-paint piece I did as Mary one Saturday night---the long dull piece with the lone figure in the left-hand section).

Sybil emerged in the fifth grade. During the previous two years, since her grandmother's death, Peggy had taken over. Sybil was so confused that she retreated; Mary took over and made the painting she wrote about in the above passage. Since Sybil could not endure the confrontation in the painting and was overtaken by fear and anxiety, Peggy emerged and destroyed it. Sybil brought the destroyed painting to Dr. Wilbur.

54. *Neighbors.* Watercolor. The two mothers in conversation with their children standing by. The touches of blue show Mary's love for her playmate (called Danny in *Sybil*). Danny, standing in front of his mother. In contrast to Danny, Mary is shyly standing behind her mother. Although Sybil felt a kinship with Danny artistically and often played with him, she knew her mother spied on them. Her fear and depression reverberate in the dark green and black foliage. The painting is simple and direct like the people of the small town, Dodge Center, where she grew up. The color scheme is predominantly medium blues and grays with touches of rust-brown. These colors are typical of many of Mary's works, blue of love, gray and brown of depression, loss, or grief. Aside from her grandmother, the only important, caring person in Mary's life was her playmate Danny. Mary was nine years old when she did this painting, which shows she felt she still had Danny even after her grandmother had died. (Shirley sent me a print of this painting.)

55. *Blue Trees and Home.* Watercolor. Cozy, warm, brown-toned houses, all similar, huddled around a grove of fluffy blue trees. Reminiscent of her grandmother's house, Mary said, "Blue is the color of love." The primitive drawing is the direct expression of Mary's heart.

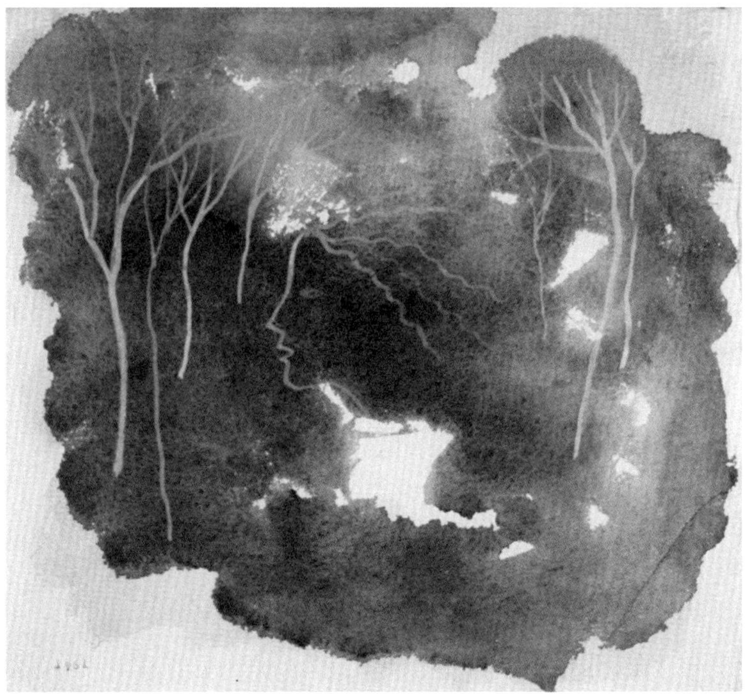

56. Grandma Lost. Watercolor. Blue for love, and muddy purple for rage and grief over grandma's death when Shirley was nine years old. The blue is shattered by dots of white space like fierce-looking eyes and a snarling mouth. A profile of a woman floats above the white space with purple grief swelling around her.

57. *Fall Trees on Grandma's Hill.* Watercolor. Warm, comforting shades of orange, brown, and beige. Mary loved sharing the beauty of nature with her grandmother. It was a time of peace when she didn't have to fear the wrath of her mother. The scene has a symmetry and balance that Mary would have liked in her own life.

58. Hills of Home. Pastel. Romantic moonlight floods the mountains and trees. Although Mary was in love with the neighborhood boy Danny, she never had that experience with a male as an adult. She tried to recapture that sensation in this romantic painting.

59. Self (Before and After). Watercolor. Illustrating the fragmentation of Shirley's personality shown as little stones. After her integration, they become a part of one large rock.

60. *Amish Farm House.* Mixed media of watercolor, chalk, pencil and ink. Conveys the unity and closeness of the Amish family. The houses and scenery form a bucolic scene of bliss. This was Mary's wish for her own family

61. Grandma's Yard. Carbon pencil on charcoal paper. The focal point is a wood-sprite looking tree reaching upwards towards the heavens. The gentle flowing lines of trees, plants, and flowers are in keeping with Mary's belief that her grandmother had gone to a more peaceful place—heaven.

62. Integration. Crayon. A drawing of Mary's concept of the integration of the sixteen personalities. Each alter possesses some unique characteristic, but joins in with the other personalities to form a whole entity.

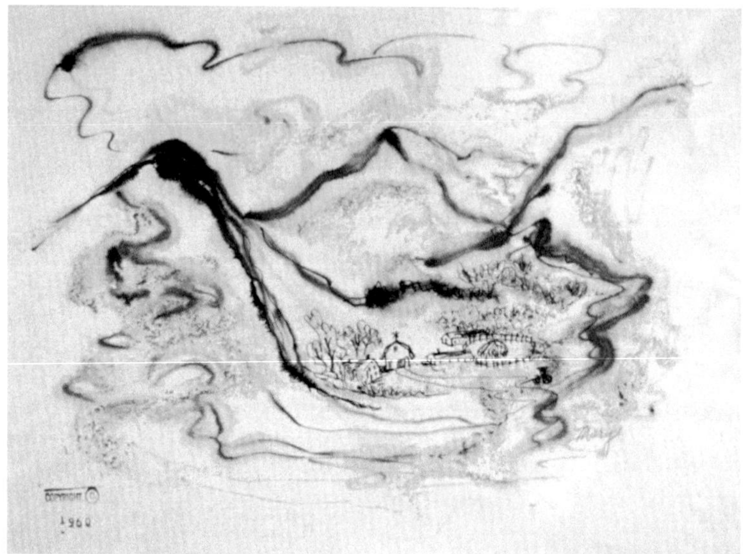

63. Amish Farm. Wash and pen drawing. A scene of an Amish homestead nestled in the valley protected by the surrounding hills. Mary's desire for safety and security.

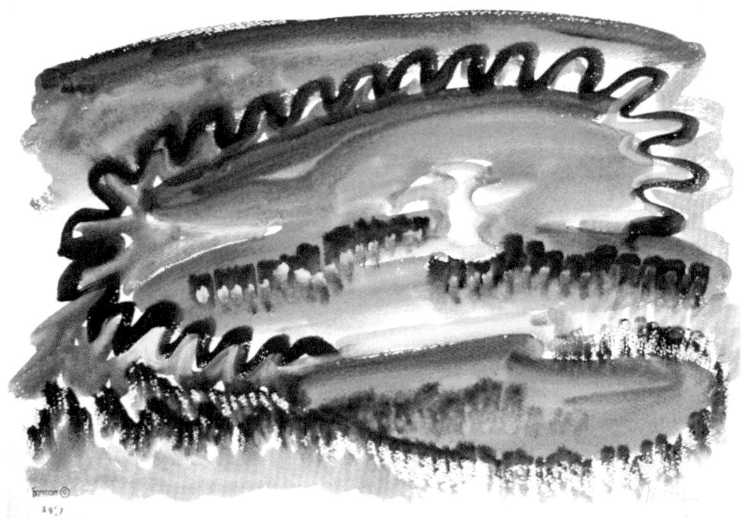

64. Finger Lakes. Tempera. Dazzling colors expose Mary's joy over visiting the Finger Lakes in upstate New York. An example of one of her rare moments of pure bliss.

CHAPTER 15

Vanessa's paintings

In *Sybil*, Vanessa is described as "a tall, slender girl with a willowy figure, dark chestnut-red hair, light brown eyes, and an expressive oval face." Her lilting voice demonstrated that she was an alter of glamour and culture. She played the piano and was full of life. Having emerged when Shirley was twelve, she felt disdain for the meager environment of Dodge Center.

Vanessa's paintings brought Shirley's unconscious feelings to the surface. She painted symbols representing events and beliefs which were instrumental in Shirley's analysis. Dr. Wilbur brought these feelings to Shirley's attention so that she could face the conflicts associated with them.

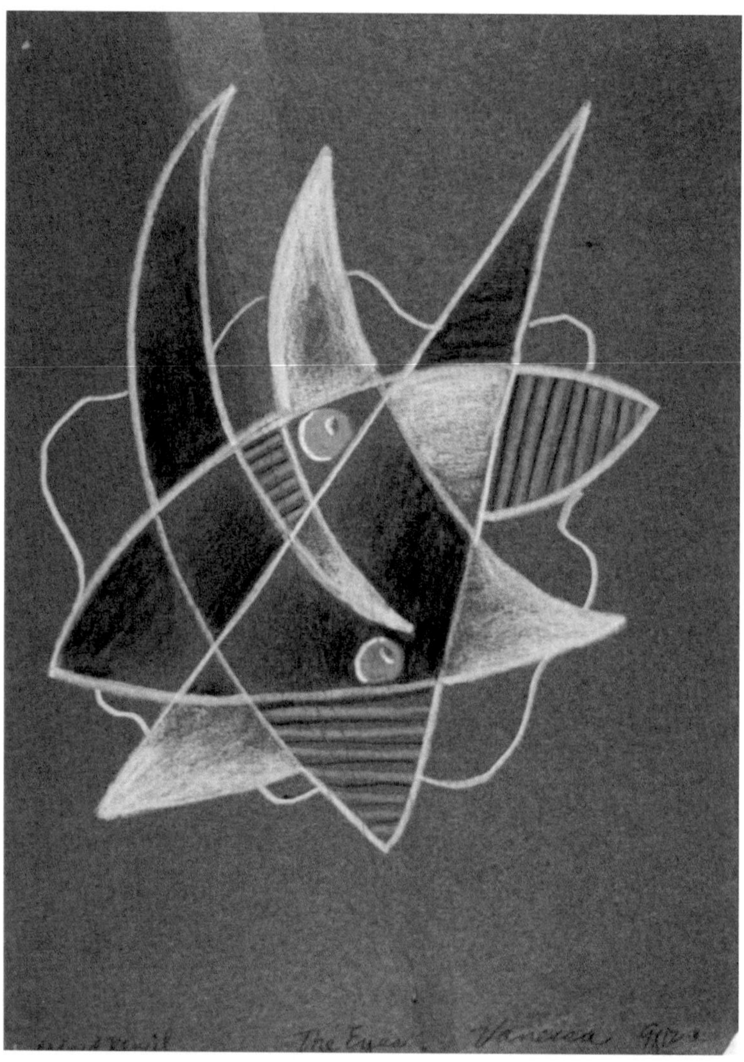

65. The Eyes. Colored pencil. The low, somber colors have a foreboding quality. Two ominous blue eyes glare at the observer. Sybil's mother's hyper-vigilant eyes. The eyes are surrounded by dangerous abstract objects with cutting, sharp edges.

66. Purple Hills and Houses. Watercolor started by Marcia and completed by Vanessa. It continues the theme of being trapped. The fence with no gate encloses the houses on a farm with barren trees. Trees on both sides of the painting contain the images within. The muted shades of blue, purple, and gray set the mood of sadness and loneliness. The grief over grandmother's death is palpable. Marcia's suicidal feelings color the painting.

67. Disjointed. Watercolor. A painting with black lines going in all different directions. In the center is a wash of cerulean blue, the color of heraldic symbols on a coat of arms. However, in Shirley's case, it was a symbol of her spirit submerged in a tangle of conflicting feelings and emotions. The wisps of pink going upward represent signs of hope.

68. Misty Dawn. Watercolor. Apartment buildings resembling castles floating in the distance. The dark tones cast a pall over what could have been a dreamy scene. Unfortunately, the buildings are encased in black lines, limiting their possibilities.

69. Road Without End. Watercolor. Clearly depicts Vanessa's trapped feelings. Facing the observer is a perilous road winding through mountains with ominous-looking trees. The road ends and threatening mountains block any escape. This was not only a feeling, but reality for the child. Her dominating mother insured that she had no one else to turn to. Her father was a more positive force in her life, but not someone she could depend upon to protect her from her mother.

70. *Floral Design.* Watercolor. Started by Peggy and finished by Vanessa. A cascade of flowers in pinks, purples, and blues intertwine and move upward. Rich full colors are ensnared by the heavy dark outlines drawn by Peggy. Vanessa's more optimistic approach toward life is dampened by Peggy's dark outlook.

71. Dutch Design. Tempera. A composition of cornflower blue and soft red shades, conveying a pleasant feeling. It is a pure expression of Vanessa's fanciful outlook on life. It has no black heavy lines.

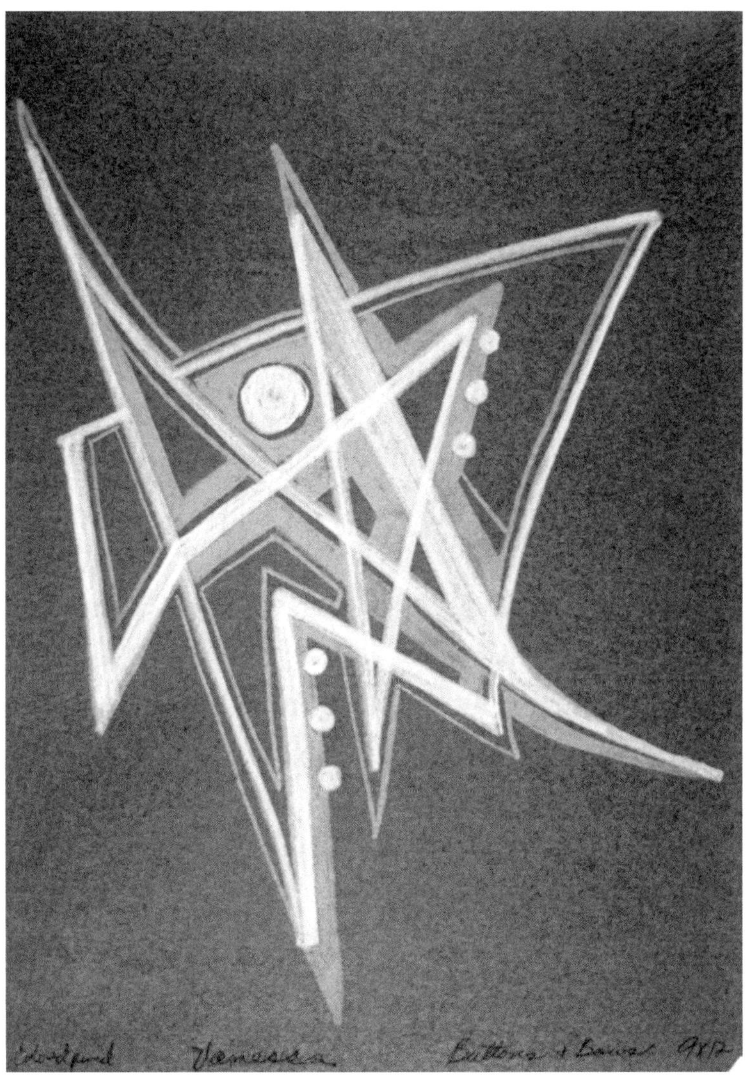

72. Buttons and Bows. Colored pencil drawing. Abstract of buttons and bows harkening back to the romantic song "Buttons and Bow." The objects are light pink and cornflower blue in keeping with the femininity expressed in the song: "where women are women."

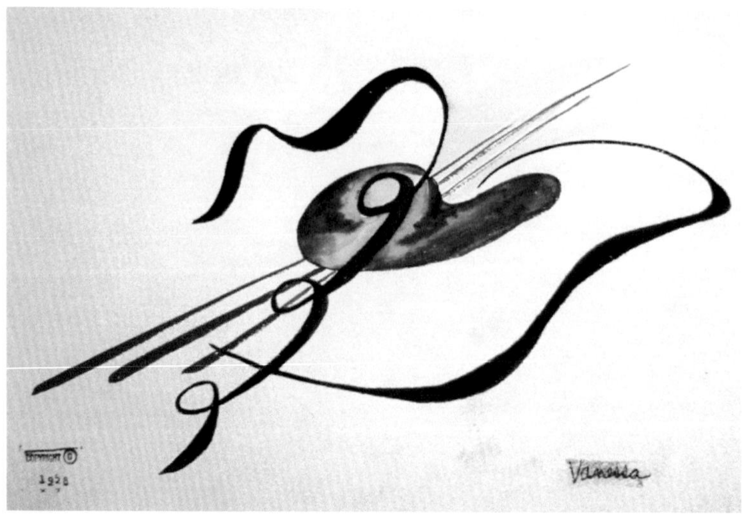

73. Flurry. Watercolor. An abstract which Vanessa gave to Dr. Wilbur. She said, "We are always bringing things none of us like. So today I am bringing a painting I did that I do like. I painted it just for you. It is not supposed to be analyzed."

CHAPTER 16

Sybil's paintings

74. The Family. Pastel drawing on a tempera-painted background. Shirley brought this to Dr. Wilbur and said, "This is just an abstract and doesn't have a meaning, but I brought it anyway, as it is the first one I have done in a long time that I like at all. I sort of like it, but I don't know why." It was painted in the third year of her analysis while examining her relationship with her parents. After disturbing dreams, once the painting was completed, she was able to sleep peacefully. Dr. Wilbur thought that it was the unconscious revelation of Sybil's existence. In the foreground is a pale yellow and gray phallic object. It represents Shirley's father standing as the passive observer. Behind him is the hovering mother figure with her hawk-like arms in fiery red. She is so overpowering that traces of her red are found on the edges of the father figure. Dr. Wilbur said, "It looks like a family of three. Why did you draw your father in two parts?" Shirley was shocked. She didn't realize she had drawn her father in two parts, displaying his weakness and unsteadiness and inability

to protect her. Off in the background is a tiny figure composed of mostly pale yellow with tinges of red, representing the lonely Sybil child. Sybil stands helpless as her mother hovers over her with her all-seeing eye. Shirley identified with her father, and therefore is the same color, but she cannot escape the influence of her mother, represented by the tiny red lines on her. A gray barren background conveys her desolation.

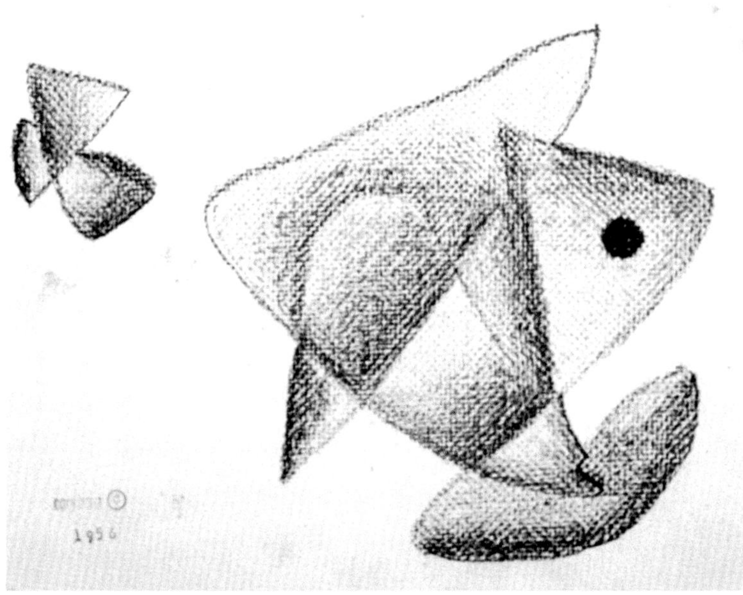

75. Mother Fish With All Seeing Eye and Self. Crayon. An abstract showing the dominant figure with sharp edges and a black dot for an eye—Shirley's ever-present mother. The tiny figure off to the left in the same low tones of dusty rose and gray represents Shirley. Her mother constantly monitored her to make sure that Shirley did not read novels or fairy tales—only The Bible. Her mother told her not to read newspapers because they had germs. This affected Shirley to such a degree that she developed the compulsion of looking at her hands for germs. Her mother threatened to cut off her hands.

76. No Exit. Tempera on illustration board. The streets run into buildings which loom above, blocking any exit. Dull blue, violet, and gray color the buildings. The windows are opaque white. Shirley said, "This is another of those things I feel compelled to do. I seem to have little conscious control over, and I feel very anxious about after it is finished. You can have it." Dr. Wilbur recognized the symbols of Shirley's defenses. In the analysis, Shirley revealed her desire to do many things, but felt trapped by her problems. Shirley said, "I felt so constricted and compelled to paint every space very carefully. I felt so tight in my throat. I don't care much for the result, but a funny thing happened. After I finished the painting, I felt a sudden relief and I have felt better ever since. Sort of free."

77. *Self and Doctor in Dr. Wilbur's Office.* Carbon pencil drawing. Sybil is sitting on the couch leaning in towards Dr. Wilbur seated in a chair next to her. They have a closer connection to each other than to the other objects in the room. The soft tones give a wistful quality to the scene. Shirley recognized that her salvation would be in her analysis with Dr. Wilbur.

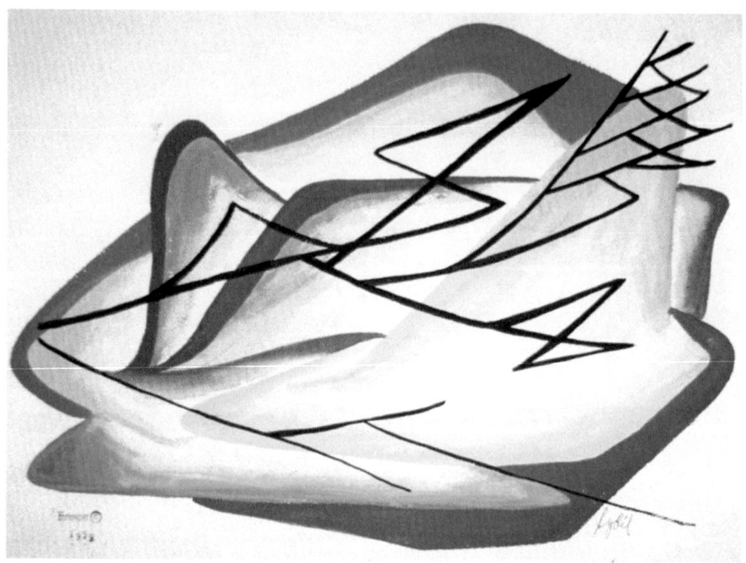

78. Abstract. Tempera wash. Early in analysis Sybil's painting also reflects Peggy's and Marcia's feelings. The aqua water, represents the life force, marred by stark hills and rocks intersected by heavy black lines. The loneliness and bleakness experienced by Shirley and her alters jumps out of the painting.

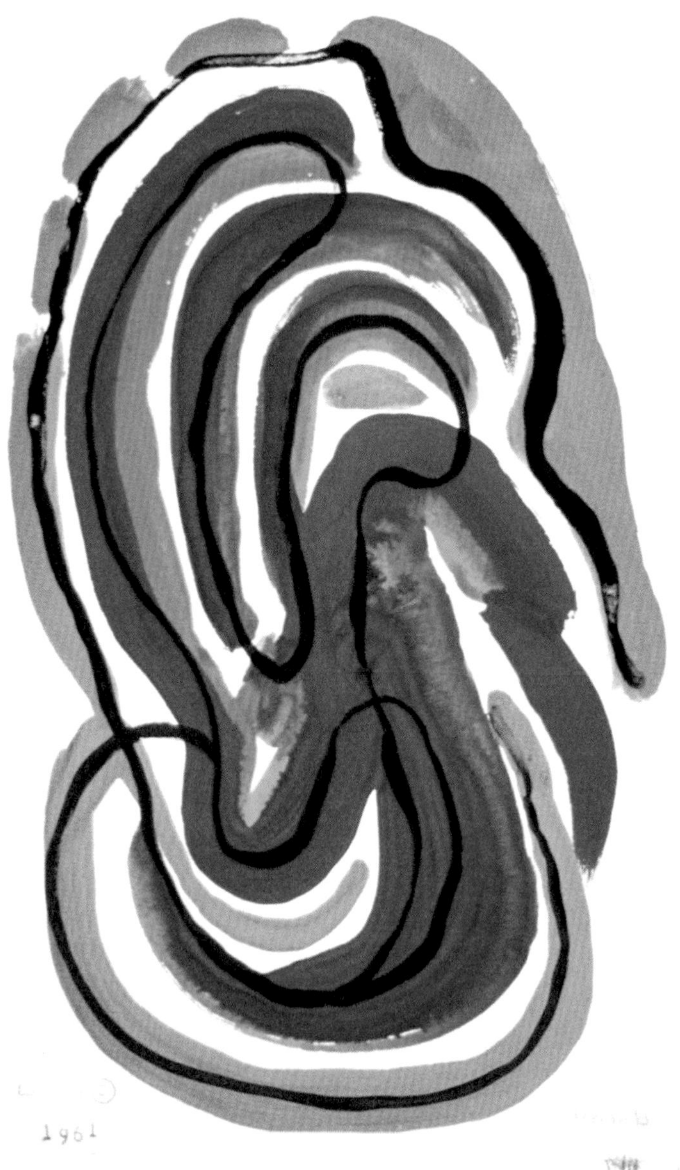

79. Womb. Tempera. A labyrinth of olive green, deep blue, and green surrounded by black lines. It reflects Shirley's perception of her origin.

80. The Wall I Can't Escape. Watercolor. A long, gray, dull brick wall. There are trees trying to break through, but they have no leaves. The threatening sky is colored deep purple and bluish-green. There are patches of white light breaking through the heavy scene, a glimmer of hope.

81. Accord. Abstract in pastel and crayon. There is a freedom in the configuration. Shirley painted this when she said that she was beginning to feel "a lot of different ways, sort of all at once." The feelings are reflected in the swirling yellow, blue and red freely blending together. Dr. Wilbur explained that the feelings of Peggy and Marcia were rising to Sybil's consciousness during the analysis. The affect and ideas of the alters were crossing the amnesic barrier from Peggy and Marcia to Shirley. She could now own the feelings which she had repressed in her past giving a greater range of expression to her painting.

82. Desert Rocks. Watercolor of boulders in vibrant yellows, reds and browns. A free-form impressionist arrangement of rocks, ground and sky. When Shirley lived in Denver, she loved to go into the Rocky Mountains and paint. Nature and solitude brought her rare moments of peace, reflected in the pleasant contemplative scene of rock formations.

83. Emotions. Watercolor. Painted by Sybil and Peggy. As they were becoming integrated, they were able to join together to express various emotions. As the blues, violets, and soft greens blend, so were their emotions and thoughts able to blend. They were beginning to exist without conflict.

84. Bus Line. Watercolor. Done by Shirley later in her analysis, after her fear of crowds had been alleviated. She shows humor in the composition of not only a bus on its route, but also the line of people waiting for the bus. This is poignant in light of her having joked to me that taking the cross-town bus to her therapy sessions was the most difficult part of the treatment.

85. Midtown Manhattan. Watercolor. "Jumble" as seen by Shirley during a distressed period. Illustrates the skyscrapers and hoards of people. There is an order to the placement of objects reaching up to a billowing sky.

86. Abstract of The Eye. Watercolor. An eye surrounded by various shapes and shades of blue. This painting shows the attempts to avoid the cruel eye of the mother. Sybil learned a coping mechanism of splitting into alternate personalities to deal with her mother's abuse.

87. Lavender Evening. Watercolor. Pleasing shades of purples, blues and greens. It attempts a lovely scene in nature despite the barren prickly trees. Shirley was able to view life more positively, even though there were still thorns in her path.

88. Self Portrait Clowns. Casein. Several clown faces with a range of expressions. Shirley felt this was the way others viewed her, and the way she came to think of herself. Self ridicule is the theme.

89. Phoenix. Tempera. A bird symbolizing Shirley's ascent from the hell she was brought up in. Her fortitude and persistence in therapy, resulting in her integration of all her alternate personalities, is shown by the phoenix rising from the ashes. The pulsating blues, greens, and yellows buoy up the bird on its journey toward freedom.

90. Chinatown. Watercolor. A delightful painting of that section of New York City. Shirley was able to capture the delicate beauty of the ornate buildings in the midst of bland skyscrapers. The pedestrians and cars are moving in an orderly fashion. She was no longer hampered by her fears and insecurities.

91. Docks. Watercolor. Painted after Dr. Wilbur took Shirley on a trip to see sailboats. Marcia painted the boat with a pristine white sail on crystal blue water. The boat is coming toward the observer. The movement of the boat and water prompted Marcia to say, "Sailing free."

CHAPTER 17

The Final Year

In 1997 I grew increasingly concerned about Shirley's health. She had fought cancer for years, but was now growing weary of the battle. In spite of that, she was so responsive about sending me material for my book. She also wanted to send me the Sybil paintings, to be used to sponsor a scholarship fund. Her enthusiasm made it hard to believe that she was dying.

An unexpected death did occur in September, 1997. My sister, Lorrine, who was 59, died. She had battled Schizophrenia since her teens. After several hospitalizations, Lorrine was able to stay at home with my mother's care. One day she was diagnosed with pneumonia. That night she collapsed and died. I wrote Shirley about it.

Shirley sent me the following letter dated November 18, 1997:

> Dear Patrick,
>
> Your letter came yesterday. I want to answer right away so you'll know I am very sorry to hear about your sister. So sudden it must have been a shock. I expect she had the lung cancer for quite awhile but since she was a heavy smoker probably didn't especially notice such symptoms as difficulty

> breathing, coughing, etc. I know it is hard on you and no doubt even more so for your mother—she'll feel as if part of her is missing. At her age she probably can't live alone much longer—that will be an extra worry for you. I am sorry about all this—please let me know sometime how things are going.
>
> I appreciated your offer (in last letter) to help me with insurance papers, etc. However, I don't have any paper work! Fortunately, I have a rare doctor who makes house calls and he signed me up with a home nursing agency who takes care of everything—medicine, insurance & all. Lucky?
>
> A nurse comes daily—sometimes twice—to change bandages and check on me. They are the very nicest nurses anyone could want. I found out what was causing my rather severe back problem—I have osteoporosis—am bent almost in half! I still get around with a cane, but barely—kitchen and back is about it. I fix my meal slowly—can't eat much due to mass in abdomen growing against my stomach.
>
> Well enough of all that! Will tell you once and not bring it up again—I do not like talking symptoms—but you did ask for an update so you have it, ha!
>
> Been very cold here—19° for so early in the year. El Nino effects, I guess—predict more than usual amount of snow.
>
> My friend Dee Sherfield still comes faithfully Mondays & Thursdays to visit and help with chores & errands. Such a good friend. She will mail this for me Thursday. I am very shaky but maybe you can read this.
>
> Always, Shirley

In accordance with her wishes, Shirley was able to stay at home rather than being hospitalized for her cancer treatment. I had to reassure her that she deserved to have Medicare pay her medical bills. She was emphatic about not wanting "charity." I told her that the problems for Medicare were not the legitimate payments for patients, but the fraudulent claims. That helped her to accept their help. She also stated, "Well, you know, my mother and father both paid in. Mother didn't use hers at all. And so these things, I figured, even out."

Shirley did have to pay for Teresa to help her at home. Shirley described her, "She's a beautiful black girl. She's just as pretty as she can be. And she's full of fun and jolly, but she can also be very, very serious. And she's really good with sick people. I look over at the little stand beside my chair, she's right there to see what I want. All I have to do is look over there…And she won't sleep nights when she comes. She says, 'Well, you might want something and not be able to tell me.' So she sits there on the couch and reads all night."

When I called on December 16, 1997, I heard pain in her voice. I asked if she could take her medicine. She replied, "Yes. I'm going to fix something hot to drink. That always makes it take effect sooner. And I'll get my wind again. I have a day like this every once in a while and thankfully the next day is better."

I repeated what she often said, "We look forward to tomorrow."

"And I get along. If I don't look ahead very far, I'm all right. I just look for what I'm doing this hour. The nurse was talking this morning about some things that could go wrong. I said, 'Well, I'd just as soon not hear about what could go wrong. I know enough about this kind of thing. I've seen enough of it in my friends. I know what can go wrong. Let's just talk about what hasn't yet gone wrong.' And we laughed about it."

"Good attitude. I'm going to write to you tonight."

She admonished, "Now listen. You are spending much too much money on phone calls to me. It's expensive."

"Oh no," I lied. I have a special plan. It isn't that expensive. So don't worry about it."

"Well, I do."

I stated emphatically, "Don't, okay. Because I enjoy talking with you."

"Well I certainly enjoy talking to you. It is a real pleasure. But I was just concerned about it."

"Don't worry. It's one of these plans for long distance calls."

"Oh, all right."

"Okay?"

"Yeah, if you say so"

"You take care now."

"I will. You too."

On January 15, 1998, Shirley had important news for me. When I called her, she was elated. She said, "I was just thinking of calling and leaving a message. We found the book of slides." She had been worried about the slides of the Sybil paintings. She had Dee look all over the house. Shirley knew that she had put them neatly in little jackets in a book.

I exclaimed, "Isn't that wonderful!"

She said, "And all the material from the Merck exhibit. Everything that I wanted. All the tapes, everything. All in a box. It's labeled on the outside what's in it. On the very shelf where I told her to look initially."

"You have a good memory."

Shirley explained, "Well, I do things logically. It didn't make sense to put that Sybil print book anywhere but with the Sybil material. I had Sybil prints and things in the closet, and Sybil paintings upstairs. So it didn't seem right to go with the other paintings. And so I put it in there. So I thought that's where it was, and I told her to look in there, and she looked. She said, 'You know, they're not in there.' And I said, 'You're sure?' And she said, 'Yes.' So a couple weeks later, after we looked everywhere else, and I couldn't understand it, I said, 'Well, will you look once more?' She looked again, you know, and she said, 'It's not in there.' So the other day I said, 'Well, I don't know anywhere else in this house to look. I've got to have that book. Without that and the list, it's no good. Nothing goes together. You're sure it's not in there in the closet on that shelf?' She said, 'I didn't find it.' And I said, 'Well, what is in there?' And she said, 'Well, I don't know. There's a couple boxes and some papers.' I said, 'Well, let's see.' So I hobbled in there and I can't see anything, so I said, 'Just list some of it, so I can think.' So she pulls out a box and listed, in great big writing, right across the top, it says "Sybil book of prints for book." And I said, 'Well, that's it, right there.' 'Oh', she said. I tell you. I tell you. Well, anyway, so I got it done up and it was mailed this morning."

I said, "Oh, thank you! I sent you pictures. You didn't get them yet?"

"Not yet."

"You'll get a kick out of them. My childhood and a couple from the play I was in at Lincoln Center. Seems like another lifetime for me."

She stated, "You know, well, it probably was. I was thinking the other day that you should write a book about you, at least the early years. Because your childhood was very typical, but dying out now. You were telling me about all of you being Catholics in the neighborhood and all being related and all going to the same school and the same church. You know, that was all over New York. That was, I guess, all over the country. There were settlements. There were people like that and I think that would be most interesting to read about and save that as history. And now you taking care of your mother."

I told her, "With Italians it's just a natural thing. You do it without even thinking about it."

"Nobody takes care of the elderly any more, I mean in a general sense. I can't complain. At least I didn't get dropped from Medicare. Over half the patients that my nurses are seeing were dropped as of February."

"Were you worried that you might get cut off?"

"Well, it crossed my mind. But the nurse reassured me immediately that I wouldn't be, because I have open wounds. The nurse said, 'Open wounds are good.' And I said, 'Well, I'm glad somebody thinks so.' She said that Medicare would pay for her to come once a day to change the dressings. It should be done twice a day, but I can't stoop down far enough. She said that the breast cancer is also an open wound, but I can dress that myself because I can reach it."

"Is the pain strong?"

"I had quite a lot of pain the last couple days. I don't know. That pain medicine doesn't seem to hold very well. I think I'll ask him for something a little stronger or different. They sent me a generic."

"Sometimes the generic is not as strong."

She related, "Well, that's what Connie used to say. They're different. They're probably different ingredients. The pain medicine might be the same but they put other stuff in it for it to stick together. I can't think of the word. Anyway, the Hydrocodone that I had, the first two prescriptions, the way they were shaped, and so on, were like the ones Connie had and they worked fine. But then the next three times they filled it they sent a different kind, a different shape. I called them and they said it was a different company. They had to take what the supplier gave them and a lot of hooey. I don't believe all that. And the nurse said no they don't have to. They have both kinds on hand and unless the doctor orders it. I think when she comes on Monday, it's about time to get it refilled. I'll see if I can't get somebody to get something different. It's just not good enough. Connie took Hydrocodone for all her fractures. Whenever she had a fracture they gave her that and she'd take it for six or seven weeks and then no more until the next time. She never got addicted to it or it never wore off and it worked. I'd give her one every six hours and it worked. But it just, it doesn't."

"Call the doctor and tell him about it and ask if he can prescribe something else."

"Well, the nurse takes care of those things. She takes care of it for me. It's part of their duty and I let them do it because they know more about everything and they can handle the doctor. It's a little hard for me to make phone calls. His office is in another town. So they don't have any trouble with it. So I'll let her—they're always wanting to do something."

She said emphatically, "Yesterday, the nurse asked me if I was sure I didn't want to go to the hospital or have the doctor come here. I told her, 'I'm sure. Just don't bother me with that. I've got all I can handle. I don't want the doctor coming over here. He makes me nervous.'"

"That's funny. He's supposed to help you."

She laughed, "He's older than I am. He dodders around. But I get the medication I need. He's a good doctor. He knows what he's doing."

"Can you up your pain medicine a little bit?"

She replied, "I could. They tell me I can. But it gets side effects, you know, if you take too much. You get dizzy and I can't afford to get dizzier than I am anyway."

I laughed, "Oh, dear."

"You know, when I have to walk around here and so on. So I can't afford to be dizzy. So I don't. But I take what I'm allowed.

Helplessly, I said, "I just wish you didn't have that pain."

She replied, "Yeah, well, it goes with the territory, I guess. I'm pulling out of this a little bit. It's up and down. Yesterday was so much worse. Now I'm getting nauseated talking. I'm going to have to go."

"Okay, you take care. Bye."

This was the first time in five years that Shirley had to cut our telephone conversation short. No matter how bad her pain, she would always rationalize that it was worse the day before and hopefully predict that it would be less tomorrow.

• • •

Shirley made me laugh during our conversation on February 8, 1998. The phone rang for a long time before she answered it.

"Hello, Shirley?" I said.

In a weak voice she replied, "Yeah, let me sit down. I'm so glad you called. I just went to the kitchen to do the dishes and now I don't have to. Like my aunt dropped a whole tray of dishes and she said she was so glad she hadn't washed them yet!"

It was comforting to know she maintained a sense of humor.

I asked, "How are you?"

"Oh, I'm pretty good. It's just so hard to walk. I just walked out there and came back and I'm out of breath. Be all right in a minute, once I sit down."

Because of a huge snow storm in Lexington, the mail had not been delivered. Shirley had not received the letter I sent her. She said she saw the post office on the TV news and the workers were stir-crazy.

She said, "It's a little sunny this afternoon and it's going to be fifty tomorrow, so it'll help. A lot of it's melting, but, oh, it's everywhere. The roofs and everything. And I looked out the back door this morning. My poor magnolia tree has so much snow on it. It was hanging all the way to the ground on one side. I realized the leaves were all turning brown. The whole thing is broken off. It's as big as the side of the house. The tree is huge. It's got to be at least fifty years old. That's how old the house is. It's way taller than my two-story house. It's a gorgeous tree."

• • •

I'm thankful that I called her on February 9th, the next day. She picked up the phone and said, "Hello, Patrick?"

"You knew it was me."

"Yes, I went out and fixed a bowl of soup, and I thought, well, I'd better hurry up with this, because he will call and if I'm in the kitchen, I can't get there quick enough. So I just sat down. Well, I didn't know, of course, what time you'd call, but I just had that kind of feeling. I get in the kitchen, and the phone rings."

"This was the only chance I would have to call. You sound so much stronger today."

"Well, I'm better. And I got your letter. It was wonderful."

I sent her a short story which I had written about a dog I found in Rome. I brought him back to New York, where he lived for twelve years. When I had to put him to sleep, I held him in my arms as the doctor injected him.

I asked, "Did you like the story?"

She sighed, "Yeah, made me cry, but I liked it."

I was touched. "Oh, that's sweet."

"The end of it. I've been through that, too. It's so hard to let them go."

"Well, I'm sending you a more cheerful story. I got the children's book and it's inscribed to you. So what's going on with you?"

Shirley said, "Well, not much of anything. The nurse came this morning and I was in quite a little pain when she came and we discussed it. She said that—well, anyway—when the doctor was here the last time he poked around in my middle—and so she said that my—he didn't say much, and I didn't ask because I didn't think it made any difference what I knew or didn't know, because, you know, I can't do anything about anything much except do what I'm supposed to do. But anyhow, she said that—she told me that my liver and my pancreas were enlarged, particularly the liver. I figured so because I'm so big across the middle, and particularly on that side. It presses up on my stomach. When I sit down, I have to, you know, press on my stomach in order to breathe. And I know I have two different kinds of pain. The pain in my back from those vertebrae rubbing around there is different from this pain that I have in my side and my ribs. And she said that I may have to have—because I made the comment that the pain medicine helps my back, but didn't do a whole lot for this other thing, and she said, well, you know, we're dealing with something else there, and she said, you may have to have two different kinds of pain medicine. But she said if I would start the morphine, it'd be a lot better, but that might control 'em both. But I would have to take considerable amounts and that's what I don't want to do—at least until after my company's been here."

"You don't want to do it yet?"

"Well, I don't want to be out of it when they're here."

Naomi, Jim and their daughter had planned a visit for quite a while. Although embarrassed by her bloated appearance, Shirley did want to see them.

Shirley continued, "The nurse said, 'My, you're a strong person.' I said, 'There's another word for it.' And the nurse said, 'What's that?' I said, 'Stubborn.'"

Shirley was hoping that Roberta might come to get her house in order for her cousins' visit. However, Roberta had sickness and deaths in her own family. Roberta told Shirley that she wanted to come to see her but was also afraid because everyone that she visited lately had died.

Shirley chuckled, "But she said she wanted to see me. She worries about me and she misses me. And we're two of a kind, I tell you. We're two of the biggest nuts you ever saw. When we get together."

"It's a good break for her, too," I said.

"That's what she said. She uses this for therapy, coming here. She's been saying that for years. And we think alike. When I start to tell her something, she finishes it. She knows what I want and she knows where everything is. She's just wonderful. It's hard for her to get here. No car and no telephone. But she's got her daughter's car now for a while."

Shirley mused, "I was sitting here after lunch and fell asleep. After a while I heard the cars going swish, swish in the water. I knew that it wasn't supposed to rain until Thursday so why is it raining today. I woke up and the sun was shining bright. And then I realized the snow was melting. Boy, it took me a long time to come to that conclusion. There's so much snow. I can see it, just sitting here and looking out the window. It's clear up to the window sill. And the neighbors' houses are just about buried. The roofs and the porch roofs, and all you can see is the chimney and some windows peeking out."

"That is so incredible," I said.

"Well, for here it is," said Shirley. "No school still. We did get mail though. A whole stack of it. I read yours first and I've got two or three I still haven't read, and a bill I didn't open. It's an electric bill."

• • •

Wishing I could go to see Shirley, I did the next best thing—I telephoned often. My calling seemed so futile now that she appeared to be nearing the end. I knew that she didn't want me to see her in that condition. Years before, she told me she didn't want me to see her that way. I was touched by her vanity. Much as I tried to convince her that her appearance was not important to me, it remained important to her.

On February 10, 1998, we spoke about Naomi's upcoming visit.

I asked, "How are you?"

She replied, "Oh, I'm a little better today. Yesterday was rough. I had to call a nurse to come back. I had to have more medicine. I had to get my friend Teresa to come and stay twelve hours overnight with me. I couldn't get to the kitchen. I couldn't get anything to eat. I hadn't had anything to eat for a long time and I was weak and shaky. And I was nauseated. The nurse came this morning. Then she came back later and she said I looked better this afternoon. She wanted to check on me and she brought me some yogurt and Gatorade. I hadn't had yogurt in years, but I used to have it when I was sick. So I ate some. A little bit at a time. My cousin called yesterday morning from North Carolina. She reminded me it was only four days until she was coming. And I told her I couldn't talk to her then—I was feeling so bad. I told her I'd talk later. So she was worried. She called Dee and talked to her. She was so afraid I wasn't going to be able to hang on. And Dee said, 'Well, K---, I promise you that she's not going to die before you get here.'

"So when Dee came this morning she told me. So she said, 'Now, you can't die, because I promised her. When I make a promise, it has to be kept.' And I said, 'Even for somebody else?' She said, 'Especially for somebody else.'"

Shirley kept the promise.

• • •

On February 13, 1998, I called but a different female voice responded, "Mason residence. May I help you?"

Surprised, I answered, "Oh, hello. This is Patrick Suraci. I just wanted to say hello to Shirley."

She said, "I tell you what. Can I say hello to her for you? She's not feeling well—she's kind of weak and she doesn't feel up to talking over the phone."

"Okay. Is this her cousin?"

She answered, "Roberta Guy."

I said, "Oh, Roberta. Hi, it's Patrick. Shirley didn't feel too well the other day when I spoke with her."

"Right."

I said, "I hope she was able to see her cousin."

Roberta informed me, "Well, she'll be here in the morning."

"Oh, good."

Roberta said, "Yeah, and she's ready for her."

"Oh, good. Just tell her I'm thinking of her and hope she'll be okay tomorrow."

"Okay, I sure will."

I didn't know then that Shirley would never be well enough to speak with me again.

CHAPTER 18

The Untidy Way of Death

On January 8, 1998, approximately six weeks before Shirley died on February 26, 1998, we spoke about her painting during the time of her Multiple Personality Disorder and after her integration.

She said, "After I got well and painted, my work was different. All my work is under my name [Shirley Mason]." Regarding the paintings previous to her integration she said, "We put those names on those paintings afterwards, you know [the names of her alters]. I painted before and after. I always claimed my own paintings. But anything that another personality did, I put aside. I kept those separate. And that's what you'll be getting. You'll get a few that say *Sybil* and that was me, but now my own work is quite different."

Shirley sent me 199 transparencies in the black book that Dee had difficulty locating, and a list of the paintings with their titles.

I said, "Well, I'd love to see your work."

"Yeah. I don't have too much of it left. I sold about sixty-five paintings a couple of years ago."

"Where are they?"

"Well, they're all over the countryside. The gallery people took them and the galleries in Atlanta, Indianapolis, and Miami. He comes and gets a load of paintings and takes off. And then he comes back a couple of weeks later with a few thousand dollars, and takes some more paintings."

"Well, that's nice."

"But that ended a couple of years ago when I got ill. Nearly out of paintings and I can't do them any more. But I kept some. I have some that I…particular ones that people want…and I had a few I want to give to my relatives."

I inquired, "Did you take photographs of them?"

"Oh, yes. I've got slides of everything. Well, I didn't do it. I had it done professionally. Because I enter exhibits at showings and you have to send in slides of what you propose to show and so forth. You've got to have professional material. I might send you some, sometime."

"Well, even just prints of them. I'd love to see the prints. It's so wonderful to paint. I wish I could do that. I tried with watercolors at one time."

"That's hard. It takes time to practice, over and over and over, doing it. Any art takes time, because you can't develop your skills or style or anything without devoting everything. It's like music. You've just got to practice."

"I loved doing it, because I would just forget about the world."

She concurred, "Yeah, oh yes, me too. Get lost in it."

Painting served several purposes for Shirley. When she was tormented as a child, she would escape the pain by fragmenting into another personality who would express her emotion by drawing and painting. When the waking self, Shirley, was present, she would paint in a different style to reflect her perceptions of the world. Her art gave a focus to her life. This was important since she had a troubled relationship with her parents and her friendships were interrupted by her fugue states [periods which she could not remember].

She was denied the pleasures of sexual activity because she was too scarred by her physical and psychological injuries from her mother's abuse. She could not engage in many behaviors that most of us take for granted. Painting also provided her with a profession, as a teacher and art therapist. But above all, she was an artist at heart and her intimate revelations were in her paintings and drawings.

Shirley said, "I had hopes of writing a book on the analysis of children's art and what it meant when they did various things. It was almost thirty years that I taught in that area. I've always been a great advocate of getting problems at an early stage. But again, I'm not able to do the book."

I wondered how Shirley's life would have been different if her abuse and mental disorder had been detected at an early age.

On January 14, 1998, Shirley said, "Don Frei, my attorney in Cincinnati, has been my attorney for years, Connie's and mine. He said the company that he's senior partner with are patent and copyright specialists. They're one of the big companies in the United States. And so he's taken care of everything, when we got sued and all that sort of thing. And he said, when I talked to him about wanting to do this art book, what I could do, because I retained the ownership of all the prints. Now Flora had the copyright to the written material in the book, but not the pictures in the book. Those are still mine. Now that is all in the name of Mason Arts. Everything is Mason Arts, Inc. All the royalty checks and everything were made out to Mason Arts and I signed it in a way that nobody ever has my name on anything. It has nothing to do with my name at all. And so of course we asked Flora to write the book for us and she said she would be glad to except for one thing. She was mad at Simon and Schuster [the publisher of her book *Shoemaker*] and she said that she had promised them her next book. She didn't want it to be ours. And so she said she'd wait and see what happened. Anyway I have tape recordings of a telephone conversation, three-way, she and Connie and I where we talked about the book. I wanted you to know that that was covered.

So many of these things, nobody knows but me and Don Frei. And so, I wanted to send you his name and address, so if later anything should come up. Because now I have to let him know what I've done with the paintings, because that was all written up, a legal agreement that Connie had with him about what to do. But the paintings came back to me. They were Connie's. She owned them for a long time. I gave them all to her, a long time ago. And she owned them, but she said she would divide everything in half with me. Then she left them to me, so that they are all mine.

Shirley continued, "I'll let you know any particulars I think you need to know. I keep Dee informed all the time as we go along, so she knows I'm sending you these paintings and why and everything. She would be the person to contact if I'm no longer around. She'll have charge of Mason Arts and whatever royalties come into that. She will disperse according to what I asked her to do, rather than putting in my will what I wanted done with it. And because I trust her completely. So that would be—she and Don Frei would be your contacts."

I said, "Okay."

Shirley responded, "But I don't see any problems at all with anything. But you might sometime be challenged whether you own these paintings or not. And the ownership of the paintings always remains with the artist, unless they've given written permission to reproduce it. So even now, when one does a textbook or anybody does anything, and they want to use prints of any of that, they have to write and get permission and pay me to do it. So that would all go, well, it's set up to go for Dee to handle. But if you own them, I guess it would go to you. I'll have to get that worked out. I'll ask Don about that. I didn't think this thing was so involved."

I said, "I'm sorry that it'll be so much trouble."

Her discourse was cut short by her pain. "I'm sorry. I'm trying to move around a little in the chair. Oh, my back is so stiff and sore and achy. I'm not in very good shape. I can't say anything because yesterday was a really bummer of a day also. Today's better. Yesterday I just sat here all day. I just hate it. I did something I've never done before. Roberta called and, you know, one of the two friends that I see regularly, and I just asked her if she could come another time. I just wasn't up to dishing with anybody. But I'm better today. So it comes and goes on different days. Well, anyway, that's why I'm moaning here."

Shirley told me that she had divided all the Sybil paintings so that they would fit into two packages according to their sizes. She put all the large ones together and the smaller ones together. She figured if one package got lost or destroyed at least I would have the other package. I was horrified at the thought of any of them being lost or destroyed. She felt certain that Dee would mail the packages to me as she had instructed.

The penultimate time I phoned Shirley's home was on February 26, 1998 at 12:07 PM. In the background I heard her weak voice pleading to Roberta, "Tell him I'm sorry. I'm sorry." Roberta informed me that Shirley was too sick to speak on the phone. I mumbled, "Please tell her that it's okay, it's okay. I'll call later." Now the reality hit me that she was in the last stages of her life. I felt helpless. I wanted to go to Lexington to see her before she died, but she had previously told me that she didn't want me to see her in her deteriorated condition. I tried to assure her that I along with her relatives and friends who loved her would not be put off by her appearance. This did not change her embarrassment.

When I called later that day at 3:01 PM Roberta stunned me with the news that Shirley had just died. I recalled Shirley's last words from my previous call, "Tell him I'm sorry, I'm sorry." I didn't know if she meant that she was sorry because the paintings were never sent to me, or because she was not physically able to call her lawyer Don Frei, or because she was sorry that she couldn't talk to me, or that she was sorry that she was leaving this life. The one thing I was certain of was that she was prepared to leave this life because of her strong faith in God.

Later that day a reporter from Lexington called John Jay College wanting to speak with Flora, who might confirm that the Shirley Mason who just died was Sybil. Also, Diane Sawyer had been negotiating with Stewart Stern to have Shirley give her an interview by phone. Shirley liked Ms. Sawyer and was seriously considering it so long as her identity would not be revealed. Now Ms. Sawyer wanted to announce on her TV show Prime Time that Sybil had died that day. I asked Ms. Sawyer's producer to please not make that announcement or the Lexington reporter would be able to make the connection to Shirley Mason. Ms. Sawyer did not make the announcement giving up her scoop and preserving Shirley's identity.

Although Shirley had died, I thought that her trusted friend Dee would send me the Sybil paintings that Shirley had designated for me. I would be able to carry out her wishes to establish a scholarship fund for needy art students. I didn't think that I would be able to part with any of the original paintings but that I could have prints made, as Shirley suggested, and sell them to provide money for the scholarships.

Since the paintings never arrived, I sent a letter dated March 2, 1998 to:

> Mrs. Delores Sherfield
> Dear Mrs. Sherfield:
>
> As you know Miss Shirley Mason wanted you to give me all the Sybil paintings and drawings in order for me to complete my book about them. I am trying to do my best to carry out her wishes. She wanted me to use the art work and the analysis of them as the basis for this book. Her intentions for this book were to show the world that early diagnosis of multiple personality disorder could be made from children's art work and that spontaneous painting during the course of therapy could be important in a successful treatment outcome.
>
> She also wanted me to show the world that Sybil was cured, since there continues to be controversy in the psychiatric world over multiple personality disorder. She wanted me to relate that Sybil never had a relapse and lived a productive life.

As her friend and executrix of her estate I hope that you will honor Ms. Mason's wishes to use Sybil's art, which was created during the most difficult part of her life, to help prevent such horrors occurring to other children. I would like to offer you $700.00 for fourteen of the paintings and drawings which she wanted me to use in the book.

Enclosed are the photographs which she sent me. They are numbered with a description and size in inches:

1. The Family—pastel on tempera 12 X 18
2. View of Manhattan—watercolor 15 X 22
3. Clown—wax crayon 14 X16
5. Tree Form in Wind—tempera 11 X 15
9. Hills in Rage—watercolor 17 X 15
34. The Eyes—watercolor 15 X 20
42. Reaching—watercolor 15 X 20
47. Alone—crayon 12 X 18
68. Neighbors—watercolor 17 X 11
76. Flurry—watercolor 12 X 17
79. Daddy's Car—tempera 14 X 19
80. Blue Trees and Home—watercolor 12 X 22
114. Self—water color 9 X 12
131. Mother Fish—crayon 8 X 10

Thank you for your consideration.

Sincerely,
Patrick J. Suraci

I received no response from Mrs. Sherfield, so I telephoned her and she told me that she would not send me the paintings because it was not stipulated in Shirley's will. Previously, she sent me the black book containing the transparencies of all the Sybil paintings at Shirley's request. After I received the black book, Shirley had asked Dee to also send the original paintings. I reminded her of this, but she maintained her position. She did not send me any paintings.

Rather than taking legal action, since I had taped conversations of Shirley telling me that she wanted me to have the paintings, I sent Dee a second letter on April 4, 1998:

> Dear Mrs. Sherfield:
>
> As we discussed on the telephone, I would like to purchase all the Sybil paintings and drawings that are not framed, since it is more convenient for you to sell them all together.
>
> I hope that I can afford to buy all of them, because I have a limited budget. I am financing the book myself and have no source of money for it. Managed care companies reducing my fees and supporting my elderly mother have placed restrictions on the amount I can spend on the book. I hope to produce a work which Ms. Shirley Mason would approve of.
>
> Will you please let me know the cost when you are able to ascertain it?
>
> Thank you for your consideration.
>
> Sincerely
> Patrick J. Suraci

I never heard from Mrs. Sherfield. I later learned that an art dealer bought the paintings which were left in Shirley's house. Since the Sybil paintings were not sent to me, Shirley's wishes for me to create a scholarship fund have not been carried out.

• • •

When I visited Naomi, she spoke with me about her final visit with Shirley. She told me that Shirley, knowing that she was dying, had given her the Sybil paintings.

• • •

In attempting to elucidate Shirley's character, Naomi said, "This is very important. Prayer played a big part in her life. And literally on her deathbed, when I was there, she asked me to sit down at the piano and play hymns for her. And I played the hymns of the faith, one after another, after another. And my girls sang for her. And the hymns of the faith, the hymns of the church, are filled with the most wonderful theology of God's power to heal. And this is a woman who attributed her wellness in part, in large part, to her faith in God. And so my reason for cooperating with you is to validate that.

"Because that is a part of therapy that I think is no longer being disputed. I mean, there has been some recent research findings that show that people who are prayed for get better. Our country was founded on the principles of God-fearing people and I want to reinforce that the Judeo-Christian values and the faith in God and prayer work in healing."

Naomi showed me a photo of Shirley which she took three days before she died. Shirley was sitting in the chair in which she had been sleeping for the past few months.

Naomi and I spoke of our happy times with Shirley. She showed me these letters from Shirley.

> September 12, 1995
> My Dear Naomi,
>
> I was happy to receive your note, although I fear it was quite some time ago. I just haven't been able to write this past summer. About the phone calls, my two local friends who call me ring twice and then hang up and call back, and if you want to do that also, I'd be delighted. I hadn't asked you to do it that way because it is more trouble for you when you're dialing a long-distance number. I sometimes turn off the sound of the phone evenings and Saturdays or if I'm resting, but I almost always have it turned on in the mornings. I'd love to hear from you and would surely answer if I knew it was you. I hope all is going well for all of you. ------ will be having his first birthday in a few days, the 21st [Naomi said that Shirley remembered every one of eleven grandchildren's' birthdays] and that should be quite a milestone for him. Give him a big hug for me. Fall colors are beginning to show up here. Always lovely in Kentucky in autumn. Please give my best wishes to Jim and also to Agnes. [Naomi said that Shirley always included Agnes, Jim's mother.]
>
> Love to all,
> Shirley

• • •

December 10, 1995

My Dear Naomi and Jim,

Your beautiful precious card arrived and as always it's the highlight of my holiday season. When I look at those wonderful smiling faces, words fail me, surely. Also received a lovely card from ---- with their good news. I got a letter off to them last week to be sure it reached them by Christmas. Well, we are getting our first snow of the season today. It's one degree temperature. Don't get much usually in Kentucky. To me, a native of Minnesota, it's not Christmas without snow, but just a light dusting will do nicely. We don't need a whole two feet of it. I want to thank you, Naomi, for the note and the packet of photos you sent me this fall. They are great. You look lovely in the rose pink formal and the children are darling. How fast they grow! Thank you so much for sending the photos. Happy holidays!

Love, Shirley.

• • •

February 20, 1996

How do I even begin to thank you for the spectacular spring bouquet that arrived on a bleak winter day? Happy birthday indeed it was, thanks to you. It was arranged with several lily buds interspersed in the bouquet so a new lily opened every day all week. We finally got past the gray and snowy days, so now we have gray and rainy days. But at least the temperatures have risen, and spirits along with them. I expect you're busy and probably traveling frequently, and looking forward to your spring cruise. I hope all is well with you both, and again many thanks for remembering me in such a lovely way.

• • •

Naomi told me her paternal grandmother, Jane, and Shirley's mother, Mattie, were sisters. Naomi's father, Virgil was born in 1901 and died when she was 13, and her mother, Ellen, died when she was 23.

In November, 1966,Shirley wrote to Naomi:

> You were right about Virgil being a wonderful person. He was my mom's favorite nephew. When I was about 4 years-old and onward, for a few years, he used to come and visit us during his summer vacations. He was always so nice to me. He talked and played and joked with me.
>
> He made a big hit with a child. My writing is so poor, hope you can make it out. I start off quite fairly, but soon deteriorate in form and thought, I fear. I've had an inoperable cancer for several years without much distress. But last spring, it spread to the lymph nodes, with swelling and pain in my left arm, and possibly to my brain more recently. I've had several vision disturbances, some loss of sight, and a couple of light strokes, with weakness in my right arm during the summer. So writing letters, although high on my priority list just didn't get written. But I still think of all of you often. I wish you'd convey my love to the girls and all, and tell them I will write. I just don't know when. I'm doing well enough just now and know God will not let me down. I have great faith, peace of mind, and I feel a closeness one can't describe. But I'm just limited in action. My spirits are good, I have a good friend to help me, Roberta, and everything I need. God has indeed been good to me. I have several times at least viewed the video you sent me. I just adore it, especially the part with those adorable children. And I'm so proud of you, Naomi. Always have been. Hope this finds everyone well and looking forward to the holidays.
>
> My love to you, Jim, and Agnes, as well as the children,
>
> Shirley

• • •

Naomi called Shirley to tell her they would like to visit, but Shirley said she just didn't feel up to a visit because she didn't like the way she looked.

Naomi tried to reassure her, "We're not looking at the outside of you. We're looking at the inside of you. We just want to hug you and let you know we love you."

Shirley told her she wanted to see her so badly, but she didn't think she was up to it. Naomi asked her to let her know if she should change her mind.

In January, 1998 Shirley did call Naomi and said, "I want to see you. I'm dying and I want to see you. And I want to see the girls."

Naomi said when she arrived at Shirley's house, Dee was present and told her that Shirley was waiting to see her before she died.

CHAPTER 19

Controversy over Sybil

While Flora Schreiber and Dr. Cornelia Wilbur were alive, no one challenged the veracity of the book *Sybil*. As interest in this spectacular case grew, many people urged them to reveal Shirley's identity. They were offered money, television appearances and media interviews. They never accepted any of those offers; they preserved Shirley's anonymity.

This anonymity made it impossible for others to verify Shirley's history or to confirm her diagnosis.

Before *Sybil* was published, there were few cases of Multiple Personality Disorder (MPD) recorded since Morton Prince's famous case of Sally Beauchamp in *The Dissociation of a Personality* (1906). The case of Chris Sizemore was written up by Corbet H. Thigpen and Hervey M. Cleckley in *The Three Faces of Eve* (1957). And then came *Sybil* in 1973, capturing public and professional interest.

Clinicians who had been unfamiliar with the symptoms of MPD now learned more about this rare disorder, which may explain the burgeoning number of MPD cases reported after the book was published. Some overzealous therapists also made incorrect diagnoses of MPD, hoping to be in the vanguard.

Criminals faked MPD in order to use it as a mitigating factor in their own defense.

Multiple Personality Disorder was changed to Dissociative Identity Disorder (DID) in the revised edition of the *Diagnostic and Statistical Manual of Mental Disorders Fourth Edition DSM IV* published by the American Psychiatric Association in 1994. The *DSM IV* states:

> The essential feature of Dissociative Identity Disorder is the presence of two or more distinct identities or personality states (Criterion A) that recurrently take control of behavior (Criterion B).
>
> Individuals with Dissociative Identity Disorder frequently report having experienced severe physical and sexual abuse, especially during childhood. (p. 484.)

After Flora died in 1988 and Dr. Wilbur died in 1992, critics began to dispute Sybil's diagnosis of MPD. Some claimed that Sybil suffered from Hysteria, which is not a current diagnosis in the *DSM IV*. They implied that Sybil had produced her symptoms of MPD to please her therapist, or they were induced by Dr. Wilbur through hypnosis. Critics attracted media attention and publicity. Not only Shirley's integrity, but also the integrity of Flora Schreiber and Dr. Cornelia Wilbur, was called into question.

• • •

Dr. Herbert Spiegel, a psychiatrist, gave an interview to Mikkel Borch-Jacobsen which was published in the *New York Review of Books* on April 24, 1997. Dr. Spiegel stated that Dr. Cornelia Wilbur asked him to examine Sybil in order to "help her clarify the diagnosis."

He said, "I examined Sybil and discovered that she was highly hypnotizable...I asked Cornelia if it was okay if I did some age regression studies on her. Cornelia said yes, so I used Sybil for a lot of studies. That's when I developed a rapport with Sybil...I was doing research with Sybil, using her as a demonstration case at our classes in hypnosis at Columbia University's College of Physicians and Surgeons...But one day during our regression studies, Sybil said, 'Well, do you want me to be Helen?' And I said, 'What do you mean?' And she said, 'Well, when I'm with Dr. Wilbur she wants me to be Helen'...That's when I realized that Connie was helping her identify aspects of her life, or perspectives, that she then called by name. By naming them this way, she was reifying a memory of some kind and converting it into a 'personality'...and they [Flora Schreiber and Dr. Cornelia Wilbur] both came to see me to ask me if I wanted to be a coauthor with them...they said they would be calling her a 'multiple personality.' I said, 'But she's not a multiple personality!' I think she was a wonderful hysterical patient with role confusion, which is typical of high hysterics. It was hysteria."

Dr. Spiegel made films of his hypnosis sessions to show his classes at Columbia University. No film of this alleged hypnosis session with Sybil was ever given to me, because Dr. Spiegel said he could not find it. It is peculiar that Dr. Spiegel would tell Flora that Sybil was not a Multiple Personality because she suffered from "hysteria." He should have known that in 1905 Morton Prince wrote in his classic *The Dissociation of a Personality* that "hysteria" was a component of Multiple Personality Disorder. It also defies logic that Flora would have thanked Dr. Spiegel in the Acknowledgements of *Sybil* if he had declared that Sybil was not a Multiple Personality. Her acknowledgement read: *Dr. Herbert Spiegel, who did age regressions on Sybil and described her as "a brilliant hysteric," gave several hours to a valuable discussion of this case, which he knew first-hand.*

Moreover, it is questionable that Dr. Spiegel, as required by the code of ethics, did not report this so-called fraudulent case which became world famous. When Dr. Spiegel was asked why he waited until 1997, twenty-four years after *Sybil* was published, to report this inaccuracy, he stated that no one had ever asked him before about Sybil.

In 1997 when I spoke with Shirley about this, she said, "Let them say what they want. It's my life and I know what's the truth." Preserving her anonymity was more important than debating people who knew very little about her.

In 1999, after Shirley had died, I sent Dr. Spiegel a letter. On Sunday, Oct. 3, 1999, at 8:56pm, he called me. He stated that he had seen Sybil when Dr. Wilbur was away. He said he was a surrogate therapist. He said it was an ethical issue that prevented him from discussing the case with me. He said, "I talked about Sybil when she was Sybil. I can't do anything now. Her identity is known. It's an ethical issue."

However, in January of that same year—nine months prior to his conversation with me—he had already given an interview to *Newsweek*—after Sybil's identity had been revealed.

Shirley's cousin Naomi Rhode discovered an audio cassette of a conversation between Shirley and Dr. Wilbur which took place on February 18, 1977. They were recording their ideas for a book about Sybil's paintings that they were planning to publish. They talked about Sybil in the third person. This tape was created for their own benefit to help them to recall pertinent incidents. During the course of their conversation they hit upon the time when Dr. Wilbur sent Shirley to "an expert in hypnosis" (Dr. Spiegel).

Dr. Wilbur said, "They say that hysterics are generally suggestible, but I don't believe that. I think that hysterics are people who are willing to enter into a contract with someone whom they trust. Now if they don't trust that individual to some extent, they may appear to enter into a contract, but they don't really.

"And as an example of that, I would like to point out that, although Sybil was very readily hypnotizable by me...An expert used her as a demonstration subject, and she agreed to this and he was disagreeable to her. As a consequence he could not really hypnotize her, even though he was a real expert in the subject. She could resist this, and she out of politeness would say certain things, but she would only go so far and no further."

Shirley added, "She [Sybil] didn't trust him as much. He tried to make her make something special out of things in her life that weren't special, like birthdays. He insisted they were important, but they had never been important in her life, nor in her home. And birthdays had gone by without even being noticed, and he was trying to say her birthdays were so important to her. And they weren't. The days that were, he didn't want to discuss, because they didn't fit into his life pattern."

Dr. Wilbur interjected, "Or they didn't fit into his system of function."

Shirley replied, "He said, 'Well, every child's birthday's important.'"

Dr. Wilbur said, "And then he insisted on using them anyhow, which created some animosity on her part, and also made her distrustful, because he asked her and she said 'No' and then he contradicted her."

Shirley said, "He always used the birthdays as the starting point for the hypnosis, and this was one of the main reasons she was resisting him so. He would say, 'Well, now, let's start with your ninth birthday' and then he would try to hypnotize her back to the ninth birthday party. Nothing had happened special on her ninth birthday, that or any other. Except there were a couple of friends for her when she was seventeen."

Dr. Wilbur said, "But he never happened to hit on that birthday."

Shirley said, "Yeah."

Dr. Wilbur said, "I don't think that the hysteric is suggestible except insofar as they really want to be, in other words, and as fits into their own psychology. You cannot suggest anything to an hysteric that doesn't fit with their own psychology and is not agreeable with them and does not come from a source in which they have confidence."

The tape has been transferred to a CD in order to preserve this conversation between Shirley and Dr. Wilbur.

• • •

In August, 1998, Robert Rieber, Ph.D. presented a research paper entitled *Hypnosis, False Memory, and Multiple Personality: A Trinity of Affinity* at the American Psychological Association Conference in San Francisco. He claimed that twenty-five years prior, (which would have been in 1973, when *Sybil* had already been published), Flora Schreiber gave him a tape of a conversation between herself and Dr. Wilbur. He claimed he had thrown this tape in a desk drawer and only recently found it. He alleged the tape showed Flora and Dr. Wilbur manufacturing the diagnosis of MPD for *Sybil.* He stated that Flora gave him this tape in order to interest him in co-authoring the book, since he had many more publications than she. *Sybil* had already been published in 1973.

In his research paper of 1998 he stated in a footnote:

> The original cassette tape recordings and complete transcripts of the protocol of these recordings have been deposited in the Oskar Dilthelm Library for the History of Psychiatry, Department of Psychiatry, New York Hospital-Cornell University Medical College. It is available to anyone who wishes to do further research on this topic.

I made yearly telephone calls to the Oskar Diethelm Library and was informed by the librarian, Ms. Diane Richardson, that Dr. Rieber had never deposited the tapes.

I finally obtained the tapes when Dr. Rieber deposited them in 2006 in the library at John Jay College of Criminal Justice. I noticed a discrepancy with the date on the tape where Dr. Rieber wrote "Given to me by F. Schreiber 1978." It stated "1978" not "1973" the year he claimed to have received it. This is what is written on the tape:

Side 1: Peggy 1st tape April 4, 1971
Side 2: Early Findings April 4, 1971

[Reorganize?] tapes of Schreiber and Wilber. Gift of RW Rieber. Given to me by F. Schrieber 1978.

After listening to the tapes I did not find any evidence to support Dr. Rieber's claims.

Dr. Rieber never knew Shirley Mason. He said in an interview in *The New York Times*, August 10, 1998: "Sybil, who vacillated on whether or not her story was true, died last December." She did not die in December 1997; she died from inoperable brain cancer at home on February 26, 1998, shortly before I called her that afternoon. From my first contact with Shirley in 1993 until her death she never "vacillated" about her life's story as portrayed in the book *Sybil.* On the contrary, she often expressed gratitude that she had been cured of the terrifying and disruptive symptoms of MPD.

In 2006 Dr. Rieber published a book repeating his theory about Sybil. Among many inaccuracies, he stated the Mayo Clinic was in Rochester, Wisconsin instead of Rochester, Minnesota and that Shirley's birthplace was Wisconsin instead of Dodge Center, Minnesota.

Regarding Flora Schreiber, he wrote:

> *As I recall, she could put over the charm but she could be a vicious bitch when she lost her temper.* (p. 108.)

Dr. Rieber also states:

> *The tapes are now on deposit with the library at John Jay College, City University of New York, and at the Archives of the History of Psychology at the University of Akron, Ohio. They are available for anyone interested in conducting research on the subject of MPD/DID in general or Sybil's case in particular.* (p. 205.)

After several trips to the library at John Jay College, I discovered the tapes still had not been deposited. Dr. Larry Sullivan, the Chief Librarian, confirmed that Dr. Rieber did not deposit the tapes. On

Tuesday, April 25, 2006, I telephoned the Archives of the History of Psychology at the University of Akron. Dr. David Baker, the director, reported that the tapes had not been deposited.

As a result of persistent calls from Dr. Leah Dickstein, both a colleague of Dr. Corneila Wilbur and a good friend of Shirley Mason, and from myself, Dr. Rieber's tapes are now in the library at John Jay College. Other researchers are finally able to come to their own conclusions.

• • •

Peter Swales gave interviews and speeches attempting to discredit Flora's book. Flora had written that Hattie, Willard, and Sybil (the names Flora used for the book to protect identities) had to move to a "chicken house." Mr. Swales claimed that this incident never occurred because he could never locate the "chicken house." (See Appendix H.)

In *Sybil*, Flora wrote:

> *For, when the Great Depression struck, Willard Dorsett suffered serious reverses, even losing his home...The only house on those forty acres of land was a one-room chicken house, which the Dorsetts made their temporary home.* (p. 142.)
>
> *Sybil thought of that autumn day when she had come here with her father and mother...Her mother did say, though, "A chicken house is only fit for chickens." Her father had replied: "It's clean, and there have never been any chickens in it." Then her mother's neck got red all over, and she had sneered: "No, we're the first. When I married you, I didn't think you'd turn me into a chicken...*(p. 145.)

The chicken house was the setting for one of Sybil's dissociations into another personality. The triggering incident was a sledding accident during which her mother injured her leg.

Flora wrote about Hattie jumping on the sled and going down the hill toward the furrow of the plowed field under the snow. Hattie laughed hysterically and shot down the hill:

> *Her mother had hit the furrow. The sled rose up and threw her off. Her mother was flying through the air, a big black bird without wings. Her shadow, moving, zigzagging, was everywhere on the white snow...*
>
> *"You shouldn't have steered the sled so hard with one foot, mother. That's what made it go sideways into the plowed field," Sybil said softly. Then, turning to her father, she asked, "How did you get her to the house alone?" Looking up in the child's face, her father dryly remarked, "Well, you helped me pull her back up the hill on the sled, didn't you?" Had she? Sybil only remembered being in the field, dropping the saw, and then being beside the stove.* (p. 148.)

On August 5, 1999, I went to the area of Shirley's birth. I settled into my hotel in downtown Rochester, Minnesota, and prepared for a meeting the next day with Dr. Daniel Houlihan from Minnesota State University at Mankato, Shirley's alma mater.

The next morning Dr. Houlihan arrived in his jeep. He explained how he had been trying to locate "the chicken house" described by Flora Schreiber in *Sybil.* This was a key piece to the puzzle to prove the authenticity of the account of Sybil's childhood. A six-year search had to date proved fruitless for Dr. Houlihan.

We went to Mantorville, the capital of Dodge County. In the General Index of Deeds, Dodge County for the past one hundred years, we found the 40 acres of land owned by Walter and Martha Mason in Claremont Township, next to the property of George Gray. Dr. Houlihan was ecstatic. His search could end if the chicken house and hill were similar to those described in the book. The clerk made a copy of the original map and the new map which showed how the property had been sold off. We set out to discover the truth.

On a stretch of country road, we stopped at a house that might sit on "the Mason 40" as the original property had been called. Even today this spot of earth is remote. Next to the house was a structure with a sign "Hamm's Welding." We introduced ourselves to the man working there—Joel Hamm, who was the owner. He stated the property was indeed "the Mason 40" and that he had burned down the chicken house six years earlier. He built a chicken house which was similar, except his had a slanting roof. The original chicken house had a pitched roof and was made of dark brown, almost purple clay blocks. Mr. Hamm allowed me to take pictures of his chicken house. A gravel road with corn and wild daises growing along the sides led up to it. At the bottom of the hill ran a narrow tributary of the Zumbro River, curving toward the road which was covered by a small bridge. I imagined how lonely life must have been for Shirley there in 1929.

The hill where Mattie took her bizarre sled ride was there, complete with the furrow covered with trees. Mr. Hamm told us that the Gray family still owned the adjacent land. One of the descendants, Don Gray, was a councilman and we could find him in town.

We proceeded there to find Mr. Gray. The main street consisted of one block of stores and a bar. The townspeople were preparing for their county fair. The main event was to be a race—a race in which one person would be inside a portable toilet on wheels which would then be pushed by another person. My schedule did not allow me to stay for the attraction—I hope to return one day to see it.

Mr. Gray invited us into his home. He verified that the property was "the Mason 40," still called that after all these years. Mr. Gray said, "Everyone always called it 'the Mason 40.'" Apparently the Masons had made an indelible impression on their neighbors.

Our next stop was Dodge Center, Shriley's birthplace. It seemed as if no one was on the streets as Dr. Houlihan and I drove towards Shirley's house. He pointed out the new school building which stood on the site of the old school that Shirley attended. The stillness and stifling heat hit me. I turned toward a house on the corner opposite the school. It was the house of Shirley's tortures. Dr. Houlihan confirmed it. I asked him if I could take pictures and he said it was permissible. I walked into the street and started to photograph the white house on the corner—all the while knowing the atrocities that had been perpetrated upon Shirley in that house. The peaked roof pierced my heart. The house looked so ordinary, so white. The black shutters, gone from the windows, were replaced by black window frames. It seemed so normal and yet so frightening. I walked the short distance to Main Street, thinking of Shirley walking that same path many years ago. I turned left on Main Street and went to the Dodge Cafe. It was now owned by an Asian woman who knew nothing about the history I was tracing. I spoke with some elderly women there who said that it had always been a restaurant run by different owners.

After lunch we went to the cemetery on a hill above the Zumbro River. There was a tombstone with faded lettering—Elias Mason—who was Shirley's grandfather. Next to it was a family plot with just MASON written on the headstone.

Shirley's mother, who died in July of 1948, is buried in Kansas City. Shirley's ashes are with her cousin Naomi.

• • •

After my trip to Minnesota, the BBC aired a documentary on November 11, 1999, called "Mistaken Identities" in which they featured the case of Sybil. This program contains many inaccuracies. A glaring example is a most basic error: they claim Dr. Cornelia Wilbur "wrote up the case of Sybil not in a medical textbook, but in a paperback to be widely distributed." If they had gone to the library or looked on the internet, they would have known that *Sybil* was written by Flora Rheta Schreiber and published by Henry Regnery Company in hardcover in 1973. The paperback was later issued by Warner Books in May 1974.

They also interviewed Dr. Herbert Spiegel, who stated that Dr. Wilbur asked him "to serve as a surrogate therapist."

Dr. Spiegel said, "When Sybil was with me she did not experience alters. It was a kind of a game that she accepted in working with Wilbur, but we joked about it when we worked together."

Dr. Spiegel gave his evaluation of MPD and it's treatment: "The danger of taking alters seriously and increasing them is to add to the confusion and the anxiety and even the depression that the person had. I see nothing therapeutic about it at all."

In that BBC documentary, Dr. David Spiegel, a psychiatrist, and the son of Dr. Herbert Spiegel, was also interviewed. Dr. David Spiegel had published *Dissociative Disorders: A Clinical Review* in 1993 and *Dissociation: Culture/Mind and Body* in 1994.

In the BBC documentary Dr. David Spiegel is in his office at the Stanford University School of Medicine. He is speaking with his patient Sue and asks her to speak with her alter "Susan." He then speaks with Susan. He gives his theory about MPD/DID and its treatment.

He said, "I believe her. I've known her for many years. I have seen her react to stress with this kind of fragmentation. This, the pattern of personality states, have been quite consistent. So yes, I believe in them. There are people that recommend just ignore it or tell it to go away and I think they've run across plenty of people who do that. And if it worked we wouldn't be seeing them."

Despite those who claim Sybil was a fraud, CBS has produced a remake of the TV movie "Sybil" with a script by John Pielmeir based on Flora Rheta Schreiber's book. Jessica Lange plays Dr. Wilbur and Tammy Blanchard plays Sybil. A terrible inaccuracy, never reported in the book, is Sybil attacking Dr. Wilbur. Their relationship was a loving one where Sybil never did such an unthinkable thing.

I include this information to further the reader's ability to form his or her own conclusion.

CHAPTER 20

Identifying with Dissociative Identity Disorder

In a sense we all have "multiple" personalities. Observe your behavior when you are completely alone, and you are sure to find that you do certain things you would never do in front of another person. As soon as you are in the presence of another person, your behavior changes. You do not become another person, but you do exhibit different facets of your personality, depending on the other person and the environment. Sometimes this is done with complete awareness and deliberation, but often it is done automatically or unconsciously. Even so, you are always aware of who you are, certain of your identity.

Although we like to think of ourselves as autonomous human beings with complete control over our behavior, the reality is that our behavior is somewhat influenced by other people and the environment. Great actors understand this principle of human behavior. In an acting class discussing her performance in Tennessee Williams' play "Sweet Bird of Youth," Geraldine Page explained her creation of her character Alexandra Del Lago. She said that she did not begin to create her character's persona until she met her co-actor, Paul Newman, who played Chance Wayne. She said her character's behavior would be formed to a certain extent by her interaction with Paul Newman's character.

While we all have "multiple" facets to our personalities, most of us do not have Multiple Personality Disorder or Dissociative Identity Disorder [MPD/DID]. We are always aware of who we are; our identity is not split or fragmented into other identities. Rather, our identity remains intact and consistent even though our thoughts, fantasies and behavior might change according to our connections to other people or to the various situations in which we find ourselves. We may be startled by our uncharacteristic thoughts or behavior, but we do not lose sight of the fact that they are our thoughts and our behaviors; we don't attribute them to another person. We do not have, as *DSM IV* defines DID: "...a disruption in the usually integrated functions of consciousness, memory, identity, or perception of the environment."

We may, however, blame others for causing our uncharacteristic behavior, especially when it is negative or aggressive. But this defense mechanism is called rationalization, not dissociation. By employing defense mechanisms such as rationalization, denial, or projection we try to avoid feeling guilty over our unacceptable behavior and its consequences.

From early childhood Shirley Mason developed a rare coping mechanism for survival. As a child she was unable to fight the verbal and physical abuse of her psychotic mother. She could not physically escape, but she could mentally escape. Whenever she experienced a traumatic event, she developed the ability to escape by splitting into another personality who did not have this hideous mother. Amazingly she developed 15 other personalities: Vicky, Marcia, Vanessa, Mary, Helen, Clara, Sybil Ann, The Blonde, Peggy Ann, Peggy Lou,

Mike, Sid, Nancy Lou Ann, Marjorie and Ruthie. Each personality was formed at a different time beginning around the age of three. Some were more fully developed than others and two were of the opposite sex. It took many years in therapy to integrate each personality one by one. Dramatic license was taken in the TV film "Sybil"; when all the personalities came together to embrace Sybil at the end of the film. In reality it took years for Shirley's integration into one whole and complete personality.

Why she developed multiple or alternate personalities instead of some other psychological disorder is unknown. Likewise, it is unknown why one person might develop a maladaptive coping mechanism such as depression, while another develops anxiety to deal with stressful situations. We are making progress in answering these questions by investigating genetic codes that might reveal predispositions to particular mental disorders.

Shirley displayed flashes of anger when MPD/DID was confused with Schizophrenia in the media. People who should have known better were sloppy in their reporting—often citing "Sybil's schizophrenic behavior." Sometimes they described any bizarre behavior as the "Sybil syndrome." MPD/DID is a split in the personality as in the fictional case of Dr. Jekyll and Mister Hyde. Two or more different personalities. Schizophrenia is a split from reality often producing hallucinations, both auditory and visual. Hallucinations are similar to vivid dreams. When we awake, for a moment, we are not sure if it was a dream or if it actually took place. A schizophrenic does not question his hallucinations. They appear to be reality.

Although Shirley "lost time" when in a fugue state, she never lost touch with reality and the world around her.

Her life can be seen as a search for love to repair the damage caused by her mother. There were glimpses of love from her grandmother and playmate Danny that gave her strength to go on. Her love for her grandmother and for her playmate could not be extinguished by the pain she endured in childhood. She even experienced moments of love for her mother when she was the "good mother" doing fun things with Shirley. Her love for her father was returned but often clouded by his inability to protect her from her mother.

However, the beginning of a special love occurred serendipitously in Omaha, Nebraska in 1945. By chance, she had been taken by her parents to Dr. Cornelia Wilbur. Even though they didn't believe in psychiatric treatment, they were persuaded to seek it upon the advice of their family physician.

Shirley felt the stirrings of affection for Dr. Wilbur when she was told that her condition could be treated. Shirley hoped Dr. Wilbur might shed light on the periods of "lost time" which greatly impeded her ability to lead a normal life.

Years later, on December 29, 1958, while in analysis with Dr. Wilbur, she wrote in her diary:

> I don't like being reminded or made to remember what it was like to be in the sixth grade on nor how I felt in the high school years nor how I felt in college nor how I felt at home. I may recall some people or incidents and dwell on them in talking with you and when I can't help it I think about some things when I am here alone. But I have so long pushed aside thinking about how I FELT that I no longer do think about it. I am sure there are things there to be thought about or the feelings would not be so strong but I hate being reminded and I feel cross and annoyed and frustrated immediately. I try to talk calmly about it, but I can't hold out very long without getting cross. I particularly HATE one feeling (or impression) because it hurts and because it seems to be wrong (sinful, not incorrect) but I can't help it recurring---I can modify it and live with it for a little while but my *first* impression is always the same---when asked about or in some way made to recall my Sybil 'feelings' during the years after Peggy in the spring of '35 until the end of high school in '41, is one quick single strong impulse of extreme unhappiness, and I mean extreme. I was told I had everything. I had this and that and more of it (clothes, toys, house, and so forth) than anyone else. And so forth and so forth---no REASON for being unhappy---and I always felt a lack of something---I would

> sit on the back porch steps or on the trunk in the attic or on the shirt-waist box in the front hall and lean my head on my knees and wonder why in the world I felt so---and I didn't even have a word for it myself---it felt real until I tried to think about it and decide what was surrounding me, but all I could get was simply that I felt sad and down and blue without cause---and this created guilt, of course, and I tried to pray for forgiveness for not being more thankful and grateful for what I had (so much of!) and for not being 'like the other kids' and running and playing and being happy. But I couldn't and I tried to pretend to be gay but I would black out---or else just feel it was impossible for me to be 'good' and appreciate all I had and that ended in guilt again---and any way I thought through the thing I lost time sooner or later depending on which line of reasoning I took.

In 1945, shortly after Shirley began seeing Dr. Wilbur in Omaha, an unfortunate incident occurred. She felt abandoned when Dr. Wilbur mysteriously left Omaha without a word. She was bewildered by the inexplicable behavior of this woman whom she thought returned her affection. At that time, Shirley did not know that her mother had lied to her about telephoning Dr. Wilbur to tell her that Shirley was not well enough to attend her session. Mattie told Shirley that Dr. Wilbur did not say anything. Actually, Mattie had never called Dr. Wilbur.

In fact, Dr. Wilbur wanted Shirley to move to Chicago, since she was going there to train in psychoanalysis.

When Dr. Wilbur moved to New York, Shirley overcame obstacles to find her and move there. In the beginning of their relationship, Shirley loved Dr. Wilbur as much as was allowed by her damaged psyche. She loved the help Dr. Wilbur provided in solving the mystery of her "lost time." She ultimately loved the uncovering of her disorder—her alternate personalities whom she was able to understand after years of therapy. She loved the moments of clarity and peace. She loved the fact that this woman took an interest in her well-being and showed her affection.

As Shirley began to heal she began to love Dr. Wilbur in a

different way. She was seeing Dr. Wilbur increasingly on the level of her other female friends. Once Shirley was fully integrated, she no longer needed to idealize Dr. Wilbur.

In the years which followed, she and Dr. Wilbur could express their love for each other as two mature women. The patient-doctor relationship ended. She could give to Dr. Wilbur as much as she received from her.

One of their ecstatic moments was when they traveled to California for the making of the TV movie "Sybil". They stopped at Naomi's house and shared their happiness and excitement with her and her husband. They were the only ones who knew that Shirley accompanied Dr. Wilbur to California. The movie company had no idea that Shirley was in the hotel room waiting for Dr. Wilbur to return from her duties as a consultant. As much as Shirley and Dr. Wilbur both would have wanted Shirley to be able to witness the filming of her life, they were too worried that Shirley's anonymity might be compromised.

Shirley would anxiously await Dr. Wilbur's return every evening to discuss the events of the day. They felt that their painful work in telling Shirley's story to Flora Schreiber for the book had culminated in this more extensive medium. They felt exhilarated knowing that their work had resulted in a successful book and could now be confident that their story had the potential to become an important film. They knew that the film would reach more people.

Shirley's friendship with Dr. Wilbur lasted for thirty-five years. She worked as the doctor's assistant, accompanied her to the theatre to see friends such as Roddy McDowall, traveled with her to new cities for conventions, and took care of their pets. Together they shared the accomplishments of Shirley's artwork and Dr. Wilbur's psychiatric work.

Shirley took responsibility for caring for Dr. Wilbur when she became ill. Never did she falter in providing complete care with the best people to treat Dr. Wilbur. Nor did she ever leave Dr. Wilbur from the moment of her stroke until she died.

Shirley's life did not end with the death of Dr. Wilbur. After a period of profound grief over the greatest loss in her life, she was able to find pleasure again in her artwork, in caring for her pets, plants, family, and friends. I met her when she was seventy years old. She amazed me with her alacrity of thought, ideas, and wit. She continued to have an avid interest in the world and remained active in her church.

Although she suffered from a painful cancer, she did not stop planning the future of her paintings. She wanted her friend to send me the paintings so I could use them to provide a scholarship fund for artists. Knowing that I would carry out her wish, she died peacefully.

As I reflect on Shirley's life, I am struck by her simplicity. She wanted to fulfill her unique potential and become self-actualized in the sense that the psychologist Abraham Maslow proposes, "the best me I can be." Reaching this highest level of development did not require her gaining fame and recognition from the world. Although Sybil had become famous, Shirley was not known to be that famous person. She was content to receive satisfaction and a sense of self-fulfillment from her teaching and painting. She was content earning enough money to live comfortably. When she received a few thousand dollars for her paintings, she was able to provide a few luxuries for herself and her pets. One luxury was a piano she loved to play.

All of Shirley's quotes in this book are her own words spoken during our frequent telephone conversations, which I had recorded to ensure their accuracy. In like manner, I also taped all the personal interviews with others in this book.

One of my intentions in first contacting Shirley in 1993 was to ascertain her psychological state. My scientific interest was to discover if she had been completely integrated. If so, then I wanted to know if she had ever had a relapse. Her own words have proved her mental stability. The continuing wholeness of her personality lasted until her death.

Dr. Patrick Suraci
New York City

EPILOGUE

APPENDIX A

Peggy Lou's Drawings of Windows and African American Woman and Four Men

(Courtesy of the Author)

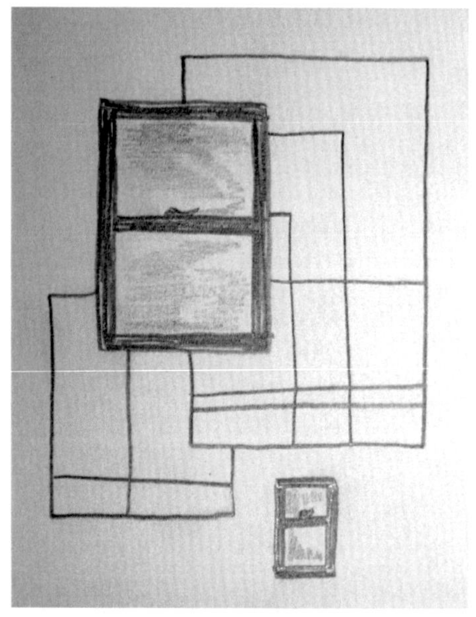

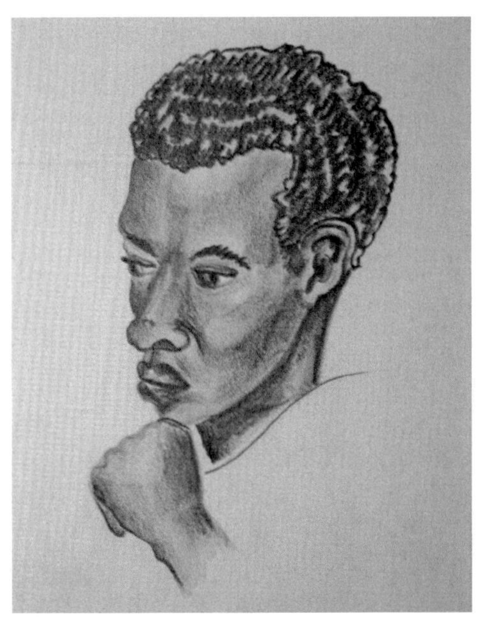

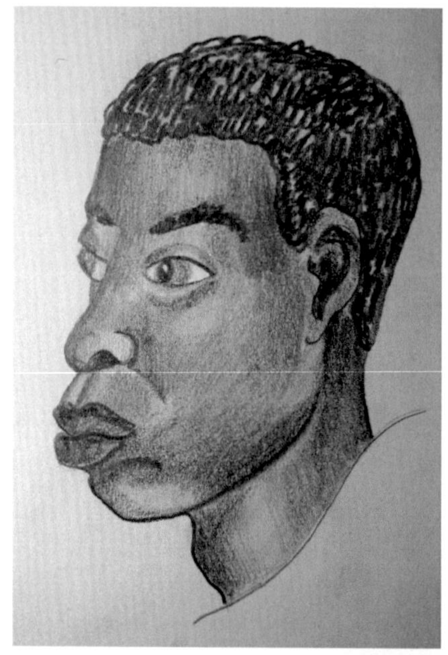

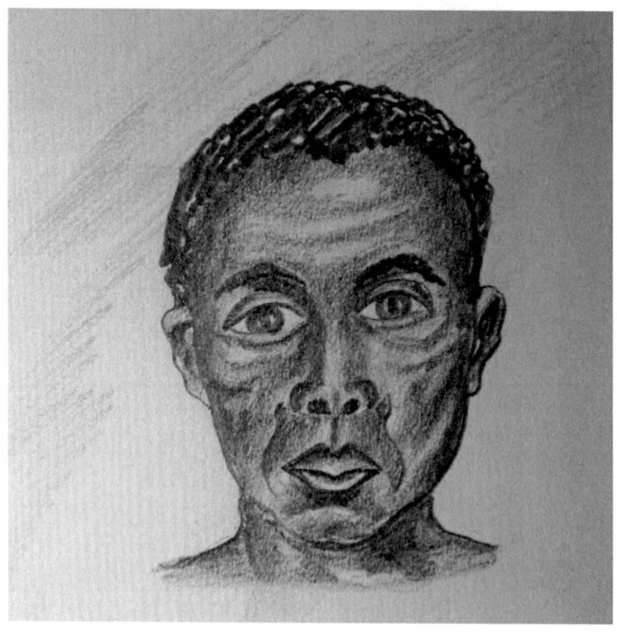

APPENDIX B

24 of Shirley's Paintings After her Integration

(Courtesy of Naomi Rhode)

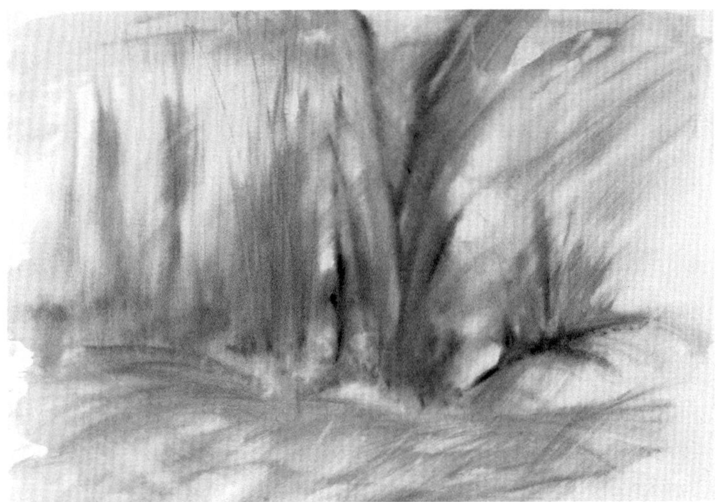

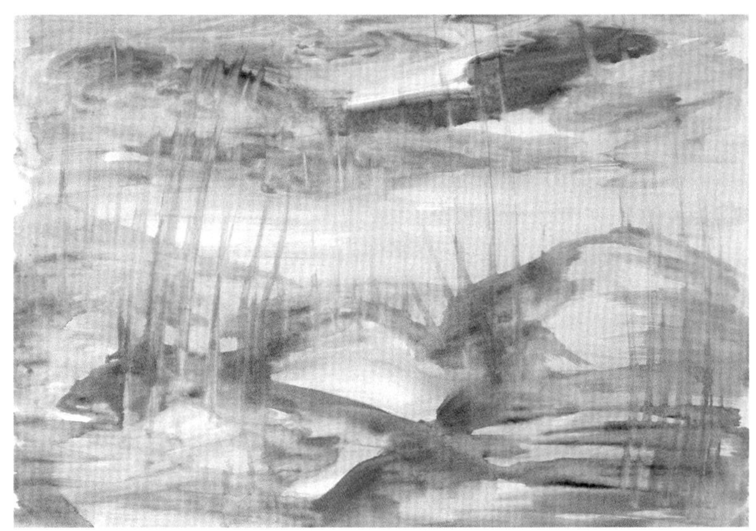

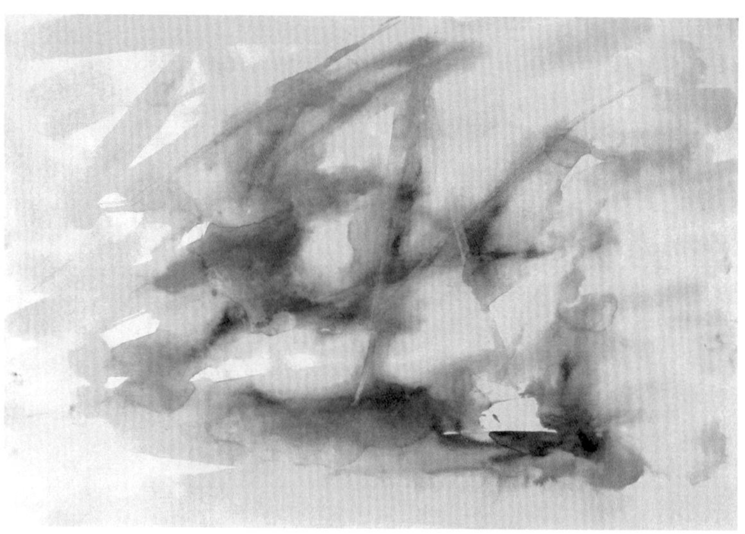

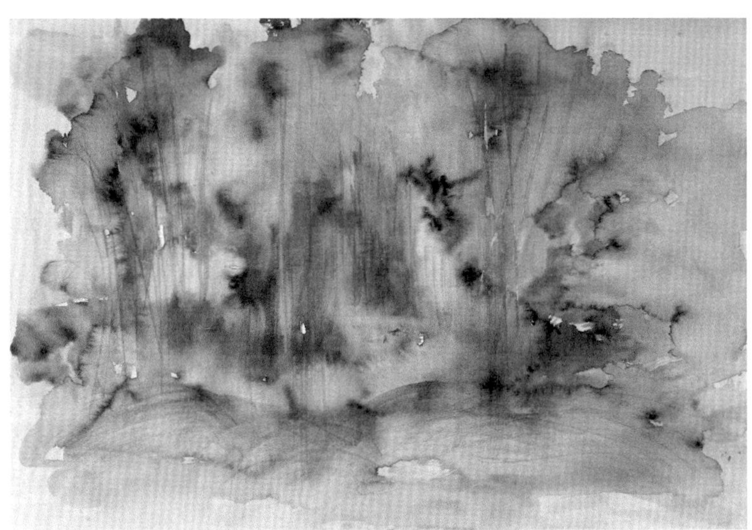

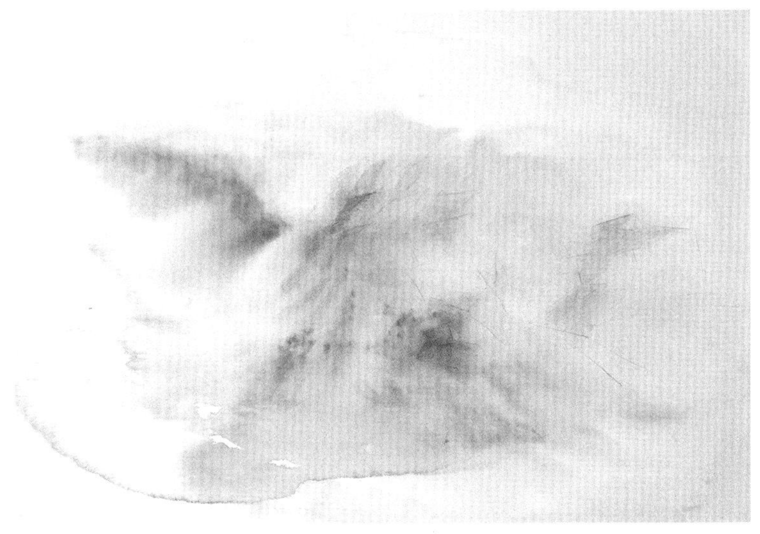

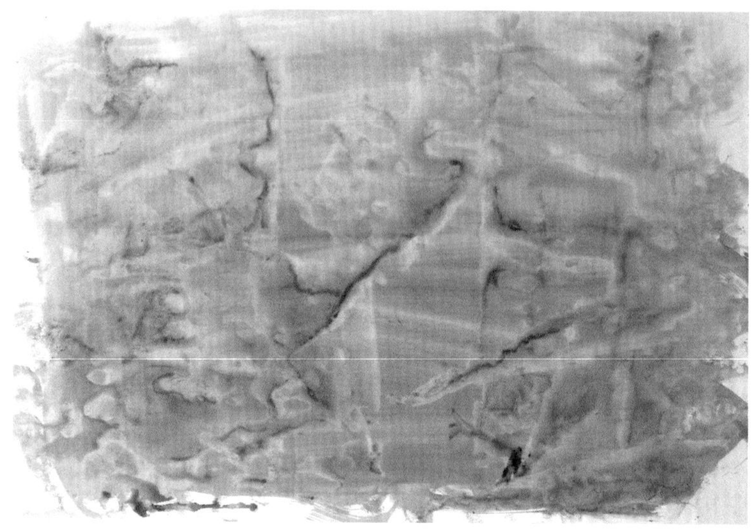

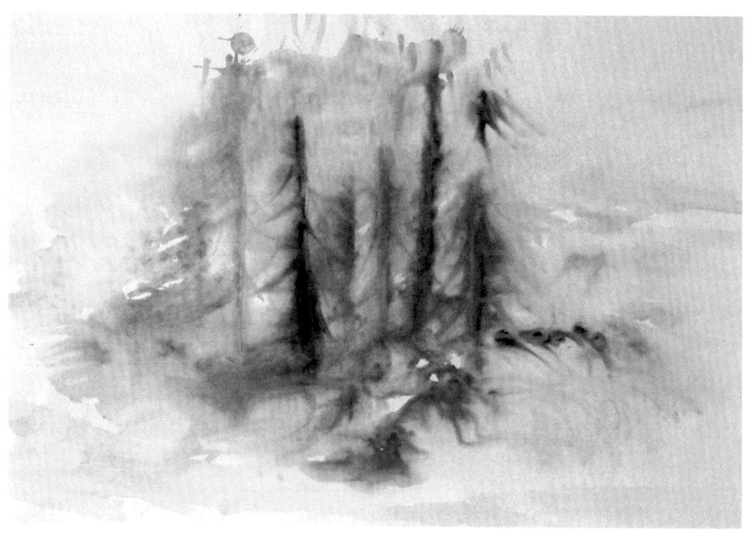

APPENDIX C

Photographs of Shirley

(Courtesy of Naomi Rhode)

Shirley at 2 years old.

Shirley's 3rd Visit to Iowa with her Grandmother, Oct. 1925.

Sept. 1925 Shirley with her doll.

Sept. 1925 Shirley with her mother.

Shirley on a rocking chair.

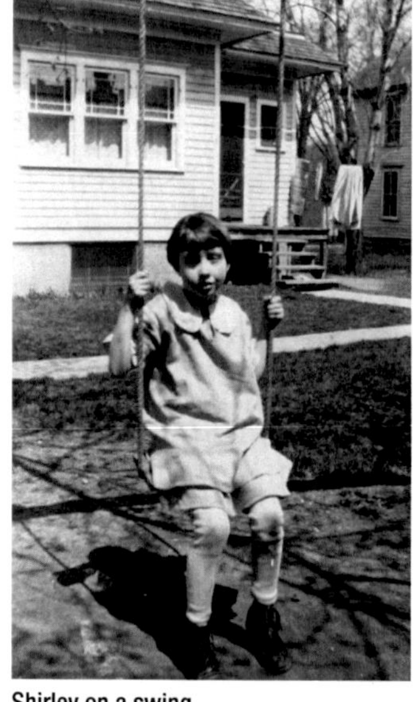

Shirley on a swing.

Shirley with her Father, Dec. 13, 1931.

Shirley with her Father.

Shirley with her Mother.

Shirley with "my pictures" 7th grade.

Shirley with her Mother and Father.

Shirley and her Mother in Rochester, Minnesota.

Shirley by the school.

Shirley, High School Graduation, 1941.

Shirley painting with brush and easel.

Shirley, College Graduation, Mankato College.

Shirley with her paintings at The National Arts Club, 1955.

Shirley with her prize-winning painting at The National Arts Club, 1955.

(far right) Shirley's winning painting at The National Arts Club.

Shirley's Graduation proof, Columbia University.

(left to right) Dr. Cornelia Wilbur and Shirley Mason.

APPENDIX D

Shirley's Painting, Christmas Card Drawings, and Letters

(From the collection of Wylene Fredericksen, courtesy of Daniel Houlihan.)

The Gulley appeared in Shirley Ardell Mason's 1949 art show at Mankato State Teachers College. She painted it while she was working at the Porter Sanitarium in Denver, Colorado. Her former art teacher, Wylene Fredericksen, was instrumental in assembling this exhibit and purchased *The Gulley*. Ms. Fredericksen was hired by Shirley's parents to teach her art while they were living in Dodge Center, mostly during Shirley's early teen years. Ms. Fredericksen lived about a block away in Dodge center and even rented a room in Shirley's house at some point. Professor Houlihan said Ms. Fredericksen gave the painting to him on her death bed. It will eventually be archived at Mankato State University.

The
Division of Fine and Applied Arts

Presents

Shirley Ardell Mason — Denver, Colorado

Phyllis Ruth Moeller — Mankato, Minnesota

in the

Annual
Commencement Art Exhibit

Mankato State Teachers College
Art Studio and Lounge

May 27 to June 3, 1949

College Lounge
Water Color Exhibit

SHIRLEY ARDELL MASON

Front Porch	1
Rural Church	2
Seclusion	3
Clark Street	4
Morning	5
Noon	6
Night	7
Interpretation	8
Inertia	9
Reflection	10
Rain	11
August	12
Gretna, Nebr.	13
Hanover Street	14
Fantasy	15
Terrace	16
Red Trees	17
The Wash	18
Barracks	19
Improvision	20
Rock Candy Mountains	21
White Horses	22
City Structures	23
Trolley Crowd	24
Omaha, Nebr.	25

PHYLLIS RUTH MOELLER

Backyard Huddle	26
Morning's Freshness	27
Gathering Clouds	28
Thunder, Lightning, and Disaster	29
Amazement and Complacence	30
T. C.'s Three	31
Dream of a Screwball	32

Art Studio
Chalk Pencil Poster Paint

PHYLLIS RUTH MOELLER

Correlations	1-3
Abstractions	4-5
Forethought	6
Analogy	7
Ceramic Study	8
Bubbles of Transparency	9
Steel Bookends	10
Comical Jacks	11
Buds of Spring	12
Seed-Pod Fantasy	13
Spacial Relations	14
Fluorescent Theme	15
The Spiral Still-Life	16
Eli	17
Autumn	18
Rondo	19
The Zipper	20
Means to an End	21
Light on Steel	22
Abstractions of a Stairway Series	23
Studies	24-28

SHIRLEY ARDELL MASON

Mountain Rhythms Series	29-31
Nature Motifs Series	32-34
8 Studies in Organization	35-42
8 Abstract Compositions	43-50
8 Monochromatic Pursuit	51-58
Jane and Joan Series	59-61
5 Impressions of America	62-66

College Lounge
Oils on Easels

PHYLLIS RUTH MOELLER

Glenwood Scene	1 A
Neighborhood	2 A
Town and Country	3 A
Still Life	4 A
Impression	5 A

SHIRLEY ARDELL MASON

Center Street Yards	6 A
Allegro	7 A
Double Pattern	8 A

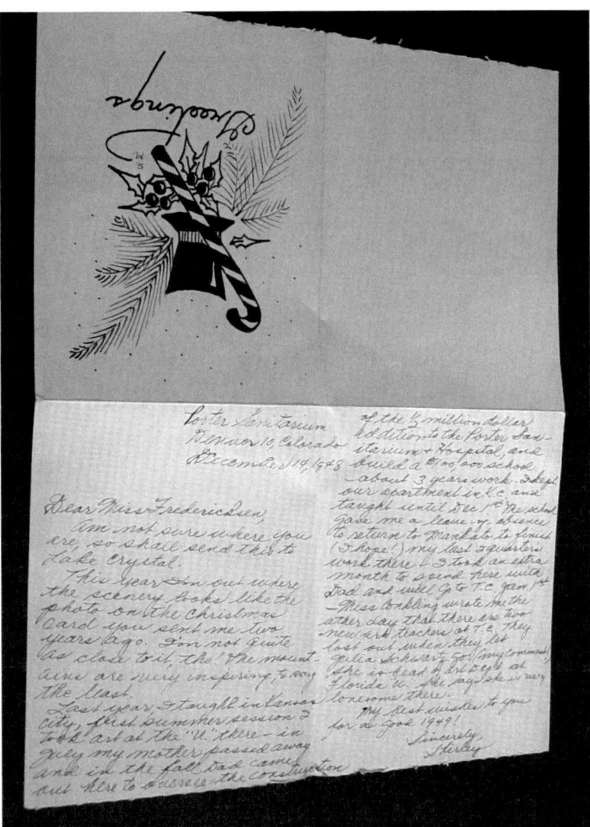

Shirley wrote about going to "T.C." (Teachers College at Mankato).

Ms. Conkling (Evie Conkling) was a well-known art professor at Mankato Teachers College. Ms. Julia Schwartz was a professor at Mankato Teachers College whom Shirley admired.

She was in contact with all three women until 1962.

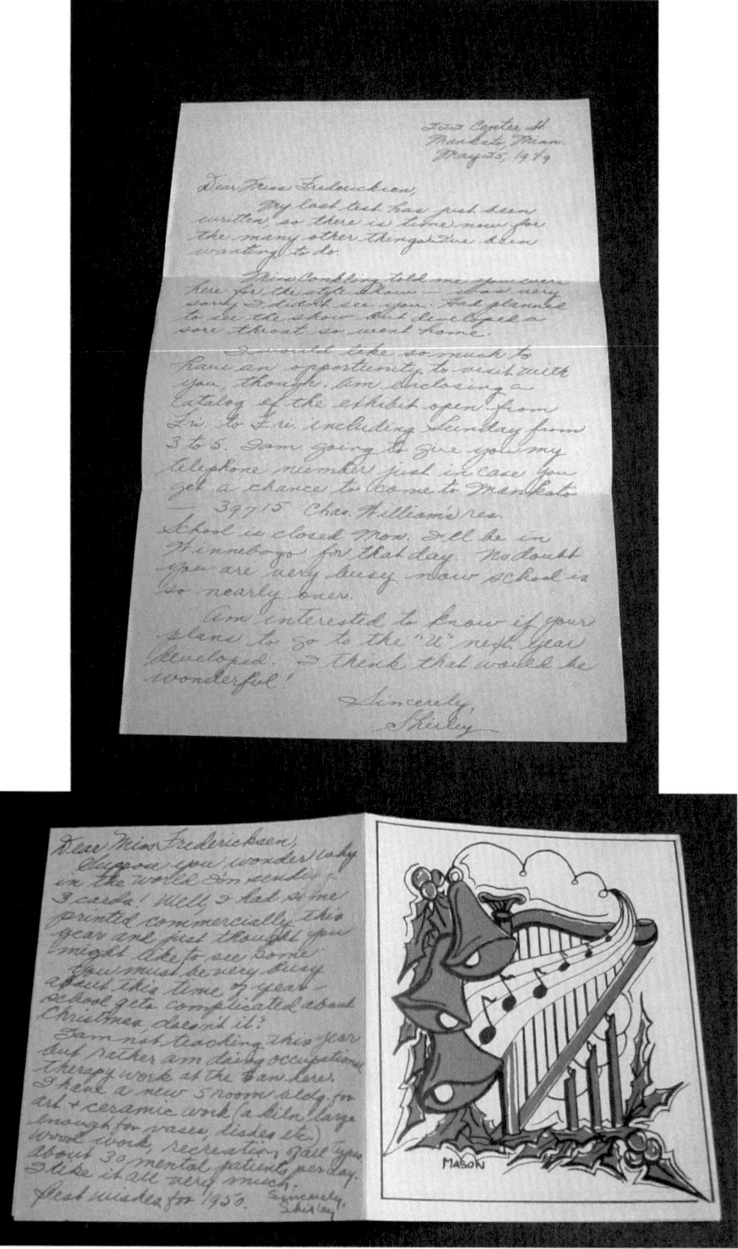

222 Center St.
Mankato, Minn.
May 25, 1949

Dear Miss Fredericksen,

My last test has just been written, so there is time now for the many other things I've been wanting to do.

Miss Conkling told me you were here for the style show — was very sorry I didn't see you. Had planned to see the show but developed a sore throat so went home.

I would like so much to have an opportunity to visit with you, though. Am enclosing a catalog of the exhibit open from Fri. to Fri. including Sunday from 3 to 5. I am going to give you my telephone number just in case you get a chance to come to Mankato — 3971S Chas. Williams res.

School is closed Mon. I'll be in Winnebago for that day. No doubt you are very busy now school is so nearly over.

Am interested to know if your plans to go to the "U" next year developed. I think that would be wonderful!

Sincerely,
Shirley

Dear Miss Fredericksen,

I suppose you wonder why in the world I'm sending 3 cards! Well, I had some printed commercially this year and just thought you might like to see some.

You must be very busy about this time of year — school gets complicated about Christmas, doesn't it?

I am not teaching this year but rather am doing occupational therapy work at the San. here. I have a new 5 room bldg. for art + ceramic work (a kiln large enough for vases, dishes etc.) wood work, recreation, all types. About 30 mental patients per day. I like it all very much.

Best wishes for 1950.

Sincerely,
Shirley

Greetings
MASON

Holiday
Greetings
MASON

APPENDIX E

Shirley Mason's Diary

When Shirley was asked if these materials from her diaries could be used, she replied that they could be used with a caveat—she wanted people to understand that "this writing was free association and that she did know how to write properly".

January, 1956.

"Grandma kept her writing tablet in a drawer and she let me use sheet after sheet of the paper for drawing. I was careful not to waste any and would draw small objects on every square inch of it on both sides. It was one of the most wonderful times I can remember---sitting there drawing and telling her all about my pictures. At home, I was forbidden to touch anything on the study desk or in Dad's office; and never, never was I to touch what Mother termed 'perfectly good paper' for just scribbling. She let me have scraps of paper, old envelopes that I could open and draw on inside, or paper sacks (I never did like the seams in them!) And when Mother would come upstairs, (usually quietly to see if I were behaving myself) and find me drawing on the writing paper, she would be very stern and yank me by the arm down off the organ stool (turned up to its height for me to reach the desk) and tell Grandma that she should not let me waste paper that way. (I always felt very guilty and also ashamed that I had in some way 'wronged' Grandma.) Grandma would change the subject and another time when we were alone let me draw some more. (A friend once said, I worried on several occasions, when, as Peggy, she gave me paper and said I could draw---she said I kept asking repeatedly if she was sure it was all right to use all the good paper---I seemed especially worried the other day about the colored sheets. I think that was due to the fact that I was taking each one out of a tablet like I had done at Grandma's). I used to draw people all the time, whole families with lots of children. I always drew the same sort of an arrangement with the oldest child a boy (big brother) and on down, each a head smaller than the previous one. I can remember Mother saying many times that she got so blamed tired of seeing drawings of families, families, families all the time. (I wonder if this is why I was surprised the other day when I was told that the person who was watching liked what I was drawing.)

My early drawings always followed a similar set-up to this.

Sometimes many more children, but almost always a boy, then a girl, then a boy, etc. The baby sat on the floor. I learned to put one child behind another, to save space."

January, 1956.

"There are certain times of day (toward evening and after supper) I don't mind too much---and at times even enjoy housework---It's O'k and there is a sense of accomplishment about some of it sometimes. But early in the morning and otherwise best parts of a day, while its raining on a rainy day or in the full sunlight of a sunny one, etc. I want overwhelmingly to paint or sketch or write or make whatever current project I am interested in (Paper mache, greeting card, sewing, clay modeling, wood carving, wire bending in mobiles), I've been so anxious to create over since we've got the fireplace wall painted, etc.

A very cryptic feeling---remark just went through my thoughts---I'll stick it in as free association, 'sometimes I even feel I like to read books'. Some ways it almost seems compulsive (not just sure of the extent of the meaning of that word) for me to do all the (was going to say 'other things first' but different words flashed through so I'll use them) 'important' household duties first---Mother would approve---in fact, insisted that they come first 'where they belong' then 'frivolous things like art and your everlasting books can be enjoyed with peace of mind that your work was well done first'!

I guess that was her neurosis. It doesn't have to stay with me and aid mine, does it? It's just that some days (if I'm tired or am worried with or without the cause being apparent, etc.) I keep hearing her constant stream of admonitions and orders in the back of my mind, but I feel condemned if I don't and damned if I do. If I don't follow and do work first, I can't paint with ease and freedom---if I do work first, I'm too tired (and also mad because I had to obey the injunction) to paint.

I'd say to Mother something to the effect 'see this picture' (or doll dress I'd made, etc.) or 'Look at the cat'. Mother would say, 'Oh, look at the cat! I can't look at the cat. I've got work to do---who do you think would get things done and meals ready on time if I stood around looking at the cat?' She said that a thousand times, or maybe even a million times years ago and it keeps running through my head and interferes with what I'm trying to do. It even interferes when I try to paint."

January 28, 1956.

"We had a faulty light fixture in the basement and as the floor was wet---shock. I finally got so scared of the basement and of light fixtures in general that I would not go downstairs nor would I turn on a light anywhere. My parents scolded me and told me how to turn on the light so I did not touch the wires---this did not help---they made me turn lights on and off and to get me over my fear, Dad would in the evenings make me go from room to room with him turning light switches on and off. I would try to cover my fright and be brave---but after a few of these tries, I would be so frightened my forehead would be all wet and my hands shake so I could hardly get the switch to turn---Dad would tell me it was perfectly silly and see it did not hurt him any and he would stand there and switch the light over and over. So brave. So smart. So perfect. So why was I so silly."

March, 1956.

"I tried to tell someone the name of your beautiful plant but I could not remember it---I knew it perfectly well---Now I think I know why I could not remember it. It clicked yesterday. I tried to tell someone the name of a flower and could not think of it. She joked, 'That, my dear, is called resistance'—Yeah, only it did not strike me funny—it struck me as being all too true---and a tune kept roaring in my ears. Finally, hours later, I recalled the flower name---and at that precise moment (now I feel so MEAN again. I HATE something---I could cry and scream---and OH---Why do I have to tell you anything?---) I feel better now. This looks like it was going to be one of THOSE days again. Oh well, when I was young, I was going to play in one of those blasted recitals my music teacher had periodically at the church (before Peggy ran away from one) and I had my heart set on playing my favorite little ditty which was a 'take-off' on Mozart's Sonata I loved. My childish version was a piece of sheet music entitled, 'Mozart's Sonatina in C' and seemed so impressive to me, and I loved the runs in it with hands crossing and so forth and so forth. I practiced and practiced and practiced and playfully day-dreamed about my playing this at the recital---BUT, I was told by the teacher that everyone was playing selections taken from our 'regular' music books---some company representative or somebody from the company would be there and give us free books for our next round of lessons because we used their material---or some fool thing. MY PIECE WAS TO BE ENTITLED 'AMRYLLIS"---although it was arranged by some guy named Whitmore Clark I never did find out who actually composed it. (It was a matter of concern to me always to know who composed the pieces), and it was long after the recital that I discovered that Amaryllis is a flower. And the name of your plant is Amaryllis!

You were asking about what Peggy was talking about when she said that letters made words and words made sentences and sentences made paragraphs. And then something about little gray boxes and rows that she had to watch and be careful. And then she had to get away. You said that at this point she often looked awfully frightened. I remembered something. I felt like a little girl. I felt as if I were a child, as if I were Peggy, one with her not like her. They were not simple 'Peggy feelings' in the sense to which we have referred to these for so long but I was Peggy remembering her childhood as if it were my childhood and feeling and recalling clearly a certain third and fourth grade experience often repeated during those years but not recalling the distress and yet not recalling just the event as I did last spring when suddenly (or so it seemed) I remembered so many things that were from the blank years. I don't know if I am being clear about this or not but what I am trying to say is this morning I was remembering vividly but without the overly intense feelings that accompany Peggy's memories. How and what I, as Peggy, had felt and done with the letters in the little gray boxes.

March 18, 1956.

"One thing that keeps coming up (just occurred to me to say 'coming up as in nausea'---guess I have been sick several times lately when thinking about some of this and in talking to you---or trying to!---about it yesterday) when I think about Mother in the fourth grade and Peggy's promise to which you referred---and that is the fact that we got a radio the year I was in the fourth grade---relatively new creation to have at that time---but even so, we would have had one sooner if Dad had not thought Grandpa would consider it a work of the devil---mother prevailed over the devil and we got the radio---never could get Grandpa to listen to it with us but we tried---Oh, dear---now I feel just awful inside---that mean, right, guilty, sickish feeling and I want to cry and I can't---and I know why the feelings---I had a thought I just don't want to ever think---let alone say or write out on paper---and I will try to do it because you said to put down what I thought and when the mean feelings occurred---well---it feels *awful*---but when I wrote a few seconds ago that Mother prevailed over the devil (she kept quoting scripture and daily telling Dad 'who else' in town had a radio because they 'were up to date AND

COULD AFFORD IT', the latter getting to Dad's ego, of course---) I mean literally she did---for I had a quick flash of a thought that followed that one just as soon as I thought 'Mother prevailed over the devil' I realized I had actually thought it with another word in there---it hurts to think it--- and I feel ashamed, but I think I feel fear and disgust more---and I know I feel sick all over---and my head hurts---well, I have sat and looked at the pigeons on the fire escape long enough now---I don't feel so sick and maybe I can finally say the sentence the way I wish I hadn't thought it---Mother prevailed over the other devil."

April, 1956.

"Mother used to say, 'Why in the world can't you behave yourself like other kids? Look at Louise and Susie and on and on infinitum. They are always full of pep and healthy and out doing things, not sitting around the house'. I could never do anything right."

April 6, 1956.

"But Mother always had to help entertain Danny. Didn't bother so much with my other friends---got rid of them all for me one way or the other. Susie (pictured with me throughout my photo albums the summer we were twelve) and two or three others---no friends for very long---none while I was in high school---then Mother hounded me because I did not go anywhere and hated parties---she used to walk with me to the very door of the house where a party was to be held to make sure I went---I either blacked-out so I did not recall a thing that occurred after I went inside the door, or else I waited on the porch until Mother was out of sight and then I walked endlessly all over town until a 'right' time to go home. Either lied about the party and felt God would never forgive me or else I said nothing and felt equally 'bad' because Mother scolded me for not being communicative. I would go to bed feeling utterly alone and so wrong and hating myself so much."

April 24, 1956.

"Mother used to scold me because I sat around drawing and painting so much when I should be doing something else---any one of a number of things which she thought important at the moment.

I feel a little bit light headed this time---it would be very typical of Dad to say at this point, 'You are always a little light headed, aren't you?' and then laugh. He was always kidding me a lot but I never before realized how it was always in a deprecatory manner---Has years of that helped to undermine my confidence in myself?"

May 5, 1956

"Mountains---I keep wanting to paint mountains---I don't know why---can't seem to get enough expressed about mountains---they meant so much to me---

Today I want to paint some pictures---I would like most of all to do some chalk drawings of the trees we saw---my mind is full of all the beautiful scenes---I think I want to do them realistically, first to preserve them and then to abstract them from that---it is like an art principle that states one must be able to draw correctly before he can distort with meaning. Only it isn't exactly that with me---I just want to do chalk on colored paper---only I can't see well enough at the moment---I ate and wanted to draw but I was too tired so I went back to bed---and this time I got up again. I decided to write because I wanted to."

May 16, 1956.

"I am worried about art now---can't finish my circus piece I felt so strong with---I wondered when that feeling left and I realize it was when I got the offer from the gallery and came home all excited and pleased (I was pleased) and thought that poster paint (as in circus pictures!) was something 'that could hang with oils' as far as medium was concerned. I lost something to fear. My anxiety is too much for me today---I can't even do my Central Park pieces---I feel very unworthy and unequal to the task of painting---I remember your saying on a few occasions that I should just go ahead and paint for myself and not for any purpose---that is the best---ISN'T IT? In fact it is just about the ONLY thing I can do---I am struggling so much (Yes, all these months) with that horse painting I am doing. I just sink inside every time I think of it---but do you see me getting right down to work on it and getting it done and out of the way for once and all? No, here I sit typing---then find a dozen other things to do."

May 18, 1956.

"You asked me yesterday why I was having trouble painting the circus scenes when I had never seen a circus before this spring and so forth---and one thing came into my mind when you asked---clowns---I answered I did not know either---and we talked on---I asked myself that again when I got home and wanted to paint---clowns again. I keep seeing compositions of clowns and can't seem to get down to doing something else---so why should I do anything else? I think I will try painting clowns and see what happens---I don't know the reasoning or the source of the feelings---just preoccupied with clowns.

2:30---Well I got him painted and matted. Wanted to show it to you---a few recurring ideas while painting so I made some notes on a scrap of paper as I painted---the ideas still come and go in that flitting manner they have all week but today was more comfortable than the other days---I mean less forced to the constant thinking. I feel much better now I have painted---have a thousand things to do and should have done them sooner because now they will not all get done.

About the notes---when I was painting I made the clown the same color as the background---I recall J telling us that was a sure was to 'lose' the main object in a painting (in other words, don't do it) and I found myself saying very emphatically to myself 'I want to lose it'. I thought this several times so maybe it means something---remember when I was little (three to four). I would get to acting up and Mother would say, 'Quit clowning!'---

Back to clowns---when I was at the circus I was especially interested in the clowns and was disappointed that they only appeared briefly between acts and paraded around---I got only one sketch of a clown---sad-looking and heavy---not what I painted---I saw much more that I wanted to paint---still want to do clowns---this one did not get it out of my system---haven't time now---and anyway at the circus we saw a fire-escape door open and some people standing out on the steps, so we went out---very high spot! I felt to myself at that moment, 'A clown would jump off here.' And then I wondered why I had that idea, but dismissed it and didn't recall it again until I was painting---in the last few weeks I have often found a sentence going through my mind: 'It is no fun to be a clown---they are unhappy'. The idea never has anything to do with my actual train of thought at the time---I think I could paint clowns all right but I can't face painting anything else about the circus before I do the clowns---the one I started last week had several clowns as the focal point but I could not get anymore painted on it---got one and do a single clown and a group of three clowns and then a composition of a whole group of clowns as in the parade---I see them all in a certain way---it is a feeling---fits how I felt lately---can't explain it in words. I painted to some music this morning---band records/Apropos!"

A Comment: *[Shirley wrote this regarding her apartment in New York.]*

"I wanted to get a coat of clean paint over that bile green (Excuse me, I guess it did say 'American Forest Green' on the painter's can but it 'sure ain't like no American forest I ever seen'---been a heck of a lot better off in a forest, though, than on this timber.) I figured if it took the painters an hour and a half to do the windows I could do them alone in one---and I did. 'Course I couldn't stop it quite as well as they, but this way it is cheaper because it takes less paint to just put it on the frame part."

June, 1956.

"In a dream last week, I walked with you (analyst) from the hallway into your office. On the way I saw a large oil painting done in dull greens, dull browned-yellows, and brown---early American style. I felt a twinge or a tug of something I guess was jealousy because I thought you were going to hang someone else's painting in the space I had been planning to do a painting for. The dark oil painting in the hallway was not hanging but rather sat on the floor leaning against the wall. It could have been on its way out as well as in but it did not occur that way to me. On thinking about it I figured it did not really relate to you and let it go at that. Then, this morning when I was deep in my French vocabulary study, all of a sudden out of the blue (to coin a NEW phrase) came this strong, strong impression with a full set of feelings---the first picture I remember from my babyhood was the dark green with dull yellows and browns of an oil painting of trees and a pale moon which hung in our sunroom where I had seen it daily since I was born and I can't recall the day I did not 'know' that it was an original oil painting, 'the real thing' as Mother would proudly point out to visitors whether they already knew it or not. Done by 'my oldest sister's girl who painted the picture in the living room and the big one in the dining room too.' I think the painter used a three-hair brush. The work was fine, detailed beyond credibility and really perfection. They were all very dark and dull even though not then old enough to be aged to that dullness---sunsets of crimson sun and dull rose and pinks on the lake reflections---I always wished I could paint like that (always until I was in college, that is) and I even tried to copy one once when my cousin sent me an oil paint set when I was about nine (the Peggy years after Grandma died). I can recall trying but not knowing how to use the paints and now knowing how to get the colors mixed the way the pictures were. I asked Mother but she did not know and said my cousin was an artist---maybe Daddy would know. I was mad. I did not want to wait for him to get home and I asked him but he was tired and after a short attempt at reading the directions he said why didn't I just experiment with them and paint anything I wanted to paint. I did not like this at all. I wanted to match the wonderful praiseworthy skill of my cousin. So I put the paints away and in later years whenever I happened to run across the set, I would get sick at my stomach. I thought it was the paint smell. When I was in high school I took private art lessons and my teacher got me started on oil painting but using a different kind of paint bought by the tube and not by the set. And we used canvas (I had been trying to use the original set on paper!) And I like it O'k but oil paints have never been my favorite medium as I prefer watercolors but they are maybe geared more to my taste as I do not like long drawn-out detailed work and was taught in college the value of being able to do a 'wash' with a few strokes and so forth in water colors and I loved it. Well, that painting in the dream was a different subject. (That is why I didn't recognize it but it had the same colors as my cousin's and the feeling was the same as it once was.)"

October, 1956.

"Many of these stereotyped ideas of my mother's [A Freudian slip? Almost every other time, Shirley wrote "Mother" with a capital "M"] existed as mine (degrees varied) more or less---I suppose because she did hold them and because she held them so tightly. That is the understatement of the year! When she held a view or opinion on anything she held it dogmatically, righteously, and uncompromisingly. I hate to admit it about my own mother but she definitely had a 'holier-than-thou' attitude toward everything and everybody and I assumed her to be superior. By the time I was in high school---began to doubt---began to have different ideas and had my inclination (so annoying to Mother) to be for the underdog. And Mother and I had loud arguments which terminated in blank spells for me. Sometimes sent for a walk or on an errand to get me out of the house. It just occurred to me that perhaps some of my intense inferiority feelings could come from my having believed Mother's opinion of herself. I think, too, that much of this was a sham because it all sort of crumbled when she became a semi-invalid."

November, 1956.

If you will read this carefully and believe and try to understand it if it is at all understandable from the hodge-podge may I write when I 'let loose' and just type with my hands and not my head---visualize that one, if you can, I can't! (That is labeled 'feeble joke'). But I was not meaning to be---nor trying to be funny---actually, I believe this kind of typing which is much faster than writing in long-hand or talking---is a type of free-association (as much as I know what that term is supposed to mean) as much so as my 'fast and thoughtless abstracts'---(that aren't always so abstract---at least after they get into your hands with your interpretations!)---Why can I type it when I cannot say it? I know that I can tear this up and never show it to you, and I can perhaps get some of the aggression worked off this way --- if I want to say it or paint it, alright for now---and if I don't choose to show you this, as at first I thought I might, then you will no doubt pick out the word 'aggression' (tying gets worse all the time---more feeling, more speed more mistakes---and say, <u>that</u> is true---<u>that</u> is good---let's look at <u>that</u>---don't you dare!!

Danny was quick and smart and wonderfully imaginative---always way ahead of me---the dolls were not dolls to him, I am sure---they were people with names and personalities and real talent (they always had talent!)---his mother had been a teacher but then was a dressmaker, so would give us scraps of material and we would sew by the hour---I liked to make doll clothes and he liked to make costumes and dress the dolls as dancers or story characters---he did a tremendous amount of reading---but he wasn't as good at drawing and did not care to draw or paint much but he thought I was so good at it, he was always asking me to make pictures for him and he had a scrapbook full of my crayon drawings when we were seven or eight years old---and he made me a large four-room dollhouse (sewed the curtains and papered the walls and got scraps of linoleum for the floor etc.,etc,!) We had so much fun when we played and never lacked for ideas of something new or different to do. We thought each other's ideas were so good.

O'k. SO I SHALL WRITE ABOUT CHRISTMAS. [See Peggy's painting #5, *Christmas Tree* in Chapter 12.] And do the black tree design that I can't seem to get rid of, very much with me this morning. But I'm feeling better---went right to sleep, probably because I did feel calmer and slept well and dreamt practically none 'til toward morning---nothing disturbing and nothing depressing. I tried to do something distracting by listening to the radio and I was painting, which did help, but it kept nagging away at me and then every so often it would reappear in full force and I couldn't manage it very well. But you understood---I felt you did---and I felt you didn't blame me. When I was a youngster and got afraid of something (and even then, sometimes without knowing what it was that frightened me) Mother always was impatient and scolded and told me to behave myself and not be silly, after all, nothing was wrong. I'd just gotten scared over imaginary things.

I wanted to talk about this Christmas business. While I was writing, I played some Christmas records and it was O'k, too. However, they are so full of memories---the other years don't seem to matter or even enter into my thoughts much, but childhood Christmas recollections do---they seem perfectly innocent and unimportant but it must be they aren't really or they would not be so persistent---the mood is low---like the drawing. I don't know where such an idea came from---certainly I never saw one like that anywhere! Not a cheerful interpretation of the holiday---I now (since yesterday) have a very insistent idea for a couple of Christmas cards—not at all what I could send to anyone that I know but I think that I will paint the designs just the same, for even though they are nudes, or practically so, they are just what I feel about the matter---don't know the words for it but I think if I can paint them the way I see them, they will express it to you so you will know what I feel. I don't think it is just Christmas, as such, nor its memories alone---it feels as if it ties up with something else. Does that make sense?

Have you ever realized what gorgeous, ethereal, multicolored, softly swirling abstracts can roam the range of a person's brain when they are sitting relaxed with closed eyes and just letting a fragrant incense burn?---(I suspect the abstracts would be better painted with the eyes open, though)."

November, 27, 1956.

"I came home yesterday and 'painted up a storm' to borrow an expression. I did two Philadelphia street scenes, one abstract, one semi-abstract of leaves, and so forth, and two moody ones based on feelings toward historical sights. I felt like painting in large and sweeping strokes, so I used big paper and a sponge and my largest brushes as backgrounds and therefore everything is too big to conveniently carry anywhere considering I am not making a direct route to your office today. But I would like to show you what I have done and I can later---I am still in a painting mood, so thought I would just wait a day or so and put everything together---I did something else too—first of all---this is different but I HAD to paint it---I just loved the dress you were wearing yesterday and the color with your hair made a perfect assemblage for color combination and I did a little portrait of you before I painted anything else as that was very much with me and had to be represented somehow.

While I painted (with lots of help from Capri, of course,) I played the record player---the ballet music I bought the other day and some Stravinsky ones. I got to thinking about music and some ideas occurred---afraid to think much along any one line of it, but did feel it could be talked about today and now that today is here I still feel I could---and in the light of what you said a couple of times lately, I feel I should get at it---immediately, some other thought come in, but that is probably distraction. I have some feelings of confusion about those papers and that one painting I brought in and did not discuss much---so I am not sure what is what, but anyway I painted freely enough yesterday---I guess more freely than in months---just did it and enjoyed it and was not concerned that the results were not perfection."

March 26, 1957.

"I bog down when I paint for a specific purpose---exhibits, individual sale, and so forth. Only when I paint for the fun of painting is this lacking---and produces best results. In spite of the fact that Dr. R. (at T.C.) says one can paint well only when painting for someone in particular whom he cares for very, very much. I do not find this true---this presentation of this idea (and he also used the word 'love') irked me a great deal that day and I haven't forgotten it. Why does this idea disturb me? It is not that way with my painting so why should I pay any attention to it? Got way off the subject---didn't know that was going to come to mind again. What do I do here?

But seriously, I am concerned about what happens and why at this particular point in my designing it should occur. The dumb stuff looks good enough until I think in terms of trying to sell it. I thought if I did not have to appear with it and have an agent---or editor---look at it (with all those accompanying feelings I have related before) I would be all right. But I am not. I am not! I am not! I get so desperate feeling about it. Sometimes hopeless and sometimes like today half hope it will be different. And half knowledge that it won't be different. I will sit down and design. I will think it is passable (or I might think even that it is a reasonable idea) that the drawing or sketching is as good as the next person's and will get by. THEN I think about trying to 'get it by' some way or another and what happens? Whole idea flunks.

I get so hot and bothered over every effort to get somewhere with my art---I worry so and I can't seem to help it. I do try. And I SIMPLY MUST get some kind of ball rolling pretty soon. But I am beginning to wonder if even the acceptance would change things any. I thought If I could just find a gallery that would take some of my paintings and try to sell them it would be a start---so what happens. This one will take oils and another one will take watercolors and what will I do? I stew because I have nothing good enough to take. I have some ready and I can't get down there with them---not physically or emotionally. Suddenly they become 'not good enough'. I argue with myself I have some successes in art that I exhibited so why not rely on that? Can't---doesn't help. I tell myself the youngsters I taught have---some of them---gone on to study art---and have done well. BUT WHAT DIFFERENCE DOES IT MAKE? NONE.

Sometimes like today I feel if I could just sell my ideas to a real artist (commercial artist that is, clever, sharp, well trained and so forth) and let them go on from there, I would be better off. But I know myself well enough by now to know that is just another dodge. I would get that panicky feeling just the same."

April 24th, 1957.

"I like your telling me I was investing in my future and that it was all right (I say all right---what you said was more positive---the thing to do as it were) to just paint this summer. That makes for peace inside---if I decided that, I would have wavered---I'd have wondered if it were right and had periods of terrific doubt and depression off and on---Mother used to scold me because I sat around painting and drawing so much when I should be doing something else---any one of a number of things depending upon which she thought was important at the moment."

July 12, 1957.

"When I worked with positive and negative problems, that used to set up a kind of chain reaction! Positive and negative, black and white, right and wrong---Peggy. (Black and white as in keys on the piano, and right and wrong as in religion?). (Painting). I have some 'Mary' feelings about painting lately and felt strongly a composition of blues, grays, and browns (which I don't often use in this combination) and pink color mixed and overlapping with pen drawing of girls drawn after the paint is dry---I can visualize every detail of it as if it were already done---the figures not exactly realistic---elusive quality where they overlap and do not match or fit the color splotches in their regular spacing---Do these figures represent me? I haven't been able to 'get around to doing the painting. Other things I felt I wanted to do or felt I should do---I feel the picture is something I would like to try and yet I am afraid of it---unsettled kind of sensation. I don't know how to express it except to say I am for it and against it."

September 22, 1957.

"Once upon a time when my dad was concerned about the odd-looking drawings, or what I called designs, that occupied so much of my time, he decided to take some of the pictures and me to an art critic---so we got an appointment and went to Chicago---etc., etc., as I've told you before---when they finished telling him what they thought, he decided I might really have some ability and amount to something if I studied art---so the next idea was art lessons---he was trying to find someone in the area to help me when he found out that the schools were going to hire an art teacher and have an art department the following fall---however, the art was to be limited to the first six grades---but both of my parents were in favor of asking the teacher if she would give me private lessons---this was one matter of which my parents agreed and always favored after the art people told them I had ability---before that time, it was a struggle and a threat in many ways, but from my fifteenth year, more or less, it was easier. The art teacher came to our house once a week for the art help, but she didn't actually begin with 'art' as such---gave me a series of lessons in pencil technique, rendering from photographs, etc., technical skills---this was interesting but not 'fulfilling' the way the wild, modern design pieces felt, and I'd do my own kind after lessons were finished---one day she saw some of these---my mother showed her---embarrassed me half to death---and the teacher then began to show me chalk and crayon techniques applied to real modern art---talked modern artists and showed me prints of work by famous painters---told me about all paints and helped me with them when my folks bought me a set---then I was happier---the teacher was a very shy person, but very nice and I liked her a lot. She was not a painter herself (had done some, of course, but for assignments, etc. in school) and often said she could not help me much because I was beyond her scope---whatever that meant---but she did talk teacher's college to the hilt! She had received her training there and she thought the teacher was the best art teacher in the whole world!! This influenced me tremendously and I wanted to study art with this teacher more than I wanted anything else at that time---English second---considering teaching was what I was gong to do (as long as everyone had long ago made it clear about the medical interest not being practical for me)---so I set my goals toward her classroom and then worried myself half sick that I'd not be good enough to get in. Well, without my knowledge, my art teacher in high school told the teacher at the college about my drawings and came back with the sword that she would be thrilled to have me enroll when I finished high school (two years hence)---then I did worry. But I hoped she would forget about me---when it was time to go to school, I went up to get the enrollment information, etc. (Mother went with me, of course) and another teacher-friend from home who was going to school there that summer met us and showed us around the campus---this person had talked to me and especially to my parents for the past several years also---these things had helped a lot in my getting to go away from home. Well, she took us into the art room and I did not know that the teacher was there, but she was, and I was introduced to her. She said, 'Oh, you're the one about whom I have been told so much' and on and on. I nearly had a heart attack on the spot! Other students standing around looking and listening---she never spoke below a holler and my mother standing there pert and prim, trying to answer everything for me (and not getting very far because the teacher could outtalk her, as few others could and they always had a mutual 'mere toleration' for each other but concealed some of it for my sake, I think, anyway, the teacher tried to), so I went home in terrific conflict, tremendously pleased and tremendously scared---NOW, SHE WOULD EXPECT ME TO GET A IN ART---I began to get sick and I was so sick I could not do my own packing and Mother did it for me. Dad declared he'd been right all the time in saying I was not physically strong enough to go to college, etc., but I insisted, and although I had to lie down in the back seat of the car, I went. The next day was better and it soon became a perfectly wonderful life, to be in college---however, I was enrolled in Art 100 which was a general course required of all students going into teaching and all others who were planning to go into the teaching of art---some of the latter, of course, had been going to city high schools and had been having instruction and practice for several years. This worried me a great deal because I felt their competition was something I'd never be able to match, therefore I'd fail. But at the dorm, a new experience unfurled itself in a hurry. I was meeting almost all the girls on second floor where I lived and I was discovering that most of them (almost all of them to be correct grammatically!) were planning to become teachers and they were all taking Art 100 and were even more afraid of the teacher than I was because they had come from small or rural schools, did not know nor care for modern art---or art---and were scared to death of her loud booming voice. And so art helped me make my first contact and I made friends by explaining and demonstrating our art lessons all over again after we had been to class each day! We had to put our work on the bulletin boards and all stand around for the criticism every day---this was terrifying for she would really say what she thought---the kids would ask me to help them and then warn me not to make it too good, 'just good enough so she wouldn't holler at it, but not so good she'll know I didn't do it myself'---of course, I never should have actually drawn on their papers, but I didn't realize that then---and I explained as I went, so later the kids did do for themselves more---they said they learned more from me than they did from her. This was possibly so in the light of their lack of fear for me. But regardless of what was what, actually, the benefit to me was great for it 'established' me and I had a reputation that spread all over the place and I had never in my life had any sense of being looked up to or accepted---as you know! And at the time, I was not able to take it either---would lose time and come to far away from the school, in the dorm---too much of everything too suddenly---too much emotion evoked by it---etc.

Well, I have said all of this to say that that teacher gave me the real insight into what art was and could be---freedom of painting as one felt---acknowledgment of the good in the piece of work that was done originally and creatively from one's own feelings---and she explained why what I did was sound in composition, technique, etc., words I had never known existed in art. She got special permission for me to enroll in the advanced classes before the second year specified by the college, later let me take the art courses at a time when I was not well enough to take 'study' courses or there was a rush of dissociating so often in this or that area of study---known but not understood by then when I 'left' the classes---or whatever---

The teacher was always the same toward me and I got so I did not fear her---she was not ambivalent with me---and I discovered she was really very soft inside! Her booming voice meant nothing to me, except that she was approaching the art department from half way down the hall somewhere! She was wonderful to her students and she would go to bat for anyone whom she felt needed it, but she was very outspoken in her opinions of people who did not try to do their best---but even in this, she was very funny—some student who had been out late the night before might possibly doze a bit in her class, and she would yell, 'If you'd stay home nights and study and get some sleep there, you'd not be dreaming in here!---Now go on to the cafeteria and get a cup of coffee, you look awful---but COME BACK when you're through! Well, go on. WHAT ARE YOU SITTING THERE FOR?'---and they'd go---and come back! We dared not laugh in class but afterwards was a very different story---but I always loved and admired her and I've come to understand much of what seemed like 'quirks' about her.

So what happened last February set me to worrying again---she wrote and asked if I could send some of my art for her to see and could she use some for the college art show in the spring at graduation time---it was a wonderful letter---long and interesting and in regular prose style---BUT Mary got the letter, read it and put it away. I found it when I cleaned the house this spring, too late for the showing---and the letter of course unanswered---I did not know about it and you said Mary told you but inasmuch as I was not able to do anything right then anyway, it was just as well not to burden myself with trying to get the art done and mailed, etc.---or something to that effect and that is right, but I was afraid of my teacher's opinion of me for not answering the letter. I took it home with me but I still did not get it answered---and last week, I did finally feel I could write and say what I wanted to without apologizing or making an issue of any of it---and so I wrote a long, friendly letter about my painting and my trip to Northport and about my gain in health (and weight: She used to fuss so about my 85 pounds! And say I had to get to 100 some day!) and that I enjoyed her letters very much and that I would consider it a privilege to send her some paintings to see for her criticism would mean a lot to me as I was considering trying for a one-woman show in the future, and (I let it slide about a show at the college as if I had not quite understood or something) that it did not seem possible it had been sixteen years this month since I had first enrolled and she had opened the whole new world of modern art for me---I wrote what I felt and nothing I did not.

She answered airmail immediately and I received the letter on Saturday."

October 26, 1957.

"Well, anyway I could play it out on the piano if I could be left alone---only so often I wasn't---so I would get 'silent' as Mother called it---and she would quiz and threaten me until I would tell her about the party or invitation or whatever---and then she would blow up! 'THEY could have had the party another day---THEY knew you couldn't do thus-and-so and so forth and so forth. Why did they even ask you?' She blamed them---then (and always under these circumstances and practically never under any others) would she become softer in her tones, more tender in her words, and attitude toward me---Her poor injured, slighted child. (I hated this!)---then she would say, 'We will do something nice---just you and Mama. Mama loves you (implying group didn't---more than implied she did) Mama will take you with her somewhere nice' (even-if-group-wouldn't-attitude)---only of course it wasn't the group's fault! And then I would struggle inside. I wanted her kindness but if I accepted it I left my 'group' still farther behind. I didn't know it then, but I can feel now just what I felt then, and it is the indecision and embarrassment and rejection. So I would end up with Mother taking me up-town to buy me a new doll or crayons, or most coveted of all, cloth to sew for my dolls. All the time we were doing this, Mother would be literally 'hot under the collar'---neck red, jaw set, taut---and sputtering at the 'kids' in one breath and telling me more soothingly in the next breath that 'you and Mama don't care what the kids do---they don't care---they don't think---they don't count anyway') only they DID. They were my life. They were school, society---seven hours a day, nine months a year, year after year---got off the track there! Mother and I would get home again and she would simmer down a bit and hover over me and tell me how much I should appreciate her and what she had just bought for me and then ninety-nine percent of the time she would begin some kind of 'sexy approach' as I called it. Some of the various things I told you before that she did---or tried to do at times. If she got a phone call or a neighbor came or when Dad came for supper, there was escape for me---I rushed immediately to the piano (phoning and most visiting done in the sun parlour---the piano was in the living room.) The music alone was mine---all mine. No kids, no gifts, no parties, no religion, no problems. The music filled everything completely. It also isolated me! No one ever got inside that shell where music and I were (and when I tried to play at recitals or for groups on other occasions you know what happened---and I had never been able to let anyone share that). But the problems arose out of situations, threatening to bring on Mother's distasteful sex ideas, and could be solved only, as far as I could see, by music. I didn't know it then but I know it now because it is still that way---I cannot think of the one without the other two crowding in. They make a unit. This makes Peggy mad, makes Mary sad, and makes Vanessa say it is hopeless and useless and mixed-up. The Vicki feelings are that music is fine so forget the rest of it. Only I can't."

November 18, 1957.

"Mother had always said what I understood to be 'lilre'---that lead me to thinking how she always talked so fast (and then scolded me for doing so---and told me no to try to tell Grandma half a dozen things at the same time) that her pronunciation suffered for the speed---I think I mentioned to you before how I thought camera factory was all one meaningless word, and some other examples---well anyway when I thought of her speed, all at once it struck me what was wrong that annoys me so terribly about these neighbors---speed, loudness, and almost hysterical yakkety-yak that I can't understand and that I fear and get so worked up about---I hear French or Italian on the bus or on the street or in any crowd and I am immediately interested, but where is the difference? I have wondered and wondered---it is in the speed and tone, I bet. I did not know <u>what</u> Mother was saying lots of times but I knew for certain a storm was headed my way."

December 26, 1957.

"Then I recalled it as a part of a set of feelings about Mother letting me talk to Grandma---telling her the important things---being timed---warned against making her tired---and feeling the cause of Grandma's going away---time and fear and loss, ideas carried over after telling her something I considered important---I lost a couple of other people I loved too---(who worked for us for so long) and then after lost the child with whom I played so much and almost exclusively for several years---"

February 18, 1958.

"Then I suddenly visioned my sixth grade teacher and in the background was my mother sneering and the sneer that Dr. A. never got (never got around to having!) was not any longer a big fear---I was so darned sure she was laughing at me behind my back or thinking I was stupid or crazy or something and that it was just a matter of time at the most before it would be revealed---just as mother was---just as I had expected my sixth grade teacher to be---but it did not work that way. (Thank goodness!)."

March 10, 1958.

"Mother would not let me touch newspapers from any other family source (a few times a neighbor or some youngsters gave me some) as naturally (to her) they would have germs (spoken with disgust and disdain I can still hear and see) on them. In later years about the time I was a junior in high school according to some entries in my diary I developed an intense fear of newspapers---would dissociate at the sight of one---sometimes for a short 'few minutes', sometimes for much longer depending on things I can evaluate---anyway I lost time (blank spells I call them for myself---never mentioned to anyone, of course) and referred to by my parents as my 'acting funny again'---or 'that foolish notion of being scared stiff' (Mother's exact words as repeated again and again and again and again---) ---it finally improved when my folks stopped their subscriptions to all newspapers and magazines---I was not afraid of magazines---in fact, loved them but could not convince Mother and Dad of this. They reasoned that if I was so 'blame afraid' of newspapers then I must be afraid of magazines also because they were 'practically the same things'. I was very glad to see the end of the newspapers and quit hearing about my silly reactions but I began to want (and secretly collect from any possible source) magazines. These I hid in the bottom of boxes with other things on top to disguise the contents and placed them all in the back of my closet---when I was alone in the house I would take out the magazines and count them and look at them and then repack before Mother got back---then I had to wash my hands with hot water, then soapy water, then with the Lava soap Dad used for paint and grease on his hands, then rinse with hot water twice and with the cold water once. This almost got rid of the fear of germs but the constant, underneath feeling was that at any moment I would develop some terrible, rare (Mother's words---her way of saying venereal) disease was always present, and I had many, many symptoms of what looked like it might become a rash or a sore, or a fever or pain, etc., etc.---I was always showing Mother a spot or a mark and asking with fear if it looked like anything serious---she always said, 'Oh of course not'.---This did not allay my fears because I felt she did not take it seriously and might not do anything to cure it until it was too late and I had developed cancer. So I worried in solitude and watched the spot or scar or whatever--- very carefully. I developed a habit of looking at my hands every little while---this, as mother said, got on her nerves and nearly drove her crazy---she would yell, 'For Heavens sake, girl, quit looking at your hands!' or 'If you don't stop looking at your hands every few minutes I will do something so you won't have any hands to look at'.

This brought back very early memories of fear that I later repressed and forgot until we talked about it the other day---so I got to the place where I would look at my hands with a quick palms-up gesture when no one was looking---or if I could not avoid my folks seeing, I would get to where I just HAD to look at my hands and if I didn't get up and go into another room and look and look and look at my hands for a while, I would 'go blank' and come-to being scolded for looking at my hands again.

Pete was our newspaper carrier for several years. When the weather was very cold, Mother would always ask him to come in and get warm and she would usually give him something to eat---sandwich, cookies, and always a glass of milk (glass to be then scrubbed and scalded and disinfected with Lysol water and rerinsed---and to think that I got scolded for washing my hands repeatedly!)---but of course that was different. He came from a 'low class' family to quote my mother.

My mother drove a car with a recklessness that was very foreign to the fussiness and care and attention to details that she gave to everything else she did---she would have SUCH CLOSE CALLS---and then would say, 'Oh that didn't hurt anything. We are still here, aren't we?' and she would laugh her silly laugh and keep on swerving around the curves on the small hills near home and on the big hills surrounding us---then came the day I refused to ride with her any more---occasionally I did declare myself and this was it---I told Dad never again---and he agreed---he had ridden with her a few times too. Then he sold the car and got a different type and did not get around to showing her how to drive it. But she just took it one day, etc. But that is another train of thought. Back to the 'big day'. Mother and I were in the car, she drove into another car at an intersection on Main Street. I was thrown against the windshield and got a bump about the size of half an egg (if there is such a thing as half an egg) on my right temple. I was terribly embarrassed about Mother's driving---her fault---a big argument, etc. so I got out of the car and went home---a couple of blocks---had such a headache and was so afraid of the bump that I was certain that it was a concussion such as I had heard about in great detail when Dad's friend sustained one from which he never fully recovered---several operations, etc., horrified me---I had a cold cloth on my head and was lying on the couch in the sun parlour feeling very, very much afraid, when Pete appeared at the window on the porch outside the sun parlour window. He had seen the accident, had come to the house to see if he could do anything for me or if I wanted him to call the doctor. I told him I was all right but I was cool to him because I was so embarrassed and wanted to be left alone. When told Mother about it she said it was extremely nice of Pete to be interested and that I should be ashamed of myself for acting that way when he wanted to help. I could recall this incident every once in a while over the years and always felt a pang of regret for having acted unfriendly. I never had before and I didn't afterwards. Pete worked nearby. This necessitated his going past our back porch numerous times a day all summer and he would linger and talk with whoever was sitting on the porch resting n the rocker---Mother did not like this---said we were getting too friendly and he made more trips than he had to and that he came from a low class family. Now I am aware that this does not tie in with how I felt she was reacting when she scolded me for being cool to him. Well I had the bump on my head, had a bad headache, got scolded, and so felt miserable. But when he came with the evening paper, I was watching to apologize to him. He brushed it aside and said he hoped I would be O'k the next day and I was. As far as the bump was concerned. But the evening paper was quite a different story, the newspaper and the accident with Mother and the bump with its accompanying pain ties in with what I had been thinking periodically about trying to avoid the newspapers. It is associated with the pain in the side of my head and now I have that sharp, mean kind of feeling too close to something that hurts."

March 15, 1958.

"My foot hurt more than I said and it is distracting, but I thought it did not look bad enough to hurt that much and you'd think just like my mother used to I guess---that I was making a big fuss over nothing---so I tried to be honest enough that you would understand how it was and yet cover enough that you would not think me a sissy or a hypochondriac or something.

Today I could face nothing. I could not visualize looking you in the eye and saying I am terribly depressed over everything. When Mother would get depressed, she would be so low and feel so badly and say she had to brace up and face things so let's take a walk around the block and get a new hold---and we would go somewhere and---sure enough she would pull out of the depression---usually be very light hearted, although silly, and very generous in her feelings toward me, even put her arms around me briefly and then shove me away and say we can't waste time we have to get to work and make up for what we did not get done when I felt low."

March 24, 1958.

"My folks used to accuse me of talking in an incoherent fashion but those accusations (as I learned when I was older and could distinguish) were times following the blank spells when I was four or five or six or seven. I would protest that I had not been talking at all or that I had not said thus-and-so as they said I had---but by the time I was in the first grade I was entirely over the 'Sybil habits' of 'talking back to your mother like that', 'saying I did not in an emphatic voice or any other kind of tone', 'telling your mother she does not know what she is talking about', (this meant she had interpreted my saying I had not been talking at all as the same thing as telling her she did not know what she was saying when she had 'stood right there and heard you, YOUNG LADY, and going off somewhere to sit and pout'). Now I hated that phrase---or word---pout. I suspect any child does that sometimes and although I had always hated it, I wondered about it an have asked my friend if any of the others did it thinking perhaps it was early relegated to another---she said, Not exactly that---more childish 'I-don't-like-anything' kind of expression---(****NOW I FEEL THAT IRKED, MEAN KIND OF SOMETHING THAT MAKES ME CRY INSIDE****)---on Peggy's face and sometimes Mary but not sulky. I dislike the word sulky as much as pout---I suppose if I were normal I had inclinations in that directions, too, but it all got lost somewhere evidently if the others don't do it, because I certainly did not after a few times of being accused and spanked for it when I was very young---three or four years old---because it was before we went to the farm---evidently my mother did not try to see things from any possible point of view except her own or she might have wondered why I protested I had not been talking and so forth and so forth. But anyway I very early learned not to 'talk back' and so forth. I did have some spirit in that direction until I was ready to go to school, because I can remember trying to tell her and trying to talk louder and faster in order to stand-up for myself---but this was always fatal and the times I tried it became farther and farther apart and finally I got it through my head that it did not do any good---this was my feeling about it until the third grade---after I came-to in the fifth grade I was convinced I must be good to my dear, sweet, thoughtful 'bought-more-things-for-than-any-other-kid-in-town-mother.' Words and phrases she used repeatedly---and echoes of the poems she made memorize."

July 6, 1958.

"I realize that much of what I had been taught as a child was, essentially true. It was the people who taught it who got it mixed for me---their inconsistency, and especially Mother's---she talked (or read much of God's care and protection) and yet she worried incessantly.

(I vividly recall the one and only time I pointed this out to her---if God could care for her so well and would as she claimed, then why was she worried about money, health, life, and death, and the heareafter?---need not tell you her response!! End of subject."

August 5, 1958.

"I did some thinking about Mother---and several things have made me wonder---of course it would be stupidly obvious to say that she was not like any of them (church people). Mother was not like anyone but Mattie Dorsett—or at least I never met anyone like her although one of my acquaintances could qualify for coming in second if one considered the race was not already long since won before the second place rated. Back to Mother---I was thinking she had friends spasmodically, never close, never for very long periods of time, but every now and then some kind of intense 'speeded up' (only expression that fits how it felt to me when she was 'in' one of these so-called friendships) relationship with someone whom she referred to as a friend---they would be very 'thick' (her word) for a while, then break off, sometimes with feelings of animosity, but usually just a kind of loss of interest or a drifting apart appearance---sometimes---usually it seems---it was a sudden need on the part of my mother to 'take up' with someone of more interest to her than the existing friendship---it looked fairly all right on the surface, but we knew there was some kind of trouble causing it---sometimes never again relationships, and sometimes a casual seeming acquaintance and at times a fervent renewal that would relive the original intense friendship with the usual 'cooling off' sure to follow. This was particularly true of one woman over the years. When the family first came to WC to live, they moved in across the street from us---had four children then---two more later---they were exceedingly poor people. Mother went to bat for them with the County, went to the County Seat and told the Department they needed help and told what to do—right down to what color sweaters to give the youngsters and so forth and they did it. Mother had an in with some one at the Red Cross who operated the County Clothing Building which was open once a week. Mother would talk her into giving them certain things, different from the other people with children in the same grades so the kids would not make fun of them for wearing 'County' clothes they were forced to wear---and some other maneuvers which were really quite sensible and certainly were appreciated. They lived in different houses all over town. Mother would hot-foot it over and back a couple of times a day---or once a day depending---for a few weeks---or maybe two months, and then cool and go occasionally on Saturday afternoons for a little while---if a baby were on the way she would consider herself needed and go much more often for a while---sometimes streaks of not going for so long the woman would send for her (or on rare occasions, come herself) to see what was wrong. They considered Mother their best friend---Mother considered she was their best friend, too! She had done a lot for them, all right, and she was aware of it, pleased by it and considered it a personal victory or defeat with (or OVER) the County when she won or lost (seldom LOST). I don't think this was friendship in its true sense---she liked to hear gossip and she heard plenty there.

Mother always knew---with her everything was either right or wrong---(as Peggy would say, black and/or white), true or not true, no compromise. When anything she decided was questioned, the other person was wrong, naturally. If a friendship broke up, she was the injured party. The other person was wrong. At times I was foolish enough (or brave enough) to try to indicate there might be another side to what we were discussing besides the side she presented to me, but if I did that I was trying to start an argument and that meant I had to be punished---'put in your place, young lady'---so I gave up for many years. Then I began trying to stick up for myself and we had some pippins of arguments but I still never accomplished anything because she would throw in so many issues aside from the question, or throw at me how worthless I was, or show me I was wrong, or something---so it was no use. After that---we got by."

September 27, 1958.

"My mother always had a great regard for nice dishes, fine china, (always holding something to the light!) cut glassware, and so forth and was extremely particular about hers---seldom broke or chipped a piece, but when she did, she discarded it for she was very (and I mean VERY---could get hot on the subject) contemptuous of imperfect dishes and disdainful of anyone using them---(I just had a little 'aside' thought that is not at all nice, but this is free association, and I can say it---when I thought how she was contemptuous of cracked or broken dishes and was so careful of her own dishes, I simultaneously thought, 'But her child didn't matter'---). Well to get back to the subject if I can find it---Mother, dishes, and me. I came home from the party when I was four and I had a small cocoa stain on my dress---naturally (for me) I was very apprehensive about having soiled my 'clean, fresh (clothes were always clean and fresh and never just clean!), starched dress that Mother had worked so hard to have nicer than any other little girl in town'. (Baloney---) and even more worried less she find out I had also committed the unpardonable sin of spilling something on the tablecloth and 'disgracing her in front of everybody in town'---However, I also knew better than to lie to her and I intended to tell the truth of what had happened if I got a chance before she lowered the boom. So I started talking as I went up the front steps (she was waiting at the front door, of course) and I said, 'I spilled cocoa because it was hot and'---and she said of course it was hot, Heavens I've had cocoa before, haven't I. What was the matter with me anyway (or something very much like that---of course, I can't recall her exact words but she had certain stock phrases that somehow I am sure I wouldn't know how) seem to be seared into my memory (soft memory, I guess)---well, back again, I think to the dishes---(never did like doing them) and Mother (Well)---Mother did let me get it said that the cups didn't have any handles and I took hold of the cup that was hot and---but that is all I ever got said---then OR later---she jumped to a conclusion I had not foreseen. She immediately assumed that the child's aunt had served us with cups that had the handles broken off in as much as we were 'just kids' and she had thought we would 'hurt her old dishes' so she did not use any that she did not want broken---I was amazed and I tried to explain that the cups were tall and not like ours but I didn't get it all explained but---Looking back, I don't believe it would have made any dent in her feeling even if I had but---

Jumping again, my mother did not like Mrs. T (few did). I do not know the reasons but I suspect it would not take a lot of brain power to deduct it from her references to her as being a snob---and after all she didn't have any children. (I heard this a million times, I bet) because she thought she was 'too good to have children to bother with and after all everyone knew what kind of a family she came from (this I never did find out, but everyone knew it!) And WHO was he anyway. All he ever did was work in the post office carrying mail on a RURAL route (significance of that word rural was that it was degrading.)---and just because she, Mrs. T., had a house that was bigger than two people needed, she did not have to sling on the dog the way she did'. Mother always avoided meeting her.

I can see Mother's antagonism and I see some reasons---I could not forget about it---it kept nagging---it began with the cups and soon ended with my feelings---I went home from the party fully expecting Mother's disapproval---I nearly got it, when she suddenly latched onto the broken cup idea which was entirely her own and then because she did not like Mrs. T, I suppose, she clung to that idea and did not let me explain---it gave me an out and I took it---however, she told another lady about it the next day or so and then she told this person and that person until I had heard it repeated numerous times and always with the SAME slant---'How stupid of

Mrs. T. to give kids hot cocoa in cups without handles'---but the real injustice she had done the children was to consider them so inhuman (this is a laugh) as to give them old broken dishes---of course the woman who heard this took up the mourning with poor disgraced mother of me---I would over-hear this as I played nearby or if in another's home, usually sitting near Mother, I knew good and well this was not true about the cups being broken---in essence the story had some truth, but the part Mother stressed was not true.

And before long I began to feel very guilty for letting Mother tell people a lie about those cups---but I could not bring myself to say so, but I did ask Mother to please not tell anybody else about my spilling cocoa at the party, but she said she would tell what she wanted to when she wanted to---(that I already knew)---This morning when I quit trying to get Mrs. T. out of my mind, I remembered the reason and the guilty 'scary' feelings from way back.

I no longer feel guilty about the situation---I don't think it was right for me to let Mother tell an untruth and imply something about the woman that was false, but I also feel it was not fair for Mother to have jumped to conclusions and not listen to my explanation---I was afraid but I was intending to be honest and it was her fault if she read into it what she wanted to instead of what I tried to say---it was not right for me to let it go and take that as a way out, but I also feel it was understandable to avoid her wrath which could have come fully onto me---as I had expected---and which would not have been fair either. It was all really a very trifling matter, but it got all out of proportion in my feelings as so many events seemed to have done. However, even though the event was small, I think where the importance came was not in that, but in Mother's attitude---or more specifically, as you say it, the relationship between Mother and me. If that had been different, so would I."

UNDATED.

"Mother was always very, very busy from morning until night with her everlasting washing and scrubbing, ironing, and cleaning whether things were dirty or not. (Others must have known this, for when I was born, one of her sisters wrote and told her not to wash me to death.) And Dad was always preoccupied with thoughts of his work until his sickness had developed when I was four and a half. Their idea of entertaining a child was to buy everything available for 'safe' play. That included dolls, doll furniture that Dad made for me in his spare time (but under demand that I be kept out of the carpenter shop while he was trying to work---I wanted so much to see him making my doll's furniture), toy stove, and iron, and ironing board, and washboard, tricycle, wagon, books by the dozens, paper dolls (I got the mean feeling again when I mentioned the books---don't know why) and many other toys. They considered unsafe such things as a bicycle, ice skates, swimming lessons, skis, toboggan, sled, and roller skates. (However, I got the roller skates when I was seven when sick with scarlitina; Dad felt sorry for me and told me I could have anything I wanted to play with so although it was the middle of the winter, I got the skates!) I loved the skates and the next summer became a really good skater---it was the one and only sport at which I showed any skill, and although I was never allowed to go to 'so worldly' a place as a skating rink, I skated all over town and had the admiration of the other youngsters who always lost a race. As I look back over that, I see it as one of the very few triumphs I ever had---I suppose that is why I liked the sport so much. I think I could have done better in other things if I had had an opportunity.

March 20, 1961.

"We begun, at your instigation, to consider and try and find the time when the first alternation occurred---first we got back to a four-year-old one I recalled rather (just rather) easily, and several months or maybe a year later, we found (or rather you did) one partial or faint, or something one, when I was about eighteen months. I think that is how it was. We discussed my having the first due to Mother's unbearableness---I believe that did precipitate it---

Although I believe the unearthly 'things' mother did to me, her unfair kind of reasoning, etc. did cause me to alternate into those who could express feelings such as Peggy and later live a more normal life such as Vicki with a mother (who loved her) and father and brothers and sisters, all well and satisfactorily explained and accounted for elsewhere, but who would come for her and so forth. I think those things came from those reasons---yet it felt partly true---and all this confused me---now, about clarifying that other before I proceed---anxiety in regard to dishes, mother figures, dish towels, music (somewhat), and so forth felt as if they arose from what Mother had done, but then we'd get into the school situation and her drilling and drilling on math, spelling and so forth and expecting <u>her</u> daughter to be perfect---it didn't <u>feel</u> right. It sounded and reasoned right and I tried to accept it but at times I rebelled. I got confused---Well, she wasn't always on the subject of religion and she wasn't too enthusiastic about some things regarding it, that is especially the 'sundown' situation---she got <u>so</u> uneasy and anxious over Sabbaths, with 'nothing to do' and hated the long summer ones. In winter it was a 'short day'---also tension-producing---She would always get more and more agitated as days wore on and drew me into it. When I was young it was not a problem for me. But I was well aware of her restlessness and she complained to me of nothing to do and we'd end up with my leaving what I was enjoying to go with her for a walk 'just to get out of here' and/or 'call' on someone. It can still be Mother and her attitudes.

My first introduction to learning (as called 'studying') came at two or two-and-a-half in relation to separation from Mother---studying something I think was beyond my comprehension, hence the boredom (I recall the feeling of boredom and disinterest) and connected with school which had 'classes' (I am and have been aware of for some months that I am far less anxious of going to a 'lecture' than to a 'class').

My earliest and most vivid recollection is standing on the rocker and wiggling all over the place while Mother tried to read the 'lesson' to me. I was bored---she told me 'for land's sake to stand still'. I couldn't---it was the same day as the 'blow' that I was now big enough to go into the 'primary' class with a teacher who was not Mama and with (so I thought) nothing to do as they sat on little benches around little tables and folded their hands on top (where I could easily be cracked on the knuckles, although no one ever did that---outside of Mother at home---it was my fear). I talked about the 'lesson' and had no sandbox. I discovered they had crayons and color books (of the day's lesson) but this came only after the lesson and it was not new to me to color---and the teacher collected the books and colors and kept them for the next week. The object was to keep within the lines when we colored. This I could do better than anyone else---I can remember---and I was praised---but I wanted to take the book to show Mama and Daddy and Grandma---but the teacher would never let me (never can share anything? A connection? Maybe)."

APPENDIX F

Shirley Mason's Education and Work History

Education:

High School	Dodge Center High School Dodge Center, Minnesota	Diploma	1942
University	Mankato State Teachers College* Mankato, Minnesota	B. S.	1949
	University of Omaha* Omaha, Nebraska		1947
	Columbia University Columbia Teachers College* New York, New York	M. A.	1955

*Courses in Administration, Early Childhood Growth and Development, Psychology, Abnormal Psychology and Curriculum Planning.

Teaching Experience:

Omaha Junior Academy	Omaha, Nebraska	1945-7	High School English & Art Adult Art Extension Division, State Department of Education

Kansas City Junior Academy	Kansas City, Missouri	1947-9	Junior High School English & Art, Biology & First Aid Adult Art Extension Division State Department of Education
Porter Hospital & Sanitarium	Denver, Colorado	1949-51	Occupational Therapy Art & Ceramics Adult Art, Extension Division, State Education Department
Jackson Protestant Parochial School	Jackson, Michigan	1951	Grades 1-4 All Subjects
Memphis Public Schools	Memphis, Michigan	1951-4	High School English & Art. Elementary Art Adult Art, Extension Division, State Education Department
New York, New York		1956-60	Private and Group Art Instruction
Falkirk Hospital	Central Valley, N.Y.	1960-3	Art Therapy with Psychotic Patients
New York, New York		1963-5	Private and Group Art Instruction

Administrative Experience:

Omaha Junior Academy	Omaha, Nebraska	1945-7	Organization of School & Curriculum, advised on hiring of teachers, researched & purchased all texts for grades 1-10. Conducted all psychological and placement tests.
Porter Hospital & Sanitarium	Denver, Colorado	1949	Organization of Occupational Therapy Department in its entirety. Training of Personnel.
Memphis Public Schools	Memphis, Michigan	1951-4	Correlation of art with Core Curriculum through training of eight elementary teachers.

Art Experience:

Group shows, one-man show, exhibited in 18 states in approximately 90 art shows.

(Courtesy of The Papers of Flora Rheta Schreiber)

APPENDIX G

Shirley Mason gave this painting to Patricia Alcott's mother in 1953.

(Courtesy of Patricia Alcott)

APPENDIX H

The house where Shirley grew up in Dodge Center, Minnesota.

General Index of Deeds,
Dodge County

The road to the Chicken House

The front view of a chicken house

Side view of a chicken house

The furrows next to the Chicken House

The Zumbro River near the furrows

The Mason family headstone in Dodge County

About the Author

Patrick Suraci received a B.A. in Psychology from Assumption College, University of Windsor Ontario, Canada. After college, the U.S. Army sent him to Germany and gave him the opportunity to explore Europe. He later studied acting in New York city with the legendary Uta Hagen and worked in the theatre in New York and films in Rome, London and Amsterdam with Carroll Baker.

He received a Ph.D. in Psychology from the New School for Social Research. His first book was *Male Sexual Armor: Erotic Fantasies and Sexual Realities of the Cop on the Beat and the Man in the Street*.

Dr. Suraci is in private practice in Manhattan.

Made in the USA
Middletown, DE
07 June 2017